CW01670479

'The author's inimitable style and perception m
laced with practical wisdom, thought-provokin
that build over the course of the book. The aut
experience in the charity investment world to c
and does so with zest, clarity, humour and salty common sense.
Don Bawtree, Senior Adviser, BDO LLP

'I've loved listening to James speak on investments at Charity Finance Group events for many years. His written words are equally engaging and don't disappoint. Jam-packed with useful stuff, and delivered in a style that is easy to follow and makes sense, this is a great resource on charity investing.'
Caron Bradshaw, CEO, Charity Finance Group

'Cuts through all the noise and distraction by providing thoughtful and provocative tools that will be useful to any practitioner. It brings charity investors back to what really matters – using their organisation's wealth in a way that best helps their beneficiaries.'
Matthew Cox, Investment Director, Esmée Fairbairn Foundation

'I recommend this book enthusiastically for the trustees and senior staff of endowed charities. It focuses on investment for UK beneficiaries, is highly practical, non-technical and very well written.'
Professor Elroy Dimson, Chair, Centre for Endowment Asset Management, Judge Business School, University of Cambridge

'*Investing for Charities* is an invaluable guide to charity investment. It is practical, insightful and remarkably comprehensive. It is also deeply grounded in the distinctive characteristics of different types of charity and is packed full of the wisdom of James's many years of experience, thought and reflection.'
Luke Fletcher, Partner, Bates Wells

'An excellent, practical and jargon-free guide for all charity trustees, stressing the need to make and spend (wisely!) as much as you can for your beneficiaries. Given my long experience in charities and endowments – from the largest (Wellcome Trust) to a small, local charity – I know that, as James says in the book, good governance is the asset of choice. This title will be invaluable for trustees who aim to assess and implement prudent investment decisions and then to review their progress.'
Sarah Fromson, Chair of the Cambridge University Endowment Fund Investment Advisory Board

'I could have done with James's book when I arrived at the Barrow Cadbury Trust, having never managed an endowment. This is a book that puts money in its place – which is as a means to an end not an end in itself. I thoroughly recommend it to anyone with oversight responsibility for a charitable endowment; it will help you navigate not what is "right" but what is right for pursuing your particular charitable purpose both now and in the future.'
Dame Sara Llewellin, CEO, Barrow Cadbury Trust

'This book provides an invaluable reminder that charities exist to spend money not to hoard it. The better we run our investment portfolios, the more we will be able to spend. James provides a comprehensive framework in practical language for improving the way charities with investment portfolios can maximise their impact.'

Nick Moakes, Managing Partner and Chief Investment Officer, Wellcome Trust

'It was a delight to pick up a book that challenges the usual approaches that charities take to investing by focusing on spending. Bursting with ambition, insights and practical examples, this is a book for all trustees of charities lucky enough to have investments – including trustees who already have investment experience.'

David Renton, Estates Bursar, All Souls College, University of Oxford

INVESTING
for Charities

dsc
directory of social change

Published by the Directory of Social Change (Registered Charity no. 800517 in England and Wales)

Registered address: Directory of Social Change, First Floor, 10 Queen Street Place, London EC4R 1BE

Tel: 020 4526 5995

Visit www.dsc.org.uk to find out more about our books, subscription funding website and training events. You can also sign up for e-newsletters so that you're always the first to hear about what's new.

The publisher welcomes suggestions and comments that will help to inform and improve future versions of this and all of our titles. Please give us your feedback by emailing publications@dsc.org.uk.

It should be understood that this publication is intended for guidance only and is not a substitute for professional advice. No responsibility for loss occasioned as a result of any person acting or refraining from acting can be accepted by the author or publisher.

Print and digital editions first published 2024
Copyright © Directory of Social Change 2024

All rights reserved. No part of the printed version of this book may be stored in a retrieval system or reproduced in any form whatsoever without prior permission in writing from the publisher. This book is sold subject to the condition that it shall not, by way of trade or otherwise, be lent, re-sold, hired out or otherwise circulated without the publisher's prior permission in any form of binding or cover other than that in which it is published, and without a similar condition including this condition being imposed on the subsequent purchaser.

The digital version of this publication may only be stored in a retrieval system for personal use. No part may be edited, amended, extracted or reproduced in any form whatsoever. It may not be distributed or made available to others without prior permission in writing from the publisher.

The publisher and author have made every effort to contact copyright holders. If anyone believes that their copyright material has not been correctly acknowledged, please contact the publisher, who will be pleased to rectify the omission.

The moral right of the author has been asserted in accordance with the Copyrights, Designs and Patents Act 1988.

ISBN 978 1 78482 120 3 (print edition)
ISBN 978 1 78482 121 0 (digital edition)

British Library Cataloguing in Publication Data
A catalogue record for this book is available from the British Library

Cover and text design by Kate Griffith
Typeset by Marlinzo Services, Frome
Printed and bound in Great Britain by CPI Group, Croydon

FSC
www.fsc.org
MIX
Paper | Supporting responsible forestry
FSC® C013604

For Alison (and her forbearance)

Contents

About the Directory of Social Change

At the Directory of Social Change (DSC), we believe that the world is made better by people coming together to serve their communities and each other. For us, an independent voluntary sector is at the heart of that social change and we exist to support charities, voluntary organisations and community groups in the work they do. Our role is to:

- **provide practical information** on a range of topics from fundraising to project management in both our printed publications and our e-books;
- **offer training** through public courses, events and in-house services;
- **research funders** and maintain a subscription database, *Funds Online*, with details on funding from grant-making charities, companies and government sources;
- **offer bespoke research** to voluntary sector organisations in order to evaluate projects, identify new opportunities and help make sense of existing data;
- **stimulate debate and campaign** on key issues that affect the voluntary sector, particularly to champion the concerns of smaller charities.

We are a registered charity ourselves but we self-fund most of our work. We charge for services but cross-subsidise those which charities particularly need and cannot easily afford.

Visit our website **www.dsc.org.uk** to see how we can help you to help others and have a look at **www.fundsonline.org.uk** to see how DSC could improve your fundraising. Alternatively, call our friendly team at **020 4526 5995** to chat about your needs or drop us a line at **cs@dsc.org.uk**.

About the author

James Brooke Turner has worked for charities with investment portfolios for his entire career. He is currently the Investment Director of the Nuffield Foundation, where he has worked for over 20 years. Having served as a trustee of many charities including the Association of Medical Research Charities and the Association of Charitable Foundations, he is currently a trustee of the Idlewild Trust and the International Institute for Conservation.

He studied at the University of London, first the History of European Art at the Courtauld Institute and, some years later, an MA in Medieval Culture at Birkbeck, where he specialised in insolvency in England in the year 1200. James also studied at the Yale Endowment Management Programme and, subsequently, the London Business School's Endowment Management course. He has also sat on the Charities SORP Committee as an observer and has held a number of professional qualifications.

James has used all this experience to develop the discipline and practice of managing endowments. He convened a report on the Governance and Management of Endowed Charitable Foundations and has sat on the steering committee of its subsequent reports. He established a network for finance directors of endowed grant-making charities, written and spoken extensively about charities and their investments, and was recognised in 2017 by the Charity Finance Group as one of three inaugural Inspiring Leaders in the sector. In 2017, he co-founded Yoke and Company, a business that supports charity trustees in forging a more engaged relationship with their investable assets and in their capital allocation decisions.

In 2009, James was one of the sculptures of Antony Gormley's *One & Other* art project as part of the Fourth Plinth Commission in Trafalgar Square. He performed as a cycling dove in the opening ceremony of the 2012 London Olympics. James was also the founder of now-defunct Extremely Tall Cricket Club. He likes to cycle, swim in cold water and paint watercolours, ideally during the same outing.

Acknowledgements

This book is a distillation of a life spent dealing with charity finance and investments at various times – as an employee, a trustee, a client or an investment consultant. Each role brought into focus different aspects of investing for charities and the range of issues trustees and staff encounter.

My exposure to investing began at the Nuffield Foundation many, many years ago. The foundation's purpose is to use the power of evidence to help improve people's lives, and it is backed by an investment portfolio that today is valued at over £500 million. As an organisation built on curiosity, evidence and rigour, it has always encouraged me to look beyond the received wisdom of the industry to the underlying principles of investment and their implications. So this book is a testament to the Nuffield Foundation's support over the years in the pursuit of answers driven by this culture of curiosity – answers that have rewarded the foundation with returns of 10% a year for over 20 years.

The financial support from Yoke and Company, a charity-facing investment consultancy co-founded by Guy Davies and myself, has been invaluable. It has been an enduring privilege to hear the stories from clients and contacts, the issues they encounter in navigating the investment landscape and the day-to-day aspirations and confusions they have – regardless of their size. My hope is that this book might illuminate a path through some of this fog, so they can do more to help their beneficiaries.

No book is written alone, and this one reflects so many views of multiple people that I have encountered over the years; they may recognise their phrases or ideas in the following pages. I cannot thank you individually, but nevertheless I do thank you. Without the encouragement of Guy Davies and David Renton, who were very early readers, I might have abandoned this project. In an industry where charts are produced like wallpaper, it is surprisingly difficult to obtain permission for their use, so I'm very grateful to Tristram Blythe at Charity Finance, Mark Johnson and Jonathan Joiner at Legal & General Investment Management, Professor Elroy Dimson at London Business School and the Idlewild Trust for being so obliging. Without the constructive comments on various sections of Ian Allsop, Mark O'Kelly, Ruth Murphy, Nazier Hashemi, Richard Bowen and Julian Smith, this book would have had many more flaws in it than it must already carry, and any mistakes will be mine. Thanks too to John Martin and Gabi Zagnojute at the Directory of Social Change for their patience, encouragement and persistence. Finally, if language is what we use to give order to the chaos in our heads, none of this would have been possible without the orchestration of Hazel Bird of Wordstitch.

Foreword

Spending is at the heart of what defines charities and differentiates them from other financial institutions. Although the title of this book references investment as its subject, it is actually about the reverse side of the same coin – how charities can optimise spending through adopting best investment practices. This book addresses the essential, age-old question of 'are we doing enough?'

Investing for Charities is crafted with the unique needs of charities in mind, recognising the delicate balance they must maintain between generating return and preserving capital. Charities have the difficult task of solving this paradox and must navigate the volatility of financial markets with both boldness and caution. They need to ensure that their assets grow but, at the same time, are safeguarded and protected against unforeseen downturns and unanticipated inflation. Risk management is therefore a crucial sub-theme throughout the book's narrative, exploring strategies that can help mitigate risks and still ensure growth and a predictable stream of money to spend.

Sustainability and responsible investing have undoubtedly taken centre stage in recent years. Investors have the power to shape the future of not just their own financial landscapes but the world at large. A message that should be music to the ears of socially driven organisations like charities. Through responsible investing, we can contribute to a more equitable and sustainable global economy. Wrapped around this noble aim lies the need for good governance. One pivotal message of this book is that those in charge should not only develop a long-term plan based on sound advice and agreed beliefs but – importantly – stick with it through thick and thin, despite short-term noise and singing sirens.

In front of you lies a comprehensive guide that demystifies the complexities of the investment world, tailored to the fiduciary and ethical responsibilities of charitable organisations. Use it to invest more confidently, to spend more on your beneficiaries and to shape the future you want to see.

Gary Steinberg
Independent Advisor and former Chief Investment Officer at BP Pensions, The Wellcome Trust and The International Monetary Fund

Glossary

The following definitions explain how some commonly used terms and phrases are used in the context of this book. The best place to find explanations of investment terminology is the 'Dictionary' section of Investopedia.com.[1] For charity accounting definitions, a good source is the Charities Statement of Recommended Practice (SORP).[2] Additionally, the Sarasin Compendium of Investment is a useful and detailed all-rounder.[3]

Active management is where you employ a **manager** who makes decisions for you about your **investments** – specifically, which stocks are better to own than others. They have different ways of working this out, which they refer to as their 'investment process'. Active management is the opposite of **passive management.**

An **asset** is something that provides its owner with some form of advantage, normally financial. Assets can take a bewildering range of forms, some very complex. Charities usually consider assets to include their buildings, **investments** and cash, among other things. The opposite is a **liability**.

Asset allocation describes the process of deciding what proportions of your **investment portfolio** you want to invest in which types of **asset**. As a result, it defines how much **risk** and **volatility** you will be exposed to. It is central to the investing process.

Benchmarks are measures against which something can be compared. The term is most commonly used in charity **investments** to determine whether your investment **return** has met your investment objectives. For example, the benchmark Consumer Prices Index (CPI) plus 3% allows you to see whether your returns have met or exceeded increases in the CPI (see page 68) plus 3%. A benchmark will also be used to see whether you have met your financial objectives.

Capital is something you own and which will provide a benefit to you for some time to come. It is best explained as the tree that provides fruit to eat. It is the part of your charity's wealth that you might want to keep for a long time. You can spend it all if you want (unless it is a permanent **endowment**; see page 140), but then it is gone. In this book, the term **long-term reserve** is used in preference to 'capital' (because the money is there for the long term and the word 'capital' has a narrower meaning in the Charities SORP[4]). The phrases 'capital gains' and 'capital losses' simply refer to increases and decreases in the value of your capital, whether they be realised or unrealised.

Caution means care taken to avoid mistakes or unwelcome outcomes. It is similar to **risk** aversion.

Custodians are organisations that can hold your **assets** for you (as in 'custody'). Your assets will be in the name of the custodian (nominal ownership), but you will get the benefit and control them (beneficial ownership). The asset **manager** and custodian are invariably separate bodies, the former instructing the latter.

Diversification simply means not putting all your eggs in one basket. It is one of the two standard **investment** criteria (see page 138), so it is very important.

Earnings means the **income** a company generates from its various trading activities. Some (or all) of this can be distributed to investors as dividends or interest payments. Because of this, earnings is a broader measure of a company's profitability than the dividends or income investors receive.

Endowments are segments of **capital** which are intended to be kept for the long term. They are either expendable (in which case the capital can be spent) or permanent (in which case the capital, generally speaking, cannot be spent; see page 140 for more information on permanent endowments).

Equity is the same as shares or stocks. An equity usually entitles you to a share of the profits of a company and a say in how it is run. The more shares you have, the more profit you receive and the more say you have.

Funds come in two types (in relation to **investment**), depending on the context. One is an investment fund, which is a pooled vehicle that holds various **assets** that investors jointly own by buying units in a fund. The second is completely different and is a term used in charity accounting to describe various types of charity **reserves**, such as restricted funds and **endowment** funds.

Hedging refers to any activity which is designed to reduce your exposure to something, just like when people talk about 'hedging their bets'. In investing, it is most often encountered in the sense of hedging against adverse movements in currencies (where otherwise you'd lose money if the currency changed in value). Hedge **funds** are a specific **asset** class which is designed to use various hedging strategies (not just currencies) to achieve a desired outcome.

Income again has different meanings depending on the context. In investing, income refers to dividends and interest paid to investors. This can be an attribute of income **funds** in which you can invest and which pay investors a higher level of dividends and interest, rather than a normal amount. In charity accounting, income describes everything that is not **capital** – or, in other words, everything that can be spent if the trustees so choose. In this book, what the trustees have decided that they intend to spend is referred to as the 'spending reserve' to avoid confusion (because the money is there for spending). A nice definition of income (as opposed to capital) is that it is everything that you can spend without impairing your ability to spend it again next year.

Indices are groups of similar **investments** (such as equities, bonds or more complex variations) aggregated into a single named series. An example is the FTSE 100, which is the index of the 100 largest companies listed on the London Stock Exchange. Indices are used as the basis on which passive **funds** are constructed. An index can also be used as a benchmark for your own investment **portfolio**. This could be based on something like the FTSE 100, or inflation data for the past five years. The simplest definition of an index is that it is a point of reference.

Intergenerational equity describes an idea where different generations are treated fairly so current beneficiaries are not deprived of spending in order to favour future generations, or vice versa.

Investment means buying something that will give you a future **return**. An investment is an **asset**. This book concentrates on a simple choice: spending or investing. If you don't spend the money on your charitable purpose, you'll need to keep it somewhere, and that is usually an investment. Charities can also make investments to directly support their purpose.

Investment-led charities are charities where a **portfolio** of **investments** supports the substantial majority of spending. The portfolio represents the wherewithal of the charity and is a major focus for the trustees.

Liability see **asset**.

Liquidity refers to how quickly you can get your hands on your money. In a bank current account it will be instant, and in some deposit accounts it will either be instant or delayed for some defined period, with or without penalties. For charities the term 'liquidity' refers to how quickly you can raise cash from your **investments**. Some investments, such as property, can be slow to sell, so they are often able to lock in or 'gate' investors, which prevents investors having their money back for a (possibly prolonged) period while the **manager** raises enough money to meet the demand for redemptions. Others (such as private equity) can lock investors in until the investment completes its business. Illiquid investments can sometimes be sold more quickly but at a reduced price. In the context of investments that are quicker to sell, liquidity is measured by how much your shareholding in a particular company represents that day's trading (the higher your proportion, the more illiquid it is).

Long-term reserve is similar to **capital.** However, because 'capital' has a specific and narrow meaning in the Charities SORP,[5] this book uses the phrase 'long-term reserve' to describe more broadly something held to provide future benefits. Where the difference is inconsequential, these words are sometimes used interchangeably. Anything that is not in the long-term reserve would be in a short-term reserve.

Managers are **investment** professionals or firms that you instruct to help you manage your money. You may use one or more and there is a huge variety of styles, approaches and sizes. If you use more than one, you become responsible for deciding the proportions of your **assets** that each manager receives. These directions can be implemented either by a human or by a computer programmed by a human. Managers are usually given **mandates.**

Mandate literally means 'command' (from the Latin *mandatum*). As part of the investing process, you will give a **manager** an instruction as to how to manage your investments. Sometimes you will need to give the same manager more than one mandate, especially if you have more than one **risk** appetite.

Natural income includes **income** you receive from dividends, rents and interest but excludes any **capital** growth. The alternative is a **total return.** Under the Charity Commission's total return rules, natural income is an important part of the standard rules (as explained on page 59).

Nominal terms describes figures that are not adjusted for something like inflation. For example, if inflation were 2%, a nominal **return** might be 5%, but an after-inflation **real** return would be 3% (5% – 2% = 3%).

Passive management is a way of investing mechanically (i.e. without any human insight) in passive **funds.** Your money is invested in exactly the same proportions as the relative sizes of the companies in your chosen **index** (e.g. the FTSE 100). It is the opposite of **active management** and much cheaper. Choosing the right index (or indices) to follow is the only decision you have to make, so it is important to get that right. Passive management funds are also known as trackers (because they track an index).

Pooled funds are **investment** vehicles which own a collection of **assets,** such as equities or bonds. Investors in pooled **funds** own a fraction of the whole fund, and by implication a fraction of each asset in the fund. You can only buy and sell units in the whole fund – you cannot choose individual shares or companies to buy and sell. A **manager** chooses what to put into each fund (subject to the fund's rules). The opposite is a **segregated fund**.

Portfolio refers to a collection of **assets**. It is an imprecise term that can refer to a number of mandates or to a single **mandate**. Most commonly people refer to 'an **investment** portfolio', by which they mean all their invested assets. In this book, the word 'portfolio' always refers to investments (not **reserves**).

Prudence is different from caution because it involves weighing the balance of **risk** and **return**. Sometimes it is prudent to be incautious.

Real is another word with different meanings depending on its context. First it can be the opposite of **nominal** when it means that the figures you are looking at are already adjusted to take account of inflation. 'Real assets' is a phrase that refers to **assets** that are better able to protect you from inflation. The other meaning is the natural one in the sense of an asset being tangible or real, like property or a gold mine. These are sometimes called 'hard' assets because they are hard if you land on one.

Reserves is yet another term that has many different meanings, again depending on the context. For the purpose of this book, it has its natural meaning of something that is available to be used. It is always used in an accounting sense and should not be confused with **portfolio**, which always relates to **investments**. When used in the singular ('reserve'), it usually relates to a specific pot of money (although in practice charities often refer to their 'reserves' in the plural regardless of whether they are made up of one pot or multiple). The Charities SORP uses a more technical, tightly defined definition, which this book references when required.[6]

Responsible investing is a generic term implying that **investment** activities are undertaken with an intention to achieve a morally desirable outcome, with an expectation that at least some of the investment will be returned, with or without an additional financial **return**. Oddly there is no such term as 'irresponsible investing', although that does not mean it does not happen.

Return refers to the reward you receive for making an **investment**. In the case of a **total return**, it means the combination of **income** together with any **capital** gains or losses.

Risk has two completely different meanings in the **investment** world. If it is used in the context of default, misfeasance or some other irredeemable loss, it implies a bad outcome. Much more often, and more lazily, it is a synonym for **volatility** and indicates that your **income** and **asset** values could go up or down in the future. It is axiomatic in the industry that if you invest with no risk, you cannot make a **return** greater than inflation.

Security again has at least two meanings. First it means any **asset**, such as an **equity** or a bond, which is regarded as a financial investment. Second, it can refer to collateral that has been offered for a loan of some sort.

Segregated fund means a **mandate** (run by a **manager**) where you own shares and bonds entirely in your own name. The opposite is a **pooled fund**, where you own a fraction of each share in a pool alongside other investors. In a segregated fund, you can instruct your manager on how to vote; in a pooled fund, you may be able to suggest but are more likely to have to go along with whatever voting stance the manager chooses.

Stock selection is a method of analysis that aims to see what individual investments contributed to your **return**. It is related to **asset** allocation (which analyses the impact of choices between asset classes, geographies or industrial sectors).

Total return can be used in two related contexts. Investing for a total return means that you need not distinguish between the form of your **return**, either **income** or **capital** gains, because both are equally useful to you. In contrast, total return accounting is a way of accounting for **endowments** that are invested on a total return basis.

Tracker funds are the same as **passively** managed **funds**. Both are designed to mechanically replicate the **returns** of an **index**.

Trust, as in charitable trust, means in legal terms the purpose for which a charity is 'entrusted' with **assets**.

Uncertainty and **unpredictability** are better words for the concept of **risk** when people in fact mean **volatility**.

Volatility is a measure of how variable your **returns** can be. Generally speaking, the more volatile something is, the more unattractive it is and therefore the more you should be compensated for owning it with a higher expected return.

Working capital is the amount of cash you need from day to day to run your charity effectively, usually by not having to buy and sell **assets** at short notice to fill a gap in your cash flow. Working capital can be kept in a bank account or with a **manager** who has a cash **fund**.

Yield is simply the **income** received from an **asset** divided by the price of that asset. For example, if a share is worth £10 and gives you an income of £1, its yield is 10%. There are dozens of different types of yield calculations which illustrate different things.

Notes

1 See www.investopedia.com/financial-term-dictionary-4769738.
2 *Charities SORP (FRS 102)* [PDF], 2nd edition, Chartered Institute of Public Finance and Accounting, 2019, www.gov.uk/government/publications/charities-sorp-2005, accessed 20 January 2024.
3 Details of how to access the latest (2022) edition can be found at https://sarasinandpartners.com/compendium.
4 *Charities SORP (FRS 102)* [PDF], 2nd edition, Chartered Institute of Public Finance and Accounting, 2019, www.gov.uk/government/publications/charities-sorp-2005, accessed 20 January 2024.
5 Ibid.
6 Ibid.

Chapter one

Introduction

> There was a merchant who was so worried about the safety of his possessions that he sold them all and bought a lump of gold, which he buried on the outskirts of town. He had no greater pleasure than to visit it and to muse or dream. He did not own the gold – rather, the gold owned him. One day he found the gold was gone. He was distraught and told a neighbour of his loss. The neighbour told him to put a stone in its place – 'since you never meant to use it, the stone will be just as good as the gold'.
>
> Aesop, 6th century BC[1]

What is this book about?

Too often, charities' investment decisions focus on how to look after a portfolio rather than what the portfolio is for. This is inherently backwards, because what defines a charity is what it can do for its beneficiaries. The more it spends, the more it can help.

Charities have to make decisions about how much to spend and how much to keep for the future. This is one of the most important questions they have to answer, and yet – in my experience – it is rarely a topic of rigorous discussion. There are two main reasons for this. One is that many charities see their first duty as keeping the money safe rather than risking spending too much, in case they run out of money one distant day. They are like Aesop's merchant, who has lost sight of the fact that the purpose of money lies in how it is used.

The second reason is that, all too commonly, charities allow their investments to become their master rather than their servant. As such, instead of deciding how much money is enough to meet their spending goals, they become much more concerned with preserving the upward direction of a line on a graph.

The result is that the beneficiaries of many charities receive less than they might because charities can be too frightened to spend generously. One of the aims of this book is to change this mindset. Instead of seeing it as their first duty to protect their capital at all costs, charities should aim to do as much as possible for their beneficiaries, through both securing better investment returns and being more ambitious in their spending.

In other words, this book aims to shift the default from preserving capital to using investments more wisely. This will put you in charge of them, and not them in charge of you.

Who is this book for?

Anybody with any sort of responsibility for handling a charity's investments – whether stocks and shares, bonds, property, cash or anything else – should find much in this book to help them make better decisions on behalf of their charity. This includes trustees, CEOs and any staff who have input into deciding on or actioning a charity's financial strategy. No prior investing knowledge is assumed. Indeed, a lack of knowledge could even be an advantage given the unique nature of the charity investment sector, where the equal focus on spending and investment may not be best served by traditional ideas about investment success being reflected simply in a growing pile of money.

This is not a book for investment technicians; it is not full of calculations and models, but is based on sound general investment principles. If you have no investment background, these broad principles will enable you to understand how the investment industry works and why some of the common assumptions on which it operates are so important (and reliable). And, if you are a more experienced investor, you should find food for thought about how you measure financial success and whether good performance numbers are adequate metrics on their own. Whatever your background, I hope that this book's orientation towards spending, rather than accumulating money, will provide you with a fresh perspective.

Naturally, if your charity's income mostly comes from investments, you will have a stronger focus on driving investment returns than if fundraising underpins most of your spending. However, investments can still perform an important function in charities where they make up a smaller proportion of income (e.g. as the ballast for reserves), so it is important to understand how they perform. There is also no minimum level of investment at which understanding the principles starts to become relevant. For example, if you have £1,000 in a bank deposit account, understanding the principles of investing cash will be as relevant to you as to a larger investor. If investing matters to your charity's finances to any degree, it will always pay you to know how the process works.

Whatever the size of your charity, if you already have investments or are considering moving into this area, this book offers straightforward, pragmatic principles that you can put to use.

Is investing the right choice for your charity?

If you are coming to this book uncertain about whether investing is appropriate for your charity, you might want to start by turning to page 78, where you will find a discussion of how investing might sit within your charity's financial activities.

A note on investment managers

Generally, this book assumes that you will be working with an external investment manager, and chapter 10 goes into detail about the process of appointing a manager. There is nothing to stop charities handling their investments directly, and indeed some do, especially if their portfolio consists of property or they choose to invest in a pooled investment fund (see page 49). However, choosing such a fund is itself an investment decision. So, if you are considering making these decisions yourself, the Charity Commission expects you to take advice from someone – preferably impartial and experienced in investment matters – unless you have enough expertise at your charity or you are dealing with limited, low-value investments (see page 138). If you do decide to take matters into your own hands, there are four guiding principles to keep in mind:

- Regularly review the question of whether you ought to take advice and, if you should, how often that advice would be useful (the chapters in part II contain information that will help you).
- Makes sure the investments are suitable for your charity.

- Diversify, as far as is reasonable. Diversification is one of the Trustee Act 2000's standard investment criteria and so this is especially important, although note that the Act only says that you should *consider* diversifying (see page 138).
- Monitor your performance and compare it to what you'd get from other opportunities available to you (see chapter 11).

However, the reality is that the overwhelming majority of charities with any value in property, stocks and shares engage a professional investment management firm to make and manage direct investments for them.

Finally, if you are an investment manager who specialises in working with charity clients, this book will contain much to help you tailor your approach to the charity context. This is because it looks outside the narrow world of investing to the very reason that charities exist – to spend money on their beneficiaries.

What is different about this book?

There are dozens of books about investing, and beyond them a vast array of websites and publications on the topic. They are universally focused on making more money. In contrast, as outlined above, this book is as much about deciding how much to spend as it is about accumulating funds for spending. Obviously, you need to earn enough that there is something to be spent, and that is where investing comes in.

This book is also different because it is embedded in the charity sector. The existing guides about charitable investing are written by investment professionals, not charity practitioners, and tend to follow similar paths. They start with a description of the law as it relates to charities (as opposed to other investors), then outline the various asset classes and how they behave, and finally suggest how to get the best returns from those asset classes by combining them in different proportions. Most of this is generic investment knowledge rather than being specific to charities. It also ignores just how important spending is to charities as a driving factor in how their staff and trustees make decisions, especially when it comes to being ambitious for their beneficiaries. This book takes a holistic approach to the charity investing and spending journey, bringing together these different components into a system explicitly designed to earn a higher return, which is then fully spent. After all, that is a charity's purpose.

In other words, this book is written for and about charities. Its purpose is to give you – whether you are a charity trustee or staff – greater confidence in dealing with investments and questioning the investment and spending advice you are given, thus helping you to fulfil your duties of financial stewardship in a more informed and active way. For example, should your investment manager suggest that you might need to spend less in the future, this book will equip you to push back, consider a range of options and select the one that is most suitable for your beneficiaries. Even if you do in fact end up needing to spend less, at least your decision will have been robust and properly considered. After all, what is at stake is more than just investments.

How is this book structured?

This book is structured around the eight interlocking ideas shown in figure 1.1, with some additional chapters providing further information. Part I considers the four central components – the fundamentals of charity investing (at the centre of the triangle) – with a further chapter providing a grounding in the investment market:

- **Financial objectives and goals** (chapter 2) are at the heart of the book. Your financial objectives are broadly about what you want your charity's finances to look like in 10 to 20 years' time, encompassing *all* of your assets (not just your investment portfolio, which is just one contributing factor in your financial objectives). Within your financial objectives, you will also have a set of more detailed financial goals. Your success in meeting your financial objectives and goals is determined by the investment market and your policies in the three areas covered by chapters 4, 5 and 6.
- **The investment market** (chapter 3) is the ecosystem in which you will operate as a charity investor. You will need to have an overview of the various asset classes and the specifics of the charity investment market in order to make prudent decisions on behalf of your charity.
- **Spending** (chapter 4) is about deciding what you want to keep for the future and what you want to spend now. Your spending policy should maximise your ability to spend in line with your financial objectives and goals.
- **Investing** (chapter 5) concerns how you fund this spending (assuming that investments are the main driver of your spending). A successful investment strategy is based on an understanding of the constraints within which you need to operate as a charity investor, such as uncertainty and volatility.
- **Reserves** (chapter 6) measure what's left. Your policy around your desired level of reserves will reflect your financial objectives and goals. Therefore, being able to measure your reserves is a major aspect of knowing whether you have achieved the right balance between spending and investing for your charity.

Figure 1.1 The charity investment triangle

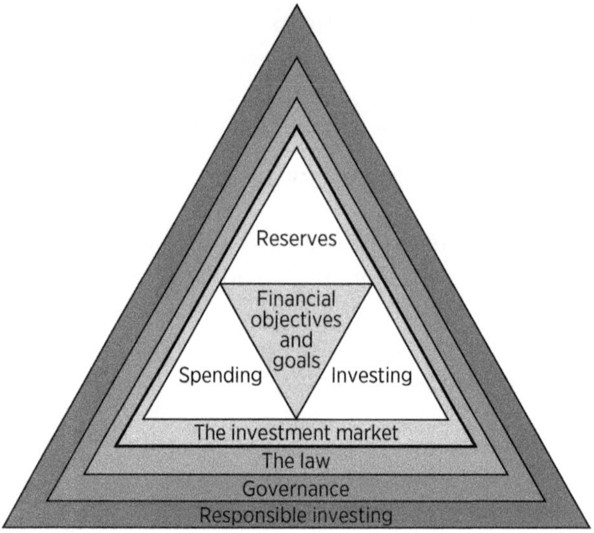

Part II of the book sets out a three-part framework that sits around your financial objectives and goals, and the fundamental approaches outlined in chapters 3–6. This framework provides the context around how your charity is organised and run. This in turn influences how your policies on spending and reserves and your investment strategy are developed and implemented, and it should be kept in mind throughout your charity's investment process:

- **The law** (chapter 7) circumscribes all of a charity's operations. This is especially relevant when it comes to developing your policies on investment, reserves and responsible investing, which are legal requirements and must be disclosed in your annual reports. This book deals with the law in England and Wales. The websites of the regulators for Scotland (www.oscr.org.uk/guidance-and-forms/charity-investments-guidance-and-good-practice) and Northern Ireland (www.charitycommissionni.org.uk) are good places to start if your charity is not based in England or Wales, although the Charity Commission for Northern Ireland refers to the Charity Commission for England and Wales website (www.gov.uk/government/organisations/charity-commission) when it comes to investment guidance.
- **Governance** (chapter 8) is about ensuring you have the people and organisational culture necessary to make good decisions and then hold fast to them, even in stressful situations. Good governance is the

cheapest aspect of investing and yet can have the greatest impact on returns.

- **Responsible investing** (chapter 9) is founded on your charity's values and beliefs. As you think about how you want to deliver your financial objectives and goals, you need to consider the relationships you want to have with the companies and people in which you invest. There is a whole range of options here, from simply excluding undesirable investments to considering your social impact more broadly.

The concepts in parts I and II are often approached as separate ideas, but in reality each one is bound into the others. Everything is linked and everything has a purpose, and that is to deliver more benefit to your beneficiaries in the best way that you see fit.

Next, part III of the book looks at two specific areas of management and implementation:

- **Appointing a manager** (chapter 10) concerns how to go about selecting your investment manager(s). This chapter walks you through the various steps of the process, including deciding what type(s) of manager you need, longlisting and shortlisting, and making and implementing your decision.
- **Performance reporting** (chapter 11) is vital as it lets you know what progress you are making towards your financial objectives and goals. This chapter sets out which questions you should ask and how to know you're getting accurate, dependable answers. After all, why set objectives and goals if you are never going to measure your progress against them?

Finally, chapter 12 summarises how all of these concepts fit together to enable you to spend as much as you can on your beneficiaries.

Fictional case studies

At the end of each chapter, you will find case studies showing how three entirely fictional charities approach three very different financial objectives (the three types of objective are fully introduced in chapter 2). These case studies put into practice the principles discussed in the chapters and illustrate how the balance between investment and spending can look very different depending on a charity's time horizon and priorities. The fictional case studies have been presented in detail to provide true-to-life examples of how different charities might approach the topic of investment.

Warden's Philanthropy

In 1860, Mr Gilbert left his entire estate of £200,000 as a permanent endowment to set up a charity to be named Warden's Philanthropy. As a self-made man, he decided to leave his entire fortune to the new charity instead of to his children, so his children could have the same opportunity that he'd had – to create their own fortune. His gift was inspired by the recently published book *The Warden* by Anthony Trollope. The book recounts how the trust deed of an almshouse named Hiram's Hospital was inadvertently written in such a way that the warden (who oversees the charity) ends up receiving more money than the beneficiaries, and Mr Gilbert is determined that no such thing will happen in his charity. Warden's Philanthropy's focus is on access and opportunity, in whatever form, for people in the Barchester area. It is now worth £40 million and has a strong sense of social purpose in how it invests its money and delivers its services. It awards a prestigious annual prize recognising effective social action.

Martello Tower Fund

The Martello Tower Fund (MTF) is one of a number of restricted funds within the charity Preserving Our Nautical Past. The charity's other income comes from fundraising and membership. The MTF is Preserving Our Nautical Past's most substantial asset but doesn't contribute to any of the charity's operational costs. The MTF was established with an endowment of £1 million to preserve a historic coastal fort. When it was set up, its endowment was given specifically so that the trustees would have sufficient money to build a higher sea wall at some future point to protect the fort against rising tides caused by climate change. It was left up to the trustees to decide when would be the best time to do this, as long as the wall is completed within 30 years. The timing will depend on whether the charity's assets grow faster than the building costs. If the assets grow well, the trustees have the option to create a lump sum that could be spent on some other project to celebrate the nautical past. Alternatively, if growth is less than planned, they may need to do a slightly less good job on the wall. In the meantime, they will have minimal spending on keeping the portfolio ticking over and monitoring whether to build now or later.

Butterworth Music Festivals

Butterworth Music Festivals was set up in 2003 by an eccentric music lover shortly before her death. It was named after her hero, George Butterworth, who was an avid collector of English folk songs and died on the day the donor was born – on 5 August 1916. Its purpose is to spend £10 million on bringing music to communities that otherwise might not enjoy any live performances. There are no instructions beyond this, but the trustees know that the donor particularly enjoyed laying on high-quality performances in villages of less than 250 people. This approach appealed to her sense of the whimsical and her dislike of the trend for 'value for money' in philanthropy – 'the worse the better', she once said. The trustees therefore have wide discretion in how to use this money, but they have to spend it all within ten years of their first grant. Otherwise, any residue at that time will be gifted to the government to advance general social well-being.

Conclusion

Books about investing invariably treat the subject as an end in itself; however, as the representative of a charity, you will ultimately be concerned with spending. As such, maximising the effectiveness of your investment portfolio is crucial, but this must always be done with an unwavering focus on your financial objectives and goals, which in turn should reflect your charitable purposes. Growing an investment portfolio should never be an end in itself, and that is what this book seeks to make clear. After all, your charitable status comes from what your charity spends, not what it saves.

Notes

1 Adapted from various versions of this tale.

PART I
Fundamentals

Chapter two

Financial objectives and goals

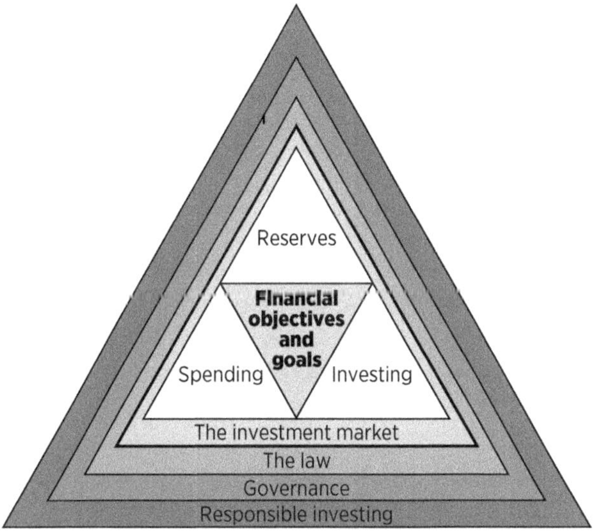

The purpose of this chapter

Your financial objectives relate to whether your charity plans to grow, shrink or stay the same size, and it is vital to begin your investment journey by understanding this most basic distinction and how it applies to your charity. This chapter is therefore the bedrock of this whole book.

The chapter sets out the three main types of financial objective and explains the difference between financial objectives and goals. It shows how having clarity around your financial objectives and goals can keep you focused on your spending (the reason for your charitable status), help you to develop your investment policy, and provide ways to measure your progress and ensure accountability. The chapter then examines the various factors that go into deciding on your financial objectives and goals.

Finally, the three case studies at the end of the chapter show how these principles might be put into practice.

What are financial objectives and goals?

Your overall financial objective is your charity's overarching drive or focus in terms of how it approaches its financial aspirations, including its investment ones. It can be helpful to think of there being three financial objectives:

- **Spender charities** want to spend as much as they can but also maintain the value of their assets far into the future.
- **Saver charities** want to accumulate enough money to reach a specific goal, after which they will spend the money on their beneficiaries.
- **Spend-out charities** want to spend everything until there is nothing left at the end of a given period.

Additionally, within your overarching financial objective of being a saver, spender or spend-outer, you will have financial goals. These are more detailed, specific statements that break down how you intend to implement your overarching financial objective. For example, if you are a spender charity, your financial goals might include some or all of the following:

- to achieve the highest return available to us;
- to grow our spending on our beneficiaries over time and in line with inflation;
- to try to maintain our assets in line with inflation as measured by the Consumer Prices Index;
- to be tolerant of volatile asset values from year to year;
- to be less tolerant of year-to-year spending volatility;
- to align our values about how we invest with our spending purpose as far as possible;
- to support and enable steadfast financial governance.

Whatever goals you choose, they should support you in achieving your overarching financial objective.

You may already have spotted that the three fictional case studies introduced in chapter 1 correspond with the three financial objectives. Throughout the rest of this book, sections at the end of each chapter will follow the three fictional charities as they work through the process of developing and implementing their different approaches to investment:

- **Spender charity**: Warden's Philanthropy is a Victorian charity set up to support access and opportunity for people in the Barchester area. It wants to do as much as it can for its beneficiaries. In line with the inspiration behind its founding, it plans not to get bigger, preferring to spend any surplus (after inflation) on its beneficiaries. In other words, it wants neither to grow nor shrink, but just spend.
- **Saver charity**: The Martello Tower Fund is a restricted fund within a larger heritage charity (Preserving Our Nautical Past). The fund is to be used to build a sea wall to protect a historic fort from rising sea levels. This needs to be completed within the next 30 years. However, until then, the fund will have no spending, so all it has to do is save as much as it can (as well as earn as much as it can to make a healthy surplus). So, for the next 30 years, it can just save.
- **Spend-out charity**: Butterworth Music Festivals is a new charity established by an elderly eccentric music lover. The donor specified that the entire sum must be spent within ten years of the first grant being made or the balance would be given to the government. Consequently, the charity is entirely focused on protecting what it has and then spending it to avoid it being given to the government.

The subsections below look at the three overarching financial objectives in more depth. The remainder of the chapter then goes into further detail about why you should have an overarching financial objective and financial goals, and how to decide which ones are right for your charity.

Spender charities

Staying about the same size is by far the most common objective of investment-led charities. It is also the mandatory approach for charities with a permanent endowment (as explored on page 140). If you are a spender charity, it means that you plan to be able to spend roughly the same amount on things from year to year (i.e. after inflation) as you do now in real terms (see box below). Sometimes this is referred to as 'intergenerational equity', which means that a charity does not plan to spend more (or less) on a future generation than the current one. Charities commonly see caution as a good thing, but being overly cautious can mean spending less on your current beneficiaries, and that can undermine the scope of your charity's current plans (this topic is explored further on page 57).

In practice, you won't ever be able to completely guarantee being able to spend the same amount in the future as you do now, because the future is unknowable. However, by understanding what uncertainties you are likely to face and how you might mitigate them (covered in chapter 5), you will give yourself the best chance of coming as close as you can to your target. The best way to combat the uncertainty is to err on the side of spending a little too much for a little too long, rather than spending too little and missing opportunities. The risk is that you will spend a little more now and end up doing more good earlier than you intended.

What does 'real terms' mean?

If you aim to have the same money in real terms in the future as you do now, it means that you aim for the value of your money to keep pace with inflation. For example, you might notice that your favourite brand of chocolate bar is now twice as expensive as it was when you were younger. If your money had kept its value in real terms, you would now have twice as much money as when you were younger, so you could still buy the same number of chocolate bars as you did before. This is a fundamental concept to understand when you are setting goals for the future.

Saver charities

Sometimes a charity will have a particular purpose that it cannot currently achieve, either because it doesn't yet have enough money or because the means to deliver the purpose is not yet available. An example might be a charity that is accumulating a fund that will enable it to rehome polar bears if the Arctic ice cap melts. If this kind of situation applies to you, you could set a target for the amount of money you want to reach and when you might need it – in other words, a target for how much you want to grow and by when (whether that is a specific date or an event that will happen at some unknown point). It is also possible to set a target to just make as much money as possible between now and your end date.

It is important to remember that when people talk about 'growing', what they generally mean is that the growth will be on top of any inflation. Chapter 4 goes into much more detail about the impacts of inflation and deflation (see page 67). The key point is that if your growth from your investments doesn't take inflation into account, you might not be growing in real terms. The result could be that your growth won't actually pay for whatever it is you wanted to buy at the end of your period of saving. Therefore, always make sure to build inflation into your plans.

Spend-out charities

Some charities have a specific mandate to spend their money (or a specific portion of their money) on their charitable purposes within a foreseeable time frame, perhaps over five to ten years. If this applies to you, it might be set out in your governing document or have been decided by your trustees, and it might apply to a particular fund or your whole charity. If it applies to all of your assets, your charity will naturally be wound up afterwards, having achieved its mission. All that will be left is your good works, and perhaps a report. Charities that have a permanent endowment (see chapter 6) are not allowed to spend out in this way.

Applying the financial objectives to suit your charity

Different objectives over time and for different funds

It is likely that you will already know which of the three financial objectives applies to your charity, but keep in mind that a financial objective is not necessarily fixed in stone. A saver charity will one day become a spender or spend-outer. Similarly, the trustees of a spender charity might decide to spend out over some future years if they believe that is the best way to support the charity's beneficiaries.

Additionally, your charity might have different financial objectives for different funds. For example, it is quite valid to grow one of your funds while spending out another (as long as you adhere to the relevant legal restrictions attached to specific endowments and donations; see chapter 7).

Investment-led versus other types of charity

It is also important to understand that these objectives apply differently to different types of charity. If your charity obtains most of its income from investments, your overarching financial objective will be closely tied to your investing and spending activities. It will determine your spending (see chapter 4) as well as your investing and attitude to uncertainty about the future (see chapter 5), and it will govern how both concepts will be supported by and reflected in your reserves (see chapter 6). Being clear about your overarching financial objective at the outset is therefore critical to your success.

Even if investments only contribute a small amount of your charity's income, the three financial objectives still apply – it is just that they will only influence a limited portion of your charity's financial activities or hold a specific purpose within your charity's balance sheet, rather than underpinning its entire approach to finance. As such, it is just as important to be clear about your overarching financial objective in these circumstances to ensure that your investments can reliably support your other activities.

For example, your charity might primarily rely on fundraising for its income but also have a small pot of investments that acts as a ballast in its reserves. In this case, the role of your investments will be to provide assurance about your ongoing solvency and liquidity by providing a fund you can draw upon as and when it is needed. In these circumstances, this pot of money's financial objective is likely to be that of a spend-out charity, which is focused on capital preservation and assumes that the money will be spent within a short period, when and if it is required. You just won't always know when the period of spending will begin, because like any reserve, the money is there for when it is needed, which in this case is when other sources of income dry up.

Why have financial objectives and goals?

Defining your financial objectives and goals will help to keep your investing focused on your charitable purpose in various ways. For example, it will help you to avoid an unthinking bias towards assuming that having more money is always better, and it will help you to measure your long-term progress and demonstrate accountability.

To avoid defaulting to a 'spend less' approach

As should be clear by now, the point of a charity is to spend as much money as it can – it is its spending that makes it charitable. Restricting your spending simply to become a bigger charity means that you are failing in your charitable purpose. It is spending, not saving, that matters.

Some charities will have a clear reason to grow their money for the time being, with the intention of delaying their spending until later – these are the genuine savers. But this should not be the default approach. For example, for a charity that wants to maintain its size in real terms, a growing balance sheet should be regarded as a measure of failure, not success.

In figure 2.1, the dark grey bars represent the amounts of money two charities have at the end of a given period and the light grey bars show how much each has spent over the same period. You can see that Charity A has more money left than Charity B because it has spent much less than Charity B. But which is more successful?

Let us assume that both charities have started with the same amount and have at least maintained their investments against inflation. Conventionally, you might assume that Charity A has been more successful because it now has more assets than Charity B. However, if both charities had chosen either spending or spending out as their financial objective, Charity B would actually be the more successful because it had spent more. Think about it from the point of view of beneficiaries: if you were a beneficiary of Charity A, you wouldn't feel that great about all that money still stuck in the charity.

Figure 2.1 Asset values: bigger is not necessarily better

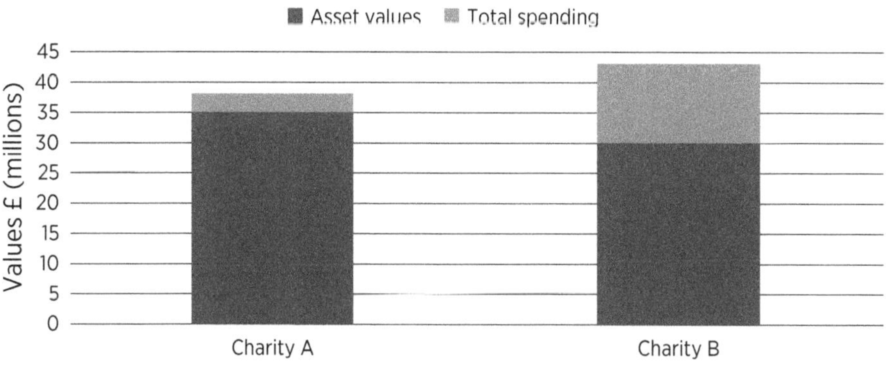

But not only has Charity A been unnecessarily frugal, it has also been a much worse investor. If you look at the combination of what each charity has spent and what it has left, you can see clearly that the stack for Charity B is much taller than that for Charity A. This means that Charity B must have earned a higher return than Charity A as well as having spent more of it.

In short, the trustees of Charity A probably feel very pleased with themselves because they have now got even more money than before, and more than Charity B, but that misses the point. It is Charity B that has been more successful because it has both earned more and spent more.

A good charity will maximise what it spends as well as what it earns – with the caveat, of course, that the money must be spent wisely, not wastefully. Having clear financial objectives and goals can help to keep you focused on what you want to achieve for your beneficiaries – and when – and avoid the common trap of unthinkingly focusing on growth.

Why shouldn't spender charities seek to grow their portfolio so they can spend more in the future?

Charities invest both in their beneficiaries (by spending) and in financial markets (by investing). Both provide returns – one social and the other financial. Spending well on your charity's purpose should generate social returns for your beneficiaries that you should expect to dwarf your long-term financial returns. But sometimes spender charities underestimate the power of this social impact and instead want to grow their portfolio in real terms – by saving money they might otherwise spend. The argument usually cited to justify this approach is that their spending is not generating a high enough social return or that they do not have the capacity to spend more. If that is the case for your charity, then you need to work out why and try to use your money more effectively. You owe it to your current beneficiaries to repurpose your resources to serve them better now, rather than putting the unknown beneficiaries of the future first, not least because avoiding the problem doesn't solve the underlying issue of not being able to spend enough, or wisely enough.

There are no circumstances where a spending charity can justify saving now simply so it can have more assets to spend more in the future. If it does seek above-inflation growth in this way, then the implication is that it has more confidence in its investing prowess than its ability to spend wisely – and that is not what should be happening in a well-run charity.

To help you develop your investment policy statement and work with your investment manager

An investment policy statement (see chapter 8) sets out what your investment goals are, who you are delegating to (i.e. an external investment manager) and the limits of that delegation. It is a key document as it forms the basis of the decisions your investment manager (covered in detail in chapter 10) will make on your behalf.

However, your financial objectives and goals are different from your investment objectives. Your financial objectives and goals will be broader than what is in your investment policy statement – and they will largely determine it – because they will tie into the whole of your charity's finances. Their purpose is to set out some charity-wide principles focusing on broad issues such as what you want to spend (or keep) across your whole charity, how stable you want your spending budgets to be, and how your approach will relate to your values and beliefs. As such, you cannot begin to formulate the details of your investment policy before you have clear financial objectives and goals.

Equally, once you get to the point of engaging an investment manager, how they approach the management of your assets will be informed by your wider plans and your financial objectives and goals. The main means of formal instruction between your charity and your investment manager will be your investment policy statement, so you will want to incorporate your wider financial objectives and goals into your investment policy statement so that your manager understands the context in which you require them to operate. For example, if you plan to spend out your entire portfolio within ten years, your investment manager will need to know that so they can build a portfolio that will give you confidence about what you can spend over that timescale. Equally, if having a stable expenditure budget from year to year is very important to you, you need to make that clear to your manager so they can find the most sustainable and stable way of distributing cash to you.

What is an investment manager?

In simple terms, an investment manager is a firm that you instruct to help you invest your money. You may have one manager or multiple ones.

Technically, a manager is always a firm, even if you always see the same rather engaging person from the firm at your meetings. Both the individual and the firm are confusingly referred to as a 'manager'. However, the reality is that the individual is simply part of the firm you have appointed and the term 'manager' is often used interchangeably to refer to firms and the people who represent them. These might include the individuals who meet clients or those who buy stocks and shares – or anything in between.

For now, as you read, just keep in mind that 'manager' may refer to an identifiable human who works for a firm or it may refer to the firm itself. You can ask either of these to help you invest your money, but this will invariably be using their own products (see page 48). Individuals cannot operate as investment managers on their own; they will always be part of a firm. People who advise you, but who do not manage money for you, are usually known as consultants.

To help you measure your progress

Surprisingly, many charities do not seem to explain to their stakeholders whether they are planning to grow, shrink or stay roughly the same size – and, if so, why. Many seem quite happy to say that they invest for 'income and capital growth' without being any more specific. This usually means that they are happy to grow a little larger every year in real terms, rather than increasing their spending. This is little better than functioning on autopilot.

An important reason to have financial objectives and goals is to help you measure your progress. This is because if you don't have a clear target, you can't know whether you have achieved it. For example, if you are committed to maintaining the value of your portfolio against inflation (or even beating inflation), you need to know what the value would have been if your portfolio had simply grown with inflation – in other words, a target. Once you have this target, all you need to do is check whether the value of your portfolio is higher or lower – after spending – to know whether you have been successful in meeting your goal.

To demonstrate accountability

If a charity had an annual fundraising surplus that grew slowly over time without being used, donors would begin to ask questions about why further gifts were necessary. A donor's assumption is that their gift is 'much needed', and a lot of fundraising messaging is developed to make that point. Investing is another form of raising funds, so why would an ever-increasing investing surplus be any more acceptable than an unused fundraising surplus?

One point to bear in mind is that some charities, especially in scientific fields, will not be able to spend everything they can if they do not have enough funding opportunities of sufficient quality. After all, funding bad science is not only wasteful but also dangerous because it can give legitimacy to poor practice. Such quality thresholds can lead to charities being unable to spend all their resources wisely and consequently inadvertently grow their asset base. Where funders do struggle with a quality shortage, part of their accountability activities should involve explaining how they are attempting to create an increased demand for their growing resources (e.g. by encouraging funding applications from high-quality applicants) rather than quietly allowing their funds to accumulate.

If you agree that the standards of accountability for gifts are the same whether the source is from a fundraising campaign or an investment portfolio, investment-led charities need to justify keeping surplus investment returns just as much as fundraising-led charities seek to justify keeping surplus fundraising income. Having clarity on your financial objectives and goals can help you demonstrate to stakeholders that there are clear reasons for your investment decisions – and that you are delivering on those decisions.

To clarify your position on responsible investing

Most charities now believe that their values should permeate all of their activities, including how they treat their beneficiaries, staff, suppliers and other stakeholders. The focus might be on protecting the charity's reputation or it might be on advancing the charity's purpose in some way. You will therefore likely want to record not only what you want to achieve in financial terms but also how you want to achieve it. This is especially true if you deliver your purpose as much through your investing (such as by building sheltered housing to rent out) as through your spending. Chapter 9 goes into much more detail on the topic of responsible investing.

Deciding on your financial objective and goals

If the bulk of your income comes from investments, it is likely that you will already have a pretty solid instinctive understanding of what your overarching financial objective is. However, if investments make up a smaller (and perhaps hitherto slightly neglected) portion of your income, you might need to think more carefully about what function you want your portfolio to have in the wider context of your charity's activities. And, whatever the main source of your income, you may find that your detailed financial goals need a bit more thought about how investments fit in.

It is important to define your financial objectives and goals and record them publicly, at least in your annual report and accounts and perhaps in a separate document, because they will form the financial backbone of how your charity operates (if you are an investment-led charity) or set out your standards for accountability for this part of your finances (if investments make up a smaller proportion of your income). Even if you already have a pretty good idea of what your objectives and goals are and how you want to go about achieving them, it is likely they will benefit from being hardened up, written down and periodically reviewed.

The following subsections look in detail at the main considerations behind your choice of financial objectives and goals.

Your charitable purposes, wider strategy, and values and beliefs

Your financial objectives are closely related to several core concepts:

- your **charitable purposes**, or the legal reason your charity exists;[1]
- your **strategy**, or the detailed plan for how you intend to enact your charitable purposes;
- your **values** and **beliefs** (which you might describe as your vision and mission), which should be consistent with your charitable purposes and strategy, and will underpin all of the decisions you make as an organisation.

Figure 2.2 shows how these concepts relate to one another. The important thing to remember is that your financial objectives summarise how your charity's money will be put to use to achieve your charitable purposes and strategy, within the guiding principle of your values and beliefs.

Figure 2.2 Relating your financial objectives and goals to the wider context of your charity

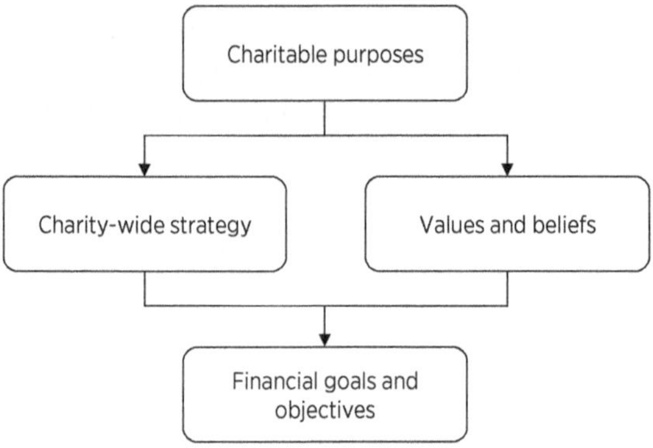

Values and beliefs will also feed into your responsible investment policy. It is becoming seen as increasingly important for charities to find alignment between how they earn their money and how they spend it.[2] This is an area you should consider carefully as it can come with significant reputational risks. See chapter 9 for more on responsible investing and your reputation.

Your time horizon, or when you will need the money back

The concept of time is inherent to all three types of financial objective:

- The **spend-out** objective is obviously defined by its timescale as the objective is to spend all the money (either across the whole charity or within a specific fund) before a specific deadline.
- In the **saving** objective, time becomes more salient the closer a charity gets to the point where it must stop saving and start spending. This becomes more complex if the saving target has no known end date (as in the polar bear example on page 16, where it is not known when the ice caps will have melted sufficiently to require polar bears to be rehomed). If this applies to your charity, you will need to agree a provisional time horizon that might be updated as events progress.
- In the **spending** objective, the time horizon is potentially infinitely long and the goal will likely be to continue to exist in perpetuity. In practice, it seems that charities' sense of their future is related to their sense of their past. If a charity was founded in 1123, it will probably expect to continue to exist for another thousand years. However, if it was founded in 1999, it might not think much further ahead than 2050 or so. There is no right answer here and the appropriate time horizon will depend on your charity's history, purposes and wider strategy.

Whatever your overarching financial objective, time matters because the nearer you are to your time horizon, the more certainty you will want to have about how much your assets are worth (see the next subsection), so you can plan your spending end game. In contrast, the further away your horizon – certainly if you are looking beyond five years – the more important the effects of inflation become (see page 67).

Volatility in your investments

The shorter your time horizon, the less uncertainty you will want about how much money you actually have, especially if you are spending out. If you might spend the money in the near future (whether on a known commitment or as a result of an unexpected problem that forces you to liquidate your reserves, such as your fundraising drying up), you will want its value to be steady, not bouncing around. In contrast, if you use your investments to generate income to spend, you might not be so worried about year-to-year volatility in what your investments are worth so long as your spending is likely to be reasonably stable. There are many ways of smoothing spending from year to year, and this removes the direct link between your annual expenditure budget and the value of your assets (see chapter 4). What matters is the trend in the growth of your portfolio and its long-term return.

Broadly speaking, the higher the return of a type of asset, the higher the associated volatility. Therefore, establishing your attitude to volatility and unpredictability early on in the process of designing your approach to investing helps to avoid the dilemma that so many investors experience between the twin emotions of fear (that they will lose a lot of money) and greed (the idea that they could be making more). Chapter 5 goes into much more detail on this balancing act.

Variation in your spending

Just as avoiding volatility in your asset values is important if you want to be confident that you will always be solvent, it is important to consider your attitude to variations in your spending. If your overarching objective is to save towards a financial goal (to spend later), then you will not be concerned about your spending going up or down from year to year because you will barely be spending anything anyway. However, if your investment income pays all of your staff members' salaries with little to spare, then you will be much more concerned about month-to-month volatility in how much you can spend. In this case, you will need to be sure you have enough to cover your needs and will have much less room to manoeuvre.

Asset value stability and spending stability are distinct from each other and have very different implications. For example, grant-making charities often find that they need spending stability more than asset value stability. It is very simple to stop making grants (i.e. control your costs) but it takes much longer to get a grant-making programme going again because you have to spend time communicating your programme to potential applicants and processing applications. In other words, grant-makers can find that their brakes work well but their accelerator is less responsive. Consequently, stopping and starting programmes and grants may be an unattractive option both for your charity and for your beneficiaries, so it is crucial that your financial objectives and goals take account of the level of spending stability that you need.

The assets that you want to include

It is important to consider which assets to include in your financial objectives and goals. The pictures here differ significantly depending on whether your charity is primarily funded by investments or whether investments make up a smaller portion of your overall financial activities.

If your charity is investment-led, the temptation might be to apply your objectives and goals narrowly, and include only your investment portfolio. A broader approach is to include all of your assets and liabilities – for example, investments, cash, property, and the grants and other commitments you have already promised to beneficiaries and suppliers but haven't yet spent. This usually gives a more accurate picture because it measures the entire wealth of your charity (as measured by its balance sheet rather than just its investment portfolio) and it tells you precisely what you have left and how much you could spend (or keep).

Alternatively, if investments perform a more limited function within your charity, it may be more appropriate to include only a specific set of assets within the remit of your financial objectives and goals. There are a number of ways to think about this and to decide which assets to include. For example, you might include the investment assets related to a particular fund within your charity that supports either general expenditure or a specific line of activity. Or you might choose to include the assets that underpin how your reserves work, such as by providing liquidity and accountability. They could be your investment assets, whether in stocks and shares or in property, or related assets such as loans or programme-related investments, where doing good is at least as important as achieving a financial return.

The point is the same as for any sort of objective or goal: if you are interested in the outcome, you will need to somehow measure it, and to do that you will need to define what you intend to measure so you can see whether you have been successful or not.

Fictional case studies

Spender: Warden's Philanthropy

Founded in 1860, Warden's Philanthropy has a permanent endowment worth £40 million. It has a strong sense of social purpose, not only in how it spends but also in how it invests, not least because of its nationally recognised prize for social action.

The key concept here is intergenerational equity. The trustees want to spend as much as they can while maintaining their ability to spend a similar amount into the future, in real terms. However, if they spend too much now, they will have less to spend for the future, and vice versa. Because they are dealing with the future, the trustees know that they will never get the balance exactly right, so they like to err on the side of confidently spending more now, rather than being seen to have accidentally built up money they could have otherwise spent (of which the charity's original donor would have profoundly disapproved). As such, over the long term, the trustees would like the charity's investment returns to cover its spending, the fees it pays its investment manager and the effects of inflation. However, they know they can't be certain that this will be the case (nothing is certain) and they accept that, so they just try their best and aim to spend wisely and monitor the outcome.

The trustees are happy for their assets to be volatile as long as they will have stable budgets from year to year – they don't want to appear disorganised by providing inconsistent levels of grants or prize money (even though it is the prestige of the award that matters, not the size).

Their requirements and financial goals are summarised in table 2.1.

Table 2.1 Requirements and financial goals for Warden's Philanthropy

Requirements	
Time horizon	More than ten years
Volatile assets	✓
Inflation protection	✓
Predictable amount to spend	✓
Growing reserves	✗

Financial goals

- To grow the charity's assets in line with inflation over the long term
- To provide a stable level of annual expenditure, sustainable into the future
- To invest with careful regard to the charity's reputation

Saver: Martello Tower Fund

The Martello Tower Fund is a substantial fund within the fundraising charity Preserving Our Nautical Past (PONP). It has £1 million to protect a historic coastal fort against rising sea levels. The trustees have appointed an investment committee, which has decided to try to grow the £1 million as quickly as possible so there will be enough money not only to build the sea wall but also to leave a surplus for other projects. They need to build their wall within 30 years.

The committee can take a very long view of their investment horizon, but eventually they will have to build the wall (at which point they will change the fund's objective to spending out). All that matters at the moment is that the value of the investments must go up more quickly than the cost of building the sea wall. The key here is inflation: if the inflation of construction costs is greater than the increase in the assets, the fund will be losing money in real terms. Because the trustees are not spending, they should be able to invest for a high return without having to worry about the year-to-year volatility of the fund's assets. And, if the assets fell in value in the next decade or so, they could wait to start the work once the value had recovered.

PONP has a number of other funds (some spending out and others saving) as well as a fundraising campaign and income from its properties. The trustees of PONP have decided that each fund should have its own financial objective so they do not get confused about the status of any individual fund. Since the work of the charity celebrates nautical engineers and designers, the trustees want to acknowledge the importance of engineering in society through an investment approach that supports and promotes the work of engineers.

The charity's requirements and financial goals are summarised in table 2.2.

Table 2.2 Requirements and financial goals for the Martello Tower Fund

Requirements	
Time horizon	Less than 30 years
Volatile assets	✓
Inflation protection	✓
Predictable amount to spend	✗
Growing reserves	✓

Financial goals

- To maximise the fund's growth over 30 years
- To exceed the rate of the construction industry's inflation over 30 years
- To be able to liquidate the portfolio with five years' notice
- To invest while recognising the engineering roots of the charity

Spend-outer: Butterworth Music Festivals

This charity was set up in 2003 and plans to spend its entire £10 million on music festivals within ten years of its first grant.

The trustees recognise that this time horizon is so short that they can have no appetite for investment losses. They will be taking money out of the portfolio every quarter and cannot afford any uncertainty about its value. The trustees accept that theirs will therefore be a low-returning portfolio, perhaps only maintaining its value against inflation, but that is a price they are happy to pay for financial certainty. The trustees haven't expressed any views on their attitude to responsible investing.

Their requirements and financial goals are summarised in table 2.3.

Table 2.3 Requirements and financial goals for Butterworth Music Festivals

Requirements	
Time horizon	Ten years
Volatile assets	✗
Inflation protection	✓
Predictable amount to spend	✓
Growing reserves	✗

Financial goals

- To spend all the assets within ten years of the first grant
- To maintain the value against inflation
- To have high and reliable liquidity
- To be able to spend quickly, wisely and decisively

Conclusion

Financial objectives and goals matter because they articulate the whole basis on which you will spend, invest and measure your progress, whether this applies to your whole charity or a single fund. Clarifying your financial objectives and goals helps you to stay focused on spending as much as you can on your beneficiaries, at the most appropriate times. This is the topic of chapter 4, but first chapter 3 outlines the environment in which you will be investing.

Notes

1 'Charitable purposes' [web page], Charity Commission for England and Wales, 2013, www.gov.uk/government/publications/charitable-purposes/charitable-purposes, accessed 20 January 2024.

2 See, for example, *Stepping Up to the Climate Crisis* [PDF], Association of Charitable Foundations, 2023, https://acf.org.uk/common/Uploaded%20files/Research%20and%20resources/Research/FCCC_report_2023.pdf, accessed 20 January 2024.

Chapter three

The investment market

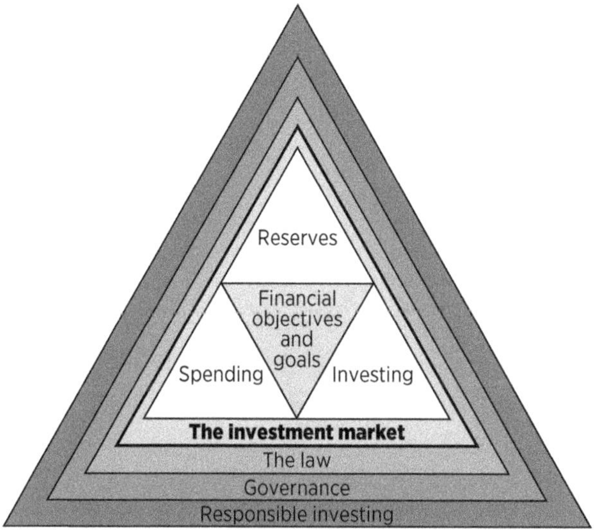

The purpose of this chapter

This chapter explains how different asset classes behave and how they interact with each other. It focuses on the crucial area of understanding how your appetite for unpredictable returns can be translated into an investment strategy (i.e. how you allocate your various assets). This will support getting your asset mix right and increase the chance that you will get the best possible result for your own circumstances. The choice between two managers, over the long term, makes little difference; it is the asset allocation that holds the power.

The chapter starts by explaining what types of asset are available to you. It then looks at fund types and the difference between passive and active management. A short section examines the contentious subject of taking advice, and the chapter then moves on to the topic of legal structures. Finally, the fictional case studies give examples of how asset choice can look in practice.

Asset types and their characteristics

There are many different ways to invest, each with their own attributes. But what matters as much as these attributes is how they are mixed together to deliver the best balance of reward and uncertainty. This section provides an outline of the five main asset classes – cash, bonds, property, public equities and alternatives. It concludes with an examination of how these asset classes can be combined within portfolios or funds, particularly focusing on mixtures of these asset types that are common investment choices for charities.

This is a simple and high-level guide to these asset types. There are hundreds, even thousands, of guides that delve into the details in more depth. If you have a deep interest, then see the start of the Glossary for some suggested starting points.

A note about expected performance

The returns figures given in the following sections for cash, bonds, property and equities are based on a history of 123 years.[1] Over that time, equities provided a 4% higher return than cash, a 3% higher return than bonds and, by extension, perhaps 1% or 2% higher than global commercial property. But remember that there will have been many periods over the 123 years that did not look like the average and where performance will have been completely different from, and even reversed, these figures. These are not laws; they are statistics. This book is dedicated to helping you understand such fluctuations and deal with them appropriately for your charity.

Cash

At its best, cash is the ultimate source of liquidity; at its worst, it is an illusion of reassurance. The only reason to invest in cash is to have secure liquidity – its real return is usually so low that there can be no other justification. Cash investors should always select their investments based on the following priorities, and only in this order:

1. **Security:** you always want access to your cash, especially in the most serious crisis, so the organisation that is holding it must not go bust. Some governments are good counterparties (see the box below) for this purpose.

2. **Liquidity:** you must be able to get your cash back when you need it, not when the borrower can repay it.
3. **Return:** too often, investors pride themselves on getting a marginally higher return by putting their money into a far less reliable bank and with a long period of time before the capital is returned. Remember that when you are taking risk, never take it with cash – that's not what it is for.

Too often people get this list precisely the wrong way round and that can be a recipe for disaster.

Types of cash investment

There are two main types of cash investment: bank deposits and cash funds. Both cash investments and bonds (see below) rely on independent institutions called credit rating agencies to pass judgement on the relative safety of counterparties, as explained in the box below.

Credit ratings and counterparties

Credit ratings are vital to understanding the creditworthiness of the person or organisation (often called a 'counterparty') to whom you are lending your money (it is important to understand that when you invest money, you are actually lending it). In investment terms, the counterparty might be the firm that holds your money or an individual company in which that firm has invested.

Counterparties are rated (assessed) by credit reference agencies such as Fitch Ratings, Moody's or S&P Global (formerly Standard and Poor's). Each agency has a slightly different labelling system, but each does the same thing: they score every publicly issued piece of debt (e.g. a bond) on a scale. From these scores, each debt issuer (e.g. a government that issues bonds or a company that issues shares) receives a rating. Generally, the more As in a rating, the better. AAA is more secure than A. BBB is the lowest form of 'investment-grade' credit. BB and lower are referred to as non-investment grade, or often as 'junk'. Ratings may change over time, with some firms becoming more creditworthy and being upgraded to investment grade, and others travelling in the opposite direction.

All other things being equal, the higher the rating, the lower the interest rate the counterparty will expect to pay to attract investors (because the counterparty will be more likely to repay the loan). And, conversely, the lower the rating, the higher the interest rate: in order to attract capital, junk bonds pay a much higher rate of interest than investment-grade bonds. At the time of writing, the most secure borrower is the US government, followed by other governments in decreasing order of safety. Many corporations (such as Amazon) are safer to lend to than many governments (such as Argentina) because they are less likely to default (i.e. not repay your money).

Bank deposits

In the UK, bank deposits up to £85,000 are guaranteed under the government's Financial Services Compensation Scheme (FSCS) (see www.fscs.org.uk). This cap covers all the deposits you might have with any one bank, and is not per account. Where relevant, you should consider having a number of deposit accounts at different banks to take advantage of multiples of the £85,000 protection. The only limiting factor in this regard is the administration involved in opening so many accounts. Most credit unions also enjoy FSCS protection.

Cash funds

Cash funds are cash deposit schemes run by investment managers. These usually offer higher rates of interest than bank deposit accounts and are highly diversified (see page 91). The most important things to look for in these funds are as follows:

- How much money is invested in it, or the **pool size**: the larger the pool, the less likely that there will be pressure on the fund's liquidity if a large investor removes their money from the fund.
- As explained in the box above, the fund's **credit rating** indicates how likely it is to be able to return your capital in a generally financially difficult environment. It is usually best to stick with a high investment grade (i.e. lots of As).
- You should be able to **access your money** within a period you can accept. Be very careful of any fund that can 'gate' you. To understand this concept, think of a farmyard gate where only one sheep (or investor) is allowed out at once. You should not invest in a fund that can prevent you from taking your cash out when you need it.

Total returns from cash

Total returns from cash tend to be just under 1% more than inflation over the long run.

Bonds

A bond generally involves an exchange of money where the borrower is obliged to pay interest to the lender (or investor) on specific dates and at an agreed rate, such as 5%, until the loan is repaid (usually up to 50 years in the future, and sometimes indefinitely). This is why bonds are also known as 'fixed-interest' investments – the interest rate is usually fixed – but they can often be referred to as 'credit' investments.

Bonds can be bought and sold by investors, either privately or on public markets, during the course of their life, with the borrower remaining unchanged and the current holder entitled to the income and repayment of the principal (i.e. the initial amount borrowed). Different bonds can give different levels of priority over other lenders (e.g. shareholders if the borrower is a company) for income and the return of their principal if the borrower becomes insolvent. In other words, they have more protection (and less risk) than other lenders.

Organisations that commonly issue bonds include governments, companies, other organisations (such as non-governmental organisations or universities) and cross-border bodies such as the European Bank for Reconstruction and Development. The public bond market is much larger than the public equity markets.

How bonds work: an example

Consider a particular bond where the income paid is fixed at £5 for every £100 issued. This is called the 'coupon'. If the bond is worth £100 and the coupon is £5, the yield will be 5%. However, if the price of the bond falls by half (to £50), that £5 coupon will now be worth 10%, so the yield (as a percentage) will go up.

In practical terms, you might buy a ten-year bond that a borrower issued nine years ago and that now only has one year left to go before the principal is repaid to the current owner (let's say the principal is £100). It would not be sensible to pay more than £100 for that bond if that was all you would get back. But in six months' time you will also receive the £5 coupon (which is the interest the issuer has promised to pay). So within the next year you will receive £105, so that is what the bond is worth, all other things being equal.

There are also situations where you can get back less than you paid for a bond because the future income you have been promised becomes less valuable for some reason. Factors that affect this include a change in the riskiness of the counterparty, or if high inflation arrives unexpectedly.

Yields

Yields for bonds are often confusing. Basically, if the yield goes up it is a bad thing because the market value of the bond has fallen and so you are losing money. Conversely, if the market value goes up, you are making money and the yield will have fallen. Unhelpfully, people invariably discuss bonds in terms of changes in their yield (where 'up' is bad), yet the same people will discuss equities in terms of their market value or price (where 'up' is good). They both mean the same thing: if the price of an asset goes up and the amount of income doesn't change, the income will represent a smaller proportion of the price (e.g. an income of £5 on a £100 bond will give you a yield of 5%, but if the price of the bond falls to £80, the income will be the same but the yield will now be higher, at 6.25%). This is because yields move inversely to market values.

There are many different ways of calculating yields depending on the question that is being asked, but happily this is beyond the scope of this book.[2]

Note that the yield (income ÷ current price) should not be confused with the coupon (the fixed £5 interest payment in the example in the box above). It also should not be confused with the total return (often just called 'return'), which will reflect your combined income and capital gains (or losses).

Duration

Simply put, duration is how long you will have to wait until you receive the principal of a bond back, so if the principal was £100, the duration would be the time from now until the £100 was repaid. The further away that moment, the riskier the bond is because there is a longer period in which unwelcome events could happen (such as high inflation, the borrower going bust or a war breaking out – the list is endless). A one-year duration is considered to have a similar level of risk to investing cash, whereas a 30-year duration is considered much riskier. When people talk about 'bond duration' without specifying the exact amount of time, they are often referring to a duration of about ten years.

Inflation

Inflation (see page 67) is a key risk for bond-holders because unlike in the case of equity or property, the income is usually fixed. As such, it cannot be increased even if inflation increases, which means that inflation can begin to gnaw away at the value of the fixed income. There are bonds where the payment is linked to the value of inflation, but these are less common.

Total returns from bonds

A total return for a global bond portfolio would usually be assumed to be about 2% more than inflation over the long run (1% more than cash). The total return for a country-specific portfolio will vary depending on the characteristics of the country.

Property

Property investments are a long-time favourite of charity investors. Property investment can be done directly (where you gain income from rents and potentially from increases in value when the property is sold) or indirectly (where you invest in a fund that buys and sells property). It is also possible to hold property as simple speculation – for example, you might hold a piece of land that is worthless now but one day might receive planning permission and be worth a fortune.

A major advantage of property investment for charities is that they do not have to pay stamp duty or any tax on the related income.[3] Additionally, if you invest directly, you have an asset that you can touch, which can be a comforting source of value that supplements the actual income the property provides.

Investing in property does, however, have some disadvantages:

- Income from property may seem high but it is not as good as it seems because, in the case of direct investing, at the end of the lease you (as the landlord) usually have to pay to update the property.
- Although both direct and indirect property provide a reasonable hedge against inflation because rents can go up periodically, since lease lengths usually have fixed rental periods for a number of years, property offers fewer opportunities to increase its earnings in line with inflation than equities (which can increase its earnings by increasing the prices of the things the company sells more frequently). This matters in times of fast-growing inflation. (Conversely, property can, to an extent, be a bulwark against the effects of falling prices, as rents don't go down as quickly as prices because rental changes are fixed in the lease.)
- Property is a classic example where liquidity can be an issue. Selling buildings is not a quick process. Furthermore, if there is a property or wider market crisis and lots of people want to sell property, the supply will increase, prices will fall and sales will become increasingly difficult to achieve. Sometimes you might be prevented from withdrawing money from a property fund (if there isn't enough cash) due to 'gating' (as explained in the section on cash above), or you

might instead have to sell at a substantial discount to the current value. As a result, you should never rely on your property holdings as a way of quickly raising cash.

Managing a property portfolio

There are several types of property in which you can invest, including offices, retail, industrial, agricultural and residential. Each of these has different characteristics and you should ensure that you understand the implications of investing across the different types.[4] If you choose to invest indirectly, your chosen property fund should provide a diversified portfolio, whether UK based or global.

If you are tempted to buy a property directly, you should feel confident that you have the time and skill to manage it effectively. Managing property directly incurs costs and requires considerable attention, including negotiations about new and existing leases, upkeep and repair, improvements, and the enforcement of rental terms. Perhaps ask yourself if you would be equally happy taking a different sort of undiversified risk, such as investing the same amount of money in the shares of a single company with a good reputation. Finally, if you sell a property, it doesn't mean you have to buy another one to replace it; the first question would be what is best in the context of your overall asset allocation.

Total returns from property

There are no reliable long-term figures for property returns (not least because of how it has been valued over the past 100 years). However, expected returns from commercial property tend to be less than equities but more than bonds – let's say 1–2% more than the returns from bonds as a very general guide. Most UK charities tend to invest in UK, not global, property.

Public equities

A public equity is a shareholding in a company listed on a stock exchange which entitles you to a share in its profits. These shares can be bought and sold by other companies, organisations and members of the public. They can be listed on a UK exchange or one overseas.

The main point about an equity is that its future returns can be unpredictable – largely because its value can go down as well as up, depending on its future prospects. Therefore, in order to attract investors away from more certain financial investments, companies with shareholders aim to offer a higher long-term return. The difference between the return on a long-term bond and the long-term return on an equity is known as the equity risk premium, and it is commonly estimated to give equities a return about 3% more than bonds.

When investing in equities, it is important to understand which market they are in, the characteristics of their industry and their market capitalisation.

Markets

Equity markets are generally considered to fall into three categories:

- **High-income countries (commonly known as 'developed markets')** include North America, Western Europe (including the UK) and parts of Asia, such as Japan.
- **Emerging markets** include other parts of Asia (such as China), South America and much of Eastern Europe.
- **Frontier markets** (also called 'pre-emerging') include countries with less developed stock markets, such as many central African countries.

Many equity companies will be listed in one area (such as London) but will draw their profits from around the globe. The markets in high-income countries are the most stable whereas the emerging markets tend to be more volatile, not least because their industries are so exposed to the health of the markets in high-income countries. The frontier markets are the most volatile.

In the days before globalisation, each individual market was said to have different characteristics, but increasingly the markets within each category move in tandem. That said, the USA is seen as being consistently more vigorous and innovative than, say, Europe.[5]

Indices

An index is a published measure of the performance of a specific group of assets (such as a particular industry or the whole market of a region of the world). All public companies are organised into a series of indices offered by different providers, such as Dow Jones, the Financial Times, Morgan Stanley and so forth. They have names like 'FTSE 100' (i.e. the 100 largest companies in the UK listed by the Financial Times) or 'MSCI WI' (i.e. the Morgan Stanley Capital International World Index, which lists companies in markets in high-income countries but not emerging markets, which come under the MSCI ACWI (All Countries World Index)).

Industries

All equity companies are allocated an industrial sector (and sub-sector) by the index providers so they can be compared with companies that have the same characteristics. For example, Shell is listed in the energy sector and Alphabet (Google) in the communications sector. The characteristics of the sectors can be used, broadly speaking, to understand how a company will fare when economies are going well or badly. For example, airlines are sensitive to market cycles (people travel less in a recession) so they are seen as cyclical whereas dog food is a consumer staple (people never economise when it comes to feeding Fido).

Market capitalisation

Companies are also segmented by their size of capitalisation ('cap' in the jargon). A company's capitalisation is the total value of all its shares based on the current price. 'Small cap' companies are usually small, local businesses, with the next levels being mid-sized all the way up to 'mega cap'. None of these is inherently better or worse – the investment strategy you adopt (see chapter 5) will naturally lead you to pick companies whose 'caps' are suitable for your financial objectives and goals (and your investment manager's approach).

Total returns from equities

Long-term returns from global equities as a whole tend to be about 5% more than inflation, as a very general guide. While these returns usually smooth out over the long term, they can be very volatile over the short term.

Alternative assets

These asset types are typically used by larger investors with very long-term horizons who invest directly into various specialist funds. These funds are rarely suitable for smaller charities because of their complexity (which usually requires the payment of large fees to a specialist investment manager) and their illiquidity (i.e. you cannot get the money back quickly). Currently in the UK, many of these products are only available to 'professional investors' (explained on page 49) as direct investments but can be accessed indirectly through publicly traded funds on recognised stock exchanges.[6]

If you are considering such investments, you will need to seek appropriate advice. However, following are basic introductions to the main types.

Hedge funds and absolute return funds

These assets vary enormously. However, broadly speaking, hedge funds use a variety of techniques to try to beat general market returns whereas absolute return funds aim for a specific return regardless of the market (although some focus on making low but safer returns). Many of these funds require long-term commitment from investors. A feature of these funds is the ability to sell assets they don't yet own in the hope of buying them later but before they have to deliver them to the purchaser (so-called 'shorting').

One of the main selling points of absolute return funds is that they are able to provide a better return than other safe assets but with lower volatility (but often with less liquidity). However, charities can usually accept the volatility of a cheaper and higher-returning asset class (such as equities), even though the ride may be less comfortable for the trustees (see chapter 8).

Venture capital and private equity

Venture capital involves investing in an invention or an early-stage business, with the intention being to cast seeds widely and nurture the ones that look promising. Private equity consists of shareholdings which are not publicly traded on a recognised stock exchange so the public cannot buy them. It is sometimes considered a separate asset class from venture capital and is focused on improving existing businesses rather than supporting new businesses. In both cases, the investment period is very long (10–15 years) and there is usually an initial loss in value as the company is built or rebuilt before the investment generates higher returns.

Charities usually access these types of investment either directly (if they are classified as professional investors) or through third-party funds (if not). There is a wide range of funds, but many are limited in the amount of direct investment they can accept from investors for their particular strategy. This is especially so for venture capital; if a fund has a good track record, there will be a queue around the block of potential investors seeking access (and pretty much all of them will be turned away because the existing investors won't want to leave). For this reason, sometimes it is jestingly referred to as an 'access class' rather than an 'asset class'.

Generally, the returns can be good (perhaps 2% above global equities with a good manager). However, properly engaging with these asset types is complex, expensive and time-consuming. A 'fund of funds' (also known as a third-party fund) combines multiple venture or private equity funds; these add an additional layer of expense, invariably eating into what you receive.

Infrastructure

Infrastructure funds tend to have more of the characteristics of bonds (with added inflation protection) than other asset classes. They tend to involve contractual payments for building and running large infrastructure projects, such as a new hospital or perhaps a road, usually backed by a government commitment. The principal risks are counterparty failure and, if you have to build the infrastructure, overspends. If the counterparty is a government, the reliability of the fund will be determined by the strength of that government.

Currency

Currency trading is very difficult and is only for the most sophisticated of investors. The received wisdom is that over the long term all currency movements eventually neutralise each other so it can be difficult to distinguish investing in currencies from simple speculation. It is best to steer clear unless you have a very specific reason for investing in this area and have taken expert advice. An example where you might become involved would be if you wanted to protect your charity against adverse movements in a foreign currency, known as currency hedging (this is very different from currency trading). Remember that currencies are a zero-sum game; if one goes down, another will immediately have to go up by an equivalent amount.

Gold, commodities, cryptocurrencies, art, wine, cars and so on

None of these generate any income so it is very difficult to work out what they are worth. It is wise to be cautious in dealing with such investments and best to take professional advice. If an asset has no income, investing in it can amount to speculation.

Investing and tax

It is beyond the scope of this book to deal with the tax implications of investing, although most charitable investing activities are taxed lightly, if at all. However, there are some more esoteric activities that can be taxed normally, such as some foreign partnerships. There are also occasions where a charity might be trading rather than investing – in other words, buying and selling solely to make a short-term profit. These can affect your charity's overall tax position and result in a tax liability.

If these situations might apply to your charity, be sure to take professional advice from a tax specialist and follow the Charity Commission's guidance.[7] HM Revenue and Customs also publishes useful material on tax exemptions for charities[8] and the Charity Tax Group is a useful resource.[9]

The room for error

Figure 3.1 shows the ranges of returns that some of the asset classes mentioned in this chapter demonstrate (based on the available data from US markets). The first thing to notice is that some of the asset classes have very wide ranges. This is in part related to the efficiency and transparency of the market in which they operate. Bond managers all produce similar returns, but getting the right private equity manager really makes the difference between an excellent outcome and a terrible one. One of the great ironies of the investment world is that the normal rules of capitalism are suspended because no one ever claims to be a cheaper but less good manager than someone else. Everyone claims to be the best, so a more expensive fund is no guarantee of better performance.

Figure 3.1 Historical dispersion of returns (showing middle 75% of outcomes)

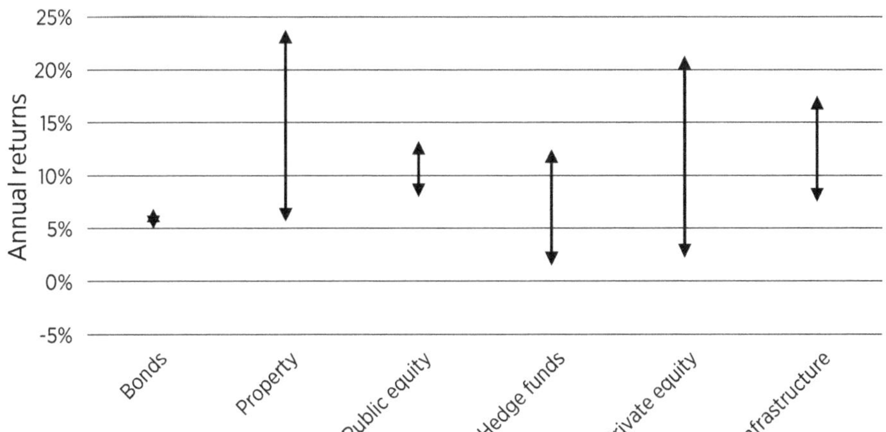

Source: Adapted from BlackRock data (as used on www.firstlinks.com.au/what-is-endowment-style-investing-and-who-should-use-it)

Mixing the asset classes together

Like any series of definitions, the ones above are simplifications. Some equities are so reliable in their dividends that they behave more like bonds, and some bonds are so unreliable that they behave more like equities. It is quite possible to create a portfolio of bonds that is as volatile as equities, and also possible (but slightly harder) to create a portfolio of equities that behaves like bonds. Investment managers understand these gradations and take care to diversify their portfolios to deliver the amount of volatility that you seek.

Chapter 5 goes into more detail about how to mix assets together to create a portfolio that will help you reach your financial objectives and goals.

The charity investment market

Fund types

There are three basic types of fund that charities can use. These are offered by numerous investment fund houses (e.g. BlackRock, CCLA and Schroders). Some firms have sub-brands – for example, BlackRock owns iShares and Schroders owns Cazenove.

Mixed funds

Mixed funds offer a complete portfolio across a wide variety of asset classes. They are designed to match a specific risk appetite (see page 81) (sometimes expressed as a particular return target, such as the Consumer Prices Index plus 3%; see page 206 for more on return targets). Investors make the decision to invest based on their assessment of whether the risk appetite and return offered are right for them. Note that a return target is not the same as an income target (the return target is usually higher and includes both the income and any capital growth).

The investment manager decides which asset classes they will invest in (equities, bonds, property, etc.) and the proportions they believe will deliver the best outcome against the return target. Mixed funds commonly appeal to charities as they are simple, diversified, cost-effective and transparent.

Single-asset-class funds

Single-asset-class funds only contain one type of asset, such as equities, bonds or property. These funds have their own investment manager, who chooses the underlying shares or properties in which to invest. Mixed funds sometimes own portions of single-asset-class funds if they think that the fund's manager can offer a level of risk, return and diversification that will complement the mixed fund's offering. The single-asset-class fund can be one of the mixed-fund manager's own funds or someone else's fund (where the latter is known as 'open architecture').

There are numerous subdivisions of single-asset-class funds. For example, within the bond category, there are government, corporate and high-yield bond funds, to name a few. There are also funds that provide more esoteric services, such as collections of private equity managers, hedge funds and other alternative assets (see page 40).

If your charity plans to invest in single-asset-class funds, you will likely need to manage the proportions you put into each asset class, leaving the manager of each fund to determine which companies to invest in. In other words, you will become responsible for your own asset allocation and therefore how likely your investment strategy is to achieve your investing goals. This is especially true if you own investment property outside a mixed fund.

Exchange-traded funds

Exchange-traded funds closely track (i.e. shadow) a selection of assets. They commonly do this by tracking indices. The indices they track can range from conventional (such as the FTSE All-Share Index, which tracks a large portion of the companies traded on the London Stock Exchange) to issue-based (such as indices of environmentally beneficial assets) through to the more niche (such as indices of 'sin stocks', or shares in industries that are considered unethical, such as tobacco). Exchange-traded funds are very cheap to buy into because they are calculated mechanically (or passively – see below).

Funds, funds and more funds

All the mentions of funds in the charity landscape can get confusing. For example, you might have an internal fund (i.e. a pot of money) set aside within your charity's accounts for a specific purpose, and you might invest in external funds of the kinds outlined above. These two types of fund may overlap – for example, you might invest your internal pot of money in one or more externally managed funds (as is the case in the Martello Tower Fund case study at the end of this chapter). Your charity may also engage in fundraising (a totally separate activity from anything described in this book) and talk generally about how it is spending its funds (i.e. money), some of which might be in restricted or designated funds. There is no simple solution here, but it can help to keep in mind that the word has different meanings in different contexts so you can clarify what is meant if misunderstandings arise.

Passive or active?

Mixed funds and single-asset-class funds can be delivered on a fairly cheap and automated basis (passive funds) or using a more expensive and skill-based approach (active funds). A perennial question is which is best.

Passive management

In passive funds, the manager simply takes a published index like the FTSE All-Share or the MSCI World Index and buys enough shares in the right weights that its portfolio performs exactly like the index that it tracks. The advantage of these funds is that they are cheap and reliable, with their cost usually being less than a third of active management. The name 'passive' is a little misleading because although your investments simply track an index, you do have to make a decision about which index to follow. Another name for passive funds is 'trackers'. All exchange-traded funds are passive.

Charities are commonly concerned with funding their spending in a cheap and sustainable way, so passive funds are a popular choice. However, it is important to understand their limitations. A passive fund will allocate most of its assets to the largest companies in the index – or, in other words, those companies that have already gone up the most in value and so have the least potential to grow further. In contrast, a shrewd investor is one who will continue to give an under-performing company more money in hope of a larger return in the long term, so long as they have confidence in their judgement that the company will go on to improve. So, investing in a passive fund means you lose the opportunity to take advantage of this potential for larger returns. However, if you (or your manager) do not have the conviction to allocate more money to under-performing companies than an index, then it may be that passive investing is a more natural home for you. (See pages 155–8 for further discussion of this trade-off between risk and reward.)

Active management

This is the opposite of passive management. In active management, managers conduct careful analysis to try to predict which companies will increase in value more than others over time. These managers might refer to indices but won't buy shares in all the companies in an index – only some. Therefore, their fund's performance will differ from that of any index they consult.

Most mixed-fund charity investment managers will use a fairly unremarkable investment approach that will suit a variety of market conditions. A manager with a more pronounced style will perform well when their style has a tailwind (i.e. when the market conditions suit their style; see page 208 for more on manager styles). This can be seen in figure 3.2, where managers A and B have different styles which wax and wane over the years depending on the market environment.

Figure 3.2 Example of variances in manager performance over time

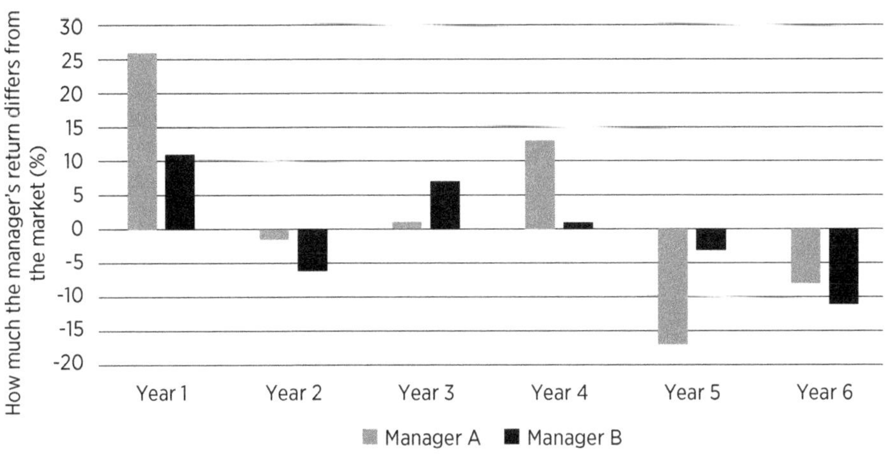

Source: Performance of iShares exchange-traded funds based on momentum and quality styles.

As the figure shows, no manager does well in all years. This doesn't necessarily mean they are a bad manager – just that markets move in cycles and that, being disciplined, a high-performing manager does not deviate from their style when they encounter a headwind. Other managers may not have a single, disciplined style and may instead attempt to adapt to a changing 'wind direction' as circumstances change. The point here is not to try to understand how specific manager styles interact with specific market conditions; there are too many potential combinations to make such an exercise helpful (and there is too little data to be able to tell which of the managers in figure 3.2 are disciplined and which are not). The point is simply to understand that the more pronounced a manager's style, the more variance there will be in their results when compared with the market – sometimes good, sometimes bad.

Active managers have other features too. Although they are more expensive, they usually provide a higher level of client care and service. Therefore, if you need someone to come to a meeting every quarter or to provide trustee training or more bespoke support, that will usually be covered by the additional cost.

Combining active and passive management

Sometimes larger charities use a passive manager to provide a core return and a more active manager to provide something extra. This is more complex and more resource intensive. It also places an additional administrative burden on the charity because it has to keep an eye on more moving parts, and adjust them to keep in line with its strategy. However, it does provide a more nuanced solution, especially if the charity is more confident about some areas than others.

Which is best?

There is no 'best manager'. There are better managers and worse managers, but your ability to stay the course with an adequate manager is an under-rated factor. Chapter 8 goes into much more detail on this topic.

There are a variety of managers, styles and approaches that you can use to invest your charity's money. If you are not sure which direction to take, it is never a bad idea to find a specialist charity manager (see chapter 10), who will be able to perform in a range of market environments.

Domestic or global portfolio?

Often, more old-fashioned investment managers preferred to invest predominantly in their domestic market. For example, a UK fund manager might have invested as much as 60% in UK equities despite the fact that the UK only represents about 5% of the global market (about the same size as Japan). The traditional argument to counter this is that UK companies trade globally and so investing in UK companies means indirectly investing in the global economy, but this is only true of some UK companies. Investing heavily in the UK market introduces distortions to a portfolio because of the lopsided nature of that market (as represented by the FTSE All-Share Index). For example, the FTSE All-Share Index includes many banks and energy companies but almost no technology companies. By comparison, a global index will lead to a global investment approach and a much more balanced portfolio. It is therefore important to make sure that if a manager proposes a large holding in UK equities (or any other specific country or region) compared to a global index, they are able to explain the advantages of this approach.

Taking advice

Investment managers cannot offer advice other than on their own funds or products. The only exception is if they have a separate agreement with a charity to offer *independent* investment advice (which is unusual). Even then, they still have to conduct a 'suitability test' to make sure they understand your investing needs accurately.[10] In a nutshell, managers cannot advise a charity on its asset allocation, just offer their own products and explain how they fit their interpretation of the charity's needs.

There are a wide variety of investment managers to choose from. They can be divided into three broad categories depending on the nature of their appointment:

- **Discretionary** management is a two-way agreement between the charity and manager where the charity delegates the entirety of the management of an investment portfolio to the manager. All the charity has to do is select the most appropriate manager based on its manager's published literature (and potentially interviews with them). The manager is then responsible for all decisions, such as what to buy and sell and in what proportions.
- **Advisory** management is similar to discretionary management, but the charity retains the overall investment decision-making power, having been given investment advice or ideas by the manager (for which the manager remains responsible). The manager will usually execute the charity's decisions through a segregated fund (see page 51).
- **Execution-only** management is where the manager executes but the charity takes full responsibility for the investment decisions, without receiving advice. In other words, the manager implements the charity's investment wishes.

These services can be delivered in different ways by different firms. Charity-specialist firms tend to be the best way to invest for all but the most expert charity investors. Generalist firms, or those without a good understanding of how charities work, will be at a disadvantage. Pension-fund specialists may just see charities as another pension fund, which can lead to problems such as misunderstanding the flexible nature of a charity's liabilities and, consequently, its tolerance of uncertainty (see page 58).

Finally, you should be alert to how an investment manager categorises your charity. This can either be 'retail' or 'professional'. If you are categorised as a professional investor, you will receive a lower level of protection from the Financial Conduct Authority (FCA) than a retail investor.[11] You are unlikely to be able to influence this categorisation.

Remember that if you make the choice yourself about which assets to invest in (including if you choose a charity investment fund), legally your charity is deemed to have made the investment decision (with all the consequences following in the Trustee Act 2000; see page 136).

Legal structures

One of the key differences between all these types of manager is whether they offer a pooled (or collective) fund or a segregated portfolio. A pooled fund is a one-size-fits-all product where everyone in the pool owns a fraction of each share, whereas in a segregated fund each investor owns their shares completely in a portfolio constructed specifically for them. Each of the types of fund discussed on page 44 (mixed, single asset and exchange traded) can be owned either on a pooled or segregated basis, or in combination.

For the most part, legal structure will make no practical difference to your experience of investing. However, it is important to understand the difference, especially if you want to exercise more discretion yourself, as segregated funds will offer you more opportunity to do this.

Pooled funds

Pooled funds are usually cheaper than segregated funds but cannot be tailored to your individual needs. If you have strong views about your tolerance for unpredictable returns, your income requirements or factors relating to responsible investment (see chapter 9), these will not be for you (unless you can find a close match from the many available funds). Most of the funds that specialise in investing for charities come with good levels of support, a named relationship manager and a range of responsible investing criteria. Decision-making is centralised with a chief investment officer, whom you may or may not meet depending on how large a client you are. Otherwise, the people you meet will tend not to make investment decisions themselves but will be well informed about the thinking behind the portfolio.

Charity authorised investment funds

Charity authorised investment funds (CAIFs) are the newest type of pooled fund. They are regulated ('authorised') by the FCA and established as charities by the Charity Commission. They are allowed to distribute a total return (see chapter 4), which can smooth income from year to year. This is very useful for permanent endowments. These funds do not have to charge VAT on their fees or pay stamp duty on UK asset purchases. The FCA has published guidance on these funds.[12]

Common investment funds

The common investment fund (CIF) is an older structure that is largely being superseded by the CAIF. A CIF is a charity in its own right with its own set of trustees. The trustees appoint the investment manager. A CIF has more limited income-smoothing powers than a CAIF and must charge VAT on its fees. Like CAIFs, CIFs do not have to pay stamp duty on UK asset purchases. These funds were established under the Charities Act 1960.

Non-charity-specific funds

Needless to say, there are legions of non-charity pooled funds that your charity is free to invest in if your trustees consider them suitable. If you are considering this type of fund, the possible starting points for information will be similar to those used by individual investors, including websites such as Morningstar.co.uk. However, if you are choosing your own funds in this way, you should be particularly mindful of your obligations under the Trustee Act 2000.

Segregated funds

A segregated fund or portfolio is one where you own your own shares, as opposed to owning a fragment of all the shares in a pool. This gives you more rights in terms of voting at meetings on your own shares – something to bear in mind if that is an important consideration for you (see page 182). A segregated fund will usually provide a more personalised service – among other things, allowing you to vet individual shareholdings – with a client director being your normal point of call, rather like a private client's stockbroker. The service can be tailored to your charity's specific needs, although this can be more expensive. Your shares are usually held for you by a 'custodian', who is responsible for dealing with all the transactions related to your shares.

The performance figures of segregated portfolios are generally less reliable as an indication of typical performance than those of pooled funds. This is because segregated portfolios differ depending on each client's preferences, so no one portfolio can be regarded as typical of a firm's own outlook.

Fictional case studies

Spender: Warden's Philanthropy

Warden's Philanthropy aims to use its investments to fund spending to support people in the Barchester area. The trustees have established two portfolios, one for the short term and one for the long term. Each has different risk appetites. They have decided to use the same manager to manage both funds so that the reporting is all in one place and the administration is simpler for the trustees.

The manager already had a CAIF that was suitable for the short-term mandate, so the charity decided to invest in that fund. For the long-term mandate, the trustees decided on advisory management via a segregated fund. This was because they wanted to be able to take a more direct interest in the assets that were in the fund, including retaining the right to exclude certain companies and state when they had particular views about how they wanted to cast their votes as shareholders. The actively managed investment style had no strong leanings in any particular direction and the client service was good (according to the references the trustees sought). The firm's performance had been reasonable – not spectacular, but consistent.

Saver: Martello Tower Fund

The Martello Tower Fund (MTF) is a restricted fund within the charity Preserving Our Nautical Past and exists to build a sea wall to protect a coastal fort. The investment committee of the MTF recommended to the trustees of Preserving Our Nautical Past that as the wall did not need to be built for 30 years, there was a high tolerance for volatility. As such, the committee recommended that a global equity exchange-traded fund would be the cheapest and most sensible choice. The committee expects that as the MTF nears the time it will start spending, it will move towards more active management, ultimately leading to all the assets being invested in a short-term portfolio.

Spend-outer: Butterworth Music Festivals

This charity, which is focused on bringing music to communities, has a short-term portfolio that the trustees have mainly invested in bonds (for stability) but also in some equities, absolute return funds and infrastructure to add to the returns. The trustees have decided to appoint an active manager because they realise they will need to keep in close touch with the manager as their spending plans change, sometimes rapidly.

Conclusion

This chapter has looked at the wide range of investment services that are available to charities. It is important background for the following chapters, which are about how you can go about implementing your financial objectives and goals.

Notes

1 Elroy Dimson, Paul Marsh and Mike Staunton, *Global Investment Returns Yearbook 2024*, London, London Business School, 2024; this expands on Elroy Dimson, Paul Marsh and Mike Staunton, Triumph of the Optimists: 101 years of global investment returns, Princeton, Princeton University Press, 2002.

2 For further information see Daniel Jark, 'Understanding the different types of bond yields' [web article], Investopedia, www.investopedia.com/articles/investing/022516/understanding-different-types-bond-yields.asp, 30 September 2022.
3 'Charities and tax' [web page], Gov.uk, www.gov.uk/charities-and-tax/tax-reliefs, accessed 20 January 2024; 'SDLT – Charity relief' [web page], Charity Tax Group, www.charitytaxgroup.org.uk/tax/stamp-duty/stamp-duty-land-tax/charity-relief, accessed 20 January 2024.
4 For further information see James Chen, 'Real estate: Definition, types, how to invest in it' [web article], Investopedia, www.investopedia.com/terms/r/realestate.asp, 20 December 2023.
5 Elroy Dimson, Paul Marsh and Mike Staunton, *Global Investment Returns Yearbook 2024*, London, London Business School, 2024.
6 'COBS 3.5 Professional clients' [web page], Financial Conduct Authority, www.handbook.fca.org.uk/handbook/COBS/3/5.html, accessed 20 January 2024.
7 'Trustees trading and tax: How charities may lawfully trade' [web page], Charity Commission for England and Wales, 2016, www.gov.uk/government/publications/trustees-trading-and-tax-how-charities-may-lawfully-trade-cc35/trustees-trading-and-tax-how-charities-may-lawfully-trade, accessed 20 January 2024.
8 'Annex I: Tax exemptions for charities' [web page], HM Revenue and Customs, www.gov.uk/government/publications/charities-detailed-guidance-notes/annex-i-tax-exemptions-for-charities, accessed 20 January 2024.
9 See www.charitytaxgroup.org.uk.
10 'Assessing suitability' [web article], Financial Conduct Authority, www.fca.org.uk/firms/assessing-suitability, 6 March 2020.
11 For an overview of the different levels of protection see the untitled article by Andy Butterworth and Paul Palmer at Honorary Treasurers, n.d., www.honorarytreasurers.org.uk/docs/PalmerandButterworth.pdf, accessed 20 January 2024.
12 See 'Charity Authorised Investment Funds' in *Handbook* [PDF], Financial Conduct Authority, 2024, www.handbook.fca.org.uk/handbook/COLL/14.pdf, accessed 20 January 2024.

Chapter four

Spending policies

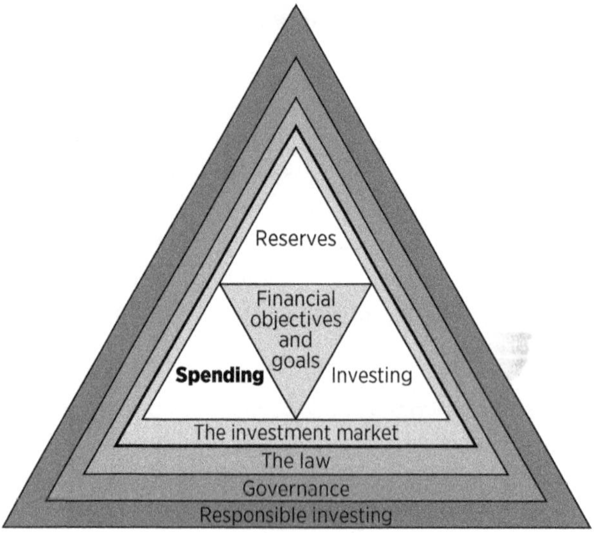

The purpose of this chapter

The success of any financial project is determined as much by what you put in as by what you take out. If you remember that what makes you charitable is what you spend, not what you save, then this chapter will help you design your spending so it supports you better in your mission. For most people a 'spending policy' simply means spending their income, but that can create its own problems. There are many other ways of deciding what can be spent and what needs to be saved for the future.

It is important to keep in mind that chapters 4, 5 and 6 cannot be considered in isolation from one another. Although you should have separate spending, investment and reserves policies, it is best to think of them as facets of one whole. The success of each depends on how well it stands up against the other two – for example, there is no point in having a spending policy that requires more income than your investment policy can deliver or that pays no heed to the reserves you require for stability.

Against the backdrop of that interrelationship, then, this chapter looks at what a spending policy is for, the differences between receiving a natural income and a total return, and various rules you can use to decide how much to spend. It then looks at how inflation affects both spending and returns, and how you can be more ambitious both in your earning and in your spending. It concludes by examining the spending policies of each of the three example charities.

What is a spending policy?

At the end of the day, all investors will want cash to spend. The question is what is the best way to get your hands on the cash you need to discharge your commitments to your beneficiaries and pay your bills when you need to do so. In investing, returns are rarely predictable and can vary wildly over time, even being negative in some years (as explored further in chapter 5). The aim of your spending policy is to help you smooth out this unevenness and make a reasonable prediction of what you might be able to spend in order to deliver your charity's financial objectives and goals (as defined in chapter 2):

- If you are a **spender charity**, delivering on your financial objectives and goals means spending as much as you can on your current generation of beneficiaries but without knowingly hampering your ability to spend in future years.
- If you are a **saver charity**, you may not need a spending policy in the immediate future, but you will certainly need to start developing one as you get closer to the date on which you plan to start putting your accumulated funds to use.
- If you are a **spend-out charity**, delivering on your financial objectives and goals means ending up with nothing on your final day of operation.

Ultimately, a spending policy is only ever an approximation of what you can spend. As such, and as indicated in the introduction to this chapter, your spending policy should be closely informed by your investment policy. It should not simply be governed by unquestioning acceptance of what you have historically been given to spend by your investment manager (if you have one) or have spent in the past. Developing a spending policy (and, more broadly, an investment policy) is an opportunity to assess whether you are creating opportunities to earn more so you can push your spending harder for your beneficiaries in a way that is consistent with your financial objectives and goals. The right policy will allow you to earn more and spend more with confidence.

The following subsections explore some of the key general considerations when developing a spending policy.

Consistency

You might want your spending policy to provide a consistent and sustainable level of expenditure long into the future so you can plan with confidence. Alternatively, if a stable level of year-on-year spending doesn't really matter to you, then you can more or less spend what you want and adjust in the light of whether your reserves are hitting their target values (see chapter 6), but your spending is likely to be quite stop–start. Some charities operate a halfway house of planning a consistent level of spending accompanied by 'bonus distributions' to reflect better-than-expected returns, which are by design unsustainable.

A 'sustainable' spending policy is only ever a best guess about the future – and of course there is no certainty about what an investment portfolio will give you in the future. A sustainable spending policy will always try to balance this equation:

Spending = Investment returns – Investment manager fees – Inflation

There are various ways of working out how much you could spend, and these are explored later in this chapter (see page 63).

Intergenerational equity

Spender charities are often concerned with the concept of intergenerational equity. This term refers to managing your spending so that you spend roughly the same amount on every generation of your beneficiaries. This is a question of fairness, and as such it is closely linked to the concept of sustainability. However, in practice, intergenerational equity is very difficult to achieve because you cannot know whether your future returns will be larger or smaller, and therefore whether you should spend more or less now.

It is also worth remembering that intergenerational equity is an artificial concept, invented by James Tobin in 1974, and has never really been challenged.[1] As such, there are unresolved questions about its implementation. For instance, does it mean that if you've had a lucky break in your investments recently, those results should be eked out in perpetuity, or can you spend your windfall as a one-off? And what about the treatment of losses – should future generations pay for losses experienced today? It is worth here remembering the capriciousness of the White Queen in Lewis Carroll's *Through the Looking Glass* (1872):

> Jam tomorrow and jam yesterday, but never jam today.

In short, treating beneficiaries fairly is an important aspiration, but ultimately it is up to individual charities to decide what to do in each specific case. The Charity Commission's guidance is silent on the matter except in the case of permanent endowments, where the stipulation is that the capital must not be spent, only reinvested, when operating under the standard rules. Alternatively, when operating under a total return order, the concept of intergenerational equity applies.[2] (See page 59 for explanations of the standard rules and total return.)

A spending policy is therefore really a best-efforts attempt to be even-handed, recognising that this is an art, not a science. And, indeed, the idea of intergenerational equity can be taken too far when trustees assume their current spending plans will survive long into the future. This sort of approach is the preserve of pension funds and should only in exceptional cases be applied to charities, as explained in the box below.

How are charities different from pension funds?

Unlike the beneficiaries of a pension fund, charity beneficiaries are not listed out with names and addresses and a legal right to their future benefits. Therefore, trustees are free to expand or reduce the scale of their charity's support depending on the financial circumstances. This is a fundamental difference between a charity and a pension fund, and it gives charities a completely different tolerance of uncertainty and volatility in their investment returns (covered in detail in chapter 5). In short, pension funds must measure their success by looking forwards whereas charities can measure theirs by looking backwards. Looking backwards is based on certain data whereas looking forwards is based on estimates. This means that charities don't have to use an actuarial approach (which is cautious, not prudent; see page 145 for a discussion of these terms). Therefore, charities don't have to proceed with so much caution in case their future returns are lower, because they can just redefine their beneficiaries when and *if* that happens.

Reputation

Chapter 9 goes into depth about responsible investing and how you might protect your charity's reputation by investing carefully. Arguably, however, there should be a far greater reputational danger to charities that fail to spend as much as they can, perhaps because their spending and investment policies are not properly fitted to their ability to tolerate volatility and uncertainty.

In other words, charities may be exposed to the reputational risk of not spending enough – and thus not achieving enough – as well as the risk of not preserving enough capital (or indeed having to reduce their spending abruptly). A very real risk that trustees infrequently consider is that they will end up with a pile of money that they could have spent on their purpose but chose not to. This is best described as 'reckless caution' and is explored more fully in chapters 7 and 8 (see especially page 145).

Spending policy types

There are two types of spending policy: one based on natural income (also referred to by the Charity Commission as 'standard rules'[3]) and a variety of other methods collectively known as 'total return'. Your spending policy relates to the overall principle that determines the characteristics of your spending needs (broadly how much and how stable you want your spending to be).

Natural income

Any investment will produce a financial return that is made up of both income and capital gains (and occasionally losses). Traditionally, investors have treated income and capital differently. A good analogy is a tree and its fruit, where you eat the fruit and as long as you nurture the tree, you should receive the same amount of fruit again the next year. Here, the fruit is your natural income. Similarly, a portfolio will provide an investor with income in the form of dividends, rents and interest (often called the 'yield'). Each one is a reward to the investor for putting their capital at risk (if there was no return, no one would put their money at risk in an investment).

Natural income remains the centrepiece of accounting for charities and many use it to work out how much they can spend. In this approach, only the income is spent and the underlying assets – be they shares, bonds, property or something else – remain untouched (or, if they are sold, the proceeds are reinvested in other assets).

It is important to understand that sometimes the term 'natural income' can also refer to a well-regarded investment management process that favours investing in companies that pay a healthy, sustainable dividend. Both uses of the term – as a method of calculating spending and as a method of choosing investments – are valid so it is vital to be clear about which one is meant in any specific context, but this chapter is obviously about spending, not investing.

Advantages of using natural income

For many charities, the simplicity and familiarity of using the natural income approach to calculate what they can spend will outweigh any disadvantages. And, as mentioned above, it is quite possible for charities to use a blended approach where they occasionally spend some of their capital when there is a particular need and it is affordable to do so (for a more regular programme of selling capital, an explicit total return method will be a better choice).

Disadvantages of using natural income

The key disadvantage of using natural income relates to the link between your spending and your investing: if you spend based on a natural income, it can encourage you (or your investment manager if you set too stretching an income target for them to achieve) to invest your portfolio in high-yielding assets, regardless of their underlying merit. This is best described as the accounting tail wagging the investing dog.

For example, many asset classes – such as private equity, hedge funds and commodities (see chapter 3) – can make healthy returns for their investors but without paying out any income as dividends, rent or interest. This lack of income makes these investments unattractive for income investors, even though they can be very good investments in terms of capital growth.

Investing for a natural income can have other perverse effects too. The UK market has traditionally offered a higher yield than the US market and this has led income-seeking investors to hold more assets in the UK than the USA, not for investment reasons but simply because the yield is higher. Complications can arise for charities because some of these high-yielding UK-listed companies are in areas that some charities might prefer to avoid, such as the oil and mining sectors (see chapter 9). In contrast, many lower-yielding but high-capital-growth US-listed companies (especially technology businesses) are more attractive investments in their own right; however, because they often don't pay a dividend, they can become very unattractive investments for a natural income investor because they don't produce any cash to be spent by the charity – it's all capital growth.

Managers who are set income targets by their clients will sometimes achieve them by selling a stock they want to own and replacing it with one that is less attractive but that is about to pay its dividend, just to harvest the dividend and hit their income target. This 'dividend-washing' may look good to a client because it produces more income, but all that is happening is that you are converting capital to income by artificially increasing the income your portfolio is generating. This is not a sustainable approach.

In short, spending your natural income does not necessarily equate to what you have earned in the year, but it is simple and well understood. It will always have a bias to spending less than you might be able to afford (because the companies in which you have invested will usually retain some earnings). It can therefore undermine intergenerational equity unless you keep a close eye on it as part of monitoring progress against your financial objectives and goals.

Spending policies for permanent endowments

The capital in a permanent endowment cannot be spent, so generally speaking any permanent endowment is only allowed by law to use the natural income approach (other than in limited, temporary circumstances known as 'recoupment', or if it has formally resolved to move to a total return basis, as described on page 278). For more information see the Charity Commission's guidance *Total Return Investment for Permanently Endowed Charities.*[4]

Total return

The alternative to spending a natural income is to spend an amount based on a 'total return'. A total return is a measure of both the income and the capital appreciation of an asset, combined into one figure. As such, total return encompasses an asset's overall gain (or loss) in a period, be it from dividends, rents, interest, and/or capital gains and losses.

See appendix 2 for a detailed practical guide to using total return accounting.

Advantages of using total return

The principal advantage of using the total return method relates to control. The trustees are the ones who decide and best understand their charity's financial objectives and goals. As such, they (with their investment manager) are best placed to look at the portfolio's overall return (rather than just its income) and decide how those earnings can most effectively be used to support the financial objectives and goals. For spender charities, this will usually involve taking an amount out to fund spending and leaving the rest to grow for the future. For savers, almost all of the return will be left to grow. For spend-out charities, the balance will depend on how imminently the spending is planned to occur.

As an example, imagine that your charity has invested in a company and the company earns a profit of £100,000, so the value of the company will increase by £100,000. Some of that money is yours because you are a shareholder, and you share in the company's profits. The company might divide this £100,000 between its shareholders as a dividend or it might reinvest the money in its own operations. If you are using the natural income approach, the amount of the dividend (which you cannot influence) is very important to you as this is what you will receive to spend. In contrast, if you are using total return, the amount of the dividend is not relevant from your point of view. Instead, you can choose the amount of money you would like to keep in the company and the amount you would like to take out, usually as a combination of receiving dividends and selling some shares. This would work particularly well if the company had made good earnings for you (and thus increased the value of your shares) but not distributed any of it to you by way of a dividend. This frees you from the restrictions on investing in low-yield companies mentioned above in the section on natural income.

Total return is regarded as the most complete measure of investment activity because it measures the true growth of an investment over time, irrespective of how much you might have been allocated as a dividend.[5] It is a measure of pure investment performance, and it places the key decisions in the hands of those who are best placed to interpret your charity's financial objectives and goals – your trustees. In contrast, in the natural income alternative, you essentially take a back seat and accept whatever the company directors wish to share with you as a dividend.

Disadvantages of using total return

As mentioned above, total return can feel less familiar and more complex, so it will not suit all charities.

What's best for you?

Natural income and total return each have their place – the choice will come down to your charity's characteristics and what feels right for you. You might find the natural income approach most suitable:

- if you want a simple, straightforward solution to your spending needs;
- if your charity has an investment portfolio worth less than £10 million;
- if your investment income only represents a small part of your total income;
- if your portfolio mainly consists of property;
- if your trustees struggle with the idea of selling capital to fund spending (sometimes referred to as 'selling the family silver');
- if you have a permanent endowment.

Conversely, you might gravitate towards the total return approach:

- if your charity is large and has more complex investment arrangements;
- if your portfolio contains a range of alternative assets (see page 40) that produce no or little income;
- if your portfolio contains a high proportion of low-yielding stocks, perhaps because it is invested in geographies that traditionally have a lower yield (such as the USA);
- if your trustees prefer to decide how much of your total return they can spend sustainably;
- if your trustees prefer to control how quickly your annual spending changes (for instance by varying the number of quarters over which market values are smoothed for the total return calculation – see page 64).

Should your charity use total return? A rule of thumb

A good rule of thumb would be to consider total return if any of the following is true:

- Investment income represents more than 70% of your total income.
- Your investment portfolio is large (perhaps more than £10 million).
- You have a permanent endowment which has grown substantially ahead of inflation and you could usefully spend some of those gains.

Spending rules

A spending rule is a formula that is used to decide exactly how much you will spend each year. This is the culmination of your spending policy, based on careful consideration of all the factors outlined so far in this chapter. Natural income is simple and is essentially a spending rule in its own right, but there is a choice of several spending rules based on total return.

Spending your natural income

This is now self-explanatory – you simply spend an amount of money equivalent to your dividends, rents and interest. There is no need to sell any assets to fund your spending.

Spending rules based on total return

If you do not use natural income to determine what you spend and what you keep, you are going to have to divide up your total return yourself. This applies especially to spender charities that want to maintain a general sense of intergenerational equity by aiming for a fair balance between what they spend and what they keep. A spending rule also helps you to deal with the fact that your total return will vary from year to year, by smoothing it out.

There are a number of spending rules that you can apply to divide up your earnings. They are all based on established expectations about what long-term returns are likely to be.

Rolling market value

This rule is based on spending a fixed percentage of the market value of your portfolio. Percentages between 3% and 5% are common for spender charities because this range is considered by the industry to be the limit of what is sustainable in the longer term.[6]

As portfolio volatility can produce widely changing annual spending budgets, this is normally smoothed over a period of time, usually three years (but sometimes five or even longer). For example, let's say over the past five years your portfolio's annual market values were £100,000, £200,000, £150,000, £300,000 and £350,000. The average would be £220,000, and 5% would give you spending of £11,000 for the forthcoming year based on those five years. If you used a three-year average, the first three years would average £150,000 so your spending would be £7,500 for the following year. It would be £10,833 for the next year and £13,333 for the next, almost doubling (and reflecting some extremely volatile assets).

The longer the period you choose, the more you will smooth out any lumps and bumps in your earnings and thus the more predictable your spending will be, but the slower any growth will be to feed through into higher spending. You can also base your calculations on quarterly valuations – for example, 12 quarters for three years or 20 quarters for five years – and this smooths out the volatility even more.

The principal disadvantage of using the rolling market average rule to determine your spending is that it can still lead to uneven budgets from year to year. If spending stability is particularly important to your charity, you might think of using a constant growth rule instead.

Constant growth

A second way of calculating your spending is to simply grow your existing spending rate, usually by an amount equal to inflation, year on year. For instance, if one year you spent £60,000 and inflation was 4%, the next year you would spend £62,400. The great advantage of this method is that you can see a reliable spending amount far into the future. This makes budgeting much easier, especially if you review your spending rate as part of your planning cycle.

However, the weakness of this approach is that it does not link your spending to the value of your assets. This means that it is possible to continue spending at a level that is no longer supported by your investments – or, vice versa, to end up with excess earnings that you are not putting to use for your beneficiaries. Consequently, every year you should reassure yourself that your spending level is consistent with the target value for your reserves (see page 113).

Other arrangements

There are myriad other hybrid arrangements. For example, one is to base 70% of the figure on the constant growth rule and 30% on rolling market values. It is also possible to vary the proportions used in the spending rule (e.g. by using 50% of last year's market value, 30% of the year before and 20% of the year before that). As a rule, simpler is better because these are all only approximations of what you can realistically spend. It is wise to keep at last half an eye on the target value for your reserves regardless of the rule you choose, as only then can you be sure your spending is in line with your financial objectives and goals.

An earnings-based spending rule is linked to what your portfolio earns. For example, let's say one year all the companies in your portfolio (worth £300,000) collectively earn £10,000 but only distribute dividends to you of £7,500, keeping the other £2,500 to reinvest in their businesses. You can spend that extra £2,500 by selling some capital even though it was not part of the dividends you were sent – you've still earned it. If the value of your portfolio subsequently went up to £400,000 but its earnings stayed at £10,000, you would still only spend £10,000 because that's all that you have earned. The advantage of this approach is that it avoids dependence on market values and concentrates on what your portfolio has actually earned, but it is only practical for simple portfolios.

Comparison of results

If we look at the results of the three main models over the last 20 years, there is little difference between the constant growth and rolling market value methods. However, following the natural income approach would have resulted in a lower spend (see figure 4.1).

Figure 4.1 Spending policies since 2002

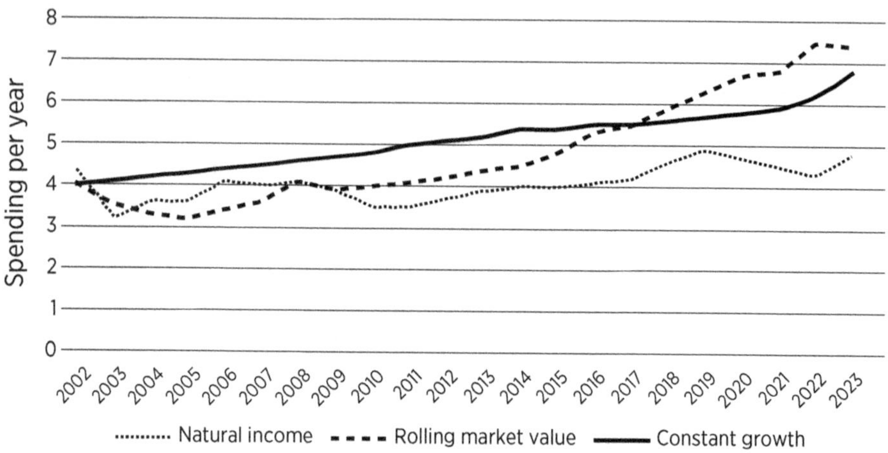

Source: Legal & General Investment Management (LGIM). Data taken from a portfolio based on 70% in LGIM's Global Equity fund and 30% in LGIM's UK Conventional Government Bond fund. Rolling market value spending at 4%. Consumer Prices Index data from the Office for National Statistics. The numbers represented by the Y axis are simply the index's way of portraying the growth of spending and have no external meaning.

The same overall position applies if we look at the results of the three main models since 2012 (see figure 4.2). Spending a natural income would have produced the lowest spending, with the constant growth method producing the next largest amount and the rolling market value method the largest. Note too that these portfolios are not specifically chosen to generate a high income but rather a sustainable one. Remember too that all spending rates are approximations of what is sustainable over the long term, and that is why they should always be reviewed in the context of financial objectives and reserve policies, and adjusted up or down as needs be.

Table 4.1 provides a summary of the major spending rules and the situations in which they can be most relevant. If stable spending is your priority, any of the rules can work well, but rolling market values is a little weaker than the others (unless you use a great many years to calculate the average). For capital maintenance, a rolling market value spending rule would be likely to suit you best (because you spend more when your assets go up). If you just want to keep things simple, you might choose natural income. And finally, as explained in the total return appendix, natural income is the best option if you want to keep your accounting simple too and in line with standard accounting practice for charities.

Figure 4.2 Spending policies since 2012

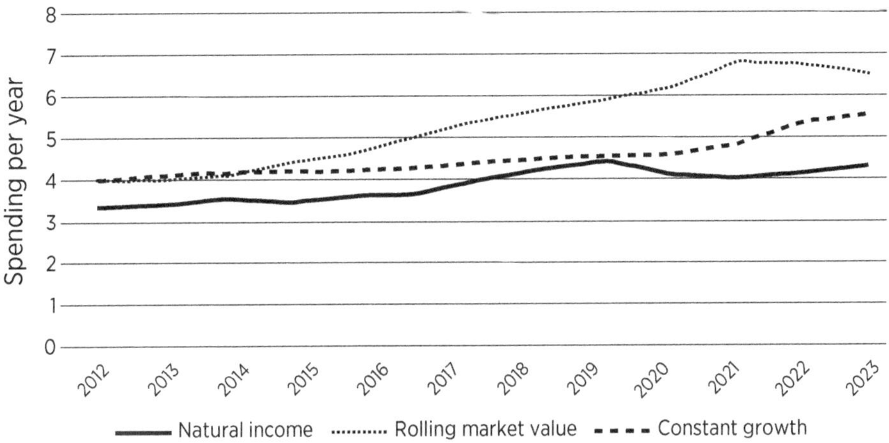

Source: Legal and General Investment Management (LGIM). Data taken from a portfolio based on 70% in LGIM's Global Equity fund and 30% in LGIM's UK Conventional Government Bond fund. Rolling market value spending at 4%. Consumer Prices Index data from the Office for National Statistics. The numbers represented by the Y axis are simply the index's way of portraying the growth of spending and have no external meaning.

Table 4.1 Summary of the major spending rules

	Most appropriate spending policy for			
Spending rule	**Stable spending**	**Capital maintenance**	**Simple cash flow**	**Charity accounting**
Natural income	✓	✗	✓	✓
Rolling market value	✗	✓	✗	✗
Constant growth	✓	✗	✗	✗

Understanding the impacts of inflation and deflation

Inflation is simply the effect of rising prices being passed on to consumers by companies to make sure their profits are maintained, not eroded. The result of inflation is that, over time, a sum of money becomes worth less than it was in the past – in other words, you can buy less with it, or, in the case of charities, you are less able to help your beneficiaries.

Returns can be measured after the effect of inflation, in which case they are called 'real returns', or they can be measured before they are eroded by inflation, in which case they are called 'nominal returns'. Whichever spending rule you choose, it is important to be aware of how you are measuring your returns, as this makes a huge difference to how sustainable your spending is, especially after several years of investing.

Indices of inflation

Inflation is measured using indices of different types of cost. Each looks at different things that charities can spend money on. There are two main types of index – consumer inflation and earnings inflation – plus a variety of specialist indices:

- **Consumer inflation** is measured using two main indices in the UK: the Retail Prices Index (RPI) and the Consumer Prices Index (CPI). The RPI is still widely used but it is no longer accepted as a valid measure of inflation (because of how it is calculated) and it is very slowly being phased out.[7] It is thought to overestimate actual consumer inflation by as much as 1% a year (see figure 4.3) and is best avoided. The CPI is the modern version of the RPI; it calculates inflation based on a basket of goods thought to be representative of what most consumers purchase in their regular shopping.[8]
- **Earnings inflation** is now measured through an index called Average Weekly Earnings, which in 2010 replaced an equivalent index called the Average Earnings Index.[9] The Average Weekly Earnings data is available with or without bonuses. You will probably find it most appropriate to refer to the data without bonuses because most charities don't pay bonuses to their staff, so these figures will most closely match the sort of salary increases your charity will have to pay. A fair assumption is that earnings inflation is 1% higher than consumer inflation (see figure 4.3).
- **Specialist indices** are also available for industries such as construction, medicine and education.

Figure 4.3 shows, by decade, that the RPI is usually higher than the CPI, and that usually earnings inflation is higher than both (in the UK, the 2010s was an unusual decade for earnings thanks to the government's austerity policies).

Figure 4.3 Comparison of different measures of inflation from 1980 to 2019

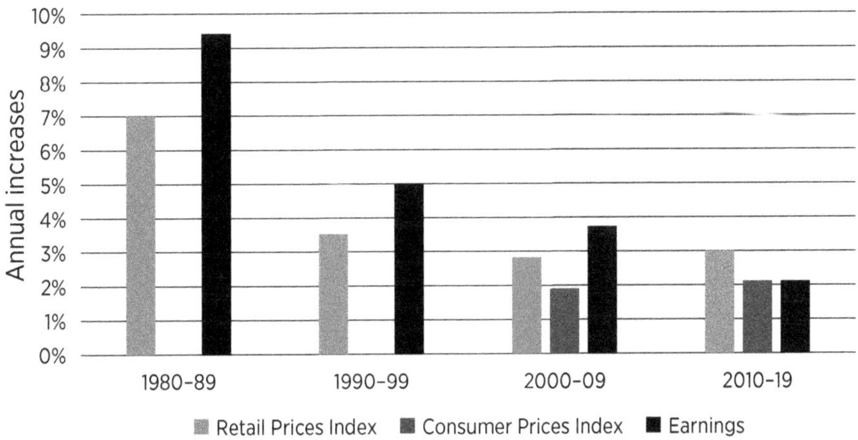

Source: Office for National Statistics data (www.ons.gov.uk). The 'Earnings' data excludes bonuses. The official Consumer Prices Index (CPI) was first published in 1997 in the UK; therefore, CPI data is not presented for the first two decades in the figure.

The rule of 72

For spender charities, and especially those with memories of the 1970s, inflation is a significant concern because it has the capacity to destroy the purchasing power of your investments. You can calculate the approximate effect of inflation using the so-called rule of 72. All you have to do is divide 72 by your chosen measure of inflation to work out how quickly your capital will halve in value. For example, at 2% inflation (the Bank of England's target rate), an amount of money will have only half its purchasing power in 36 years, assuming nothing else changes (72 ÷ 2 = 36).

Deflation

Deflation is the reverse of inflation and it means prices going down, not up. It is feared by investors (and governments) because it encourages consumers to delay purchasing based on the hope that things will get cheaper the longer they wait. This means that consumption is lower, economic growth is lower and tax revenues are lower.

The best response to a deflationary environment is to own assets that pay you a fixed return that cannot go down, such as fixed-interest assets like most bonds. For example, if you bought a bond that paid you 6% for the next 30 years, and over that time there was deflation, it would cost more and more to buy the same high level of income, and the asset would become more valuable. This is the reverse of what happens with inflation, where it is advantageous to own assets that do *not* have fixed incomes (such as equities) as they can benefit from inflation increases.

Factoring inflation into your spending decisions

Of all the risks that long-term investors face, inflation is the one they fear most. It acts like a tax on wealth, inexorably reducing its purchasing power. Some strategies are better at dealing with inflation than others, but there comes a point where it is impossible to devise an acceptable portfolio that can protect you from high long-term inflation. Most spender charities invest heavily in equities and property, which are protective, to an extent, against inflation. Consequently, the same charities that are protected against inflation will be exposed to deflation (where fixed income is their friend). This preference for inflation protection (over deflation protection) is widely considered to be an acceptable position for saver and spender charities (because inflation has been more common than deflation over prolonged periods).

Finally, remember that inflation can affect you in two different ways: global inflation will affect your investments and how they perform, but UK inflation will affect your spending. There is no reason to assume that the two rates will be the same. The difference tends to be worked out in the changing value of the currencies involved.

How to be more ambitious

The task of charities is to make as much money as they safely can and spend it as wisely as they can. To this end, there are three questions that your charity should ask itself:

- Can you earn more?
- Can you use what you earn more effectively – in other words, can you free up more of your investment income for spending?
- Can you use your assets more creatively?

Let's consider these questions in turn.

Can you earn more?

This is a matter of investment strategy and is dealt with fully in chapter 5. However, in brief, while it is easy to think that you can endlessly demand more and more from your investments, this isn't the case. The most dynamic asset class is equity investments and table 4.2 shows how an equity investor profits from this dynamism. The backbone of an investment return is based on the dividend that you receive and its prospects for increasing that payout over time. Table 4.2 shows how a company generates a growing income.

Table 4.2 Equity sources of return

Source	Amount	Explanation
Dividend	3%	The annual payment you receive from the company,
+ inflation	2%	which increases the cost of its goods by inflation
+ growing global consumption	2%	as more people buy more things (so sales increase)
+ efficiency gains	1%	and it costs less to make the same things,
Total return	**8%**	resulting in an increase in its earnings

This is a model and so all these numbers are approximate and should be taken with a large pinch of salt. They will vary over time, economic sector and geography (and will sometimes even be negative in periods of general economic recession or depression, meaning the company has zero or negative growth and so does not issue a dividend). However, the table does illustrate a simple model of how a total return is generated from an equity portfolio.

Now think about how you spend those total returns, as shown in table 4.3.

Table 4.3 Application of returns

Allocation	Amount	Explanation
Investment fees	1%	You have to pay these costs
+ inflation	2%	and you need to keep money back to protect your capital from inflation
+ saving a bit extra	1%	and if you want to grow your fund in real terms you will need to put some money aside for that
+ spending	4%	leaving a certain amount for spending,
Total allocation	**8%**	and all of this adds up to what you've earned.

If we now look at the earning and spending tables side by side (see table 4.4), you can see how small the component parts are, and how difficult they are to change in a way that will dramatically alter what you can spend.

Table 4.4 Balancing return and spending

What you receive		What you do with it	
Source	**Amount**	**Allocation**	**Amount**
Dividend	3%	Investment fees	1%
+ inflation	2%	+ inflation	2%
+ growing global consumption	2%	+ saving a bit extra	1%
+ efficiency gains	1%	+ spending	4%
Total return	**8%**	**Total allocation**	**8%**

The first thing to notice is that the two tables have the same total. The total return is 8% and the total allocated is also 8%, so everything the company has earned for you is allocated to some purpose. How then can you increase your income and spending? You can't make the population grow faster or improve company efficiency, but you can decide not to save 1% and spend it instead. You might pay less in investment fees, or find a company with a higher (but still sustainable) dividend. Conversely, you might find that the company is so badly managed that it has negative efficiency gains and the value of the dividend is in effect reduced to nil. In this situation you'd have earned nothing once you'd protected yourself against inflation. But overall, it is harder to adjust what you earn than it is to adjust how you use those earnings. And that is where spending policies come in – to make sure you are using those returns as effectively as possible for your beneficiaries.

The takeaway from the above is that the components of a long-term return are largely outside your control (such as growing global consumption), although you have some choice about investing in companies that are more efficiently run than others. The most significant decision you can make is how much to hold in high-returning assets, such as equities. The lower the proportion, the lower the amount you will generate to spend, so what was 8% might be much lower the less you hold in equities. This is why your asset choices matter so much, as does understanding whether you have the scope to live with high levels of unpredictability in your returns by choosing high-risk, high-returning assets (such as equities) over much safer but low-returning assets (such as bonds). It is the simple story that you can only take out what you put in.

In considering the question 'Can I earn more?', you will need to familiarise yourself with all of the limitations discussed in chapter 5, particularly around your tolerance for uncertainty and the time horizon on which you are operating. The answer to the question will almost certainly be 'yes' – there is almost always scope to earn more – but it would be nonsensical to pursue a path of short-term gain at the expense of your longer-term financial objectives and goals.

It is also important not to consider this question too frequently. For instance, if you decide you want to go for a high-octane portfolio to boost your earnings, but the first time you encounter a large market fall you change your mind and sell everything, you will only have damaged your portfolio. Having a policy you can live with is very important, as is having effective, steadfast governance that can give you access to higher long-term returns (see chapter 8).

Can you spend more?

This question is not about how much you can spend per se – that will be determined by how much you earn and your choice of spending rule. Rather, it is about spending more *on your charitable purpose* by carving up the cake represented by your total spending pot in the way that is most efficient and best representative of your financial objectives and goals.

There are several areas you can think about:

- **Investment management fees:** unless you are planning to invest your money yourself, or leave it in a bank, you will incur investment management fees. However, the information in chapter 10 will help you to ensure you are hiring appropriately and getting good value for money.
- **Inflation:** if you are keeping money back to match inflation, are you using the most appropriate rate? See the section on the impact of inflation on page 67.
- **Saving a bit extra:** if you are saving to protect against inflation, don't try to grow your fund faster than inflation, because you will just be saving money you could be spending.

It may seem that you have to accept the income that you are offered by your investment manager as all that you are allowed to spend, but you do have a number of levers to pull that can change what you are able to spend. How much you spend, in all cases other than a permanent endowment, is up to you, and no one else.

Can you use your assets more creatively?

You can use your assets to make social investments, which can advance your purpose as well as making a return. This is covered fully in chapter 9, on responsible investing.

Fictional case studies

Spender: Warden's Philanthropy

Warden's Philanthropy's trustees want to have a core level of spending that they can rely on year in, year out. They also want to spend as much as possible while maintaining their ability to spend a similar amount into the future. Spending volatility is an important consideration too. The trustees want to have a stable level of expenditure from year to year to help with their budgeting.

The trustees passed a board resolution to move to total return accounting and investing (the precise details of this are given in the case study at the end of appendix 2). After completing this process, the trustees discussed different spending levels with their investment manager, who suggested that 3% of their portfolio's value at the end of every year was a safe level of spending. The trustees discussed this carefully and decided that this would result in a volatile annual spending budget, and also that, considering the charity's origins, not spending enough was a worse risk than spending too much. They therefore decided on setting a 'higher than safe' spending policy based on 5% of their long-term target value of £32 million (a concept discussed in chapter 6) and monitoring it periodically to see how this turned out. Happily, this also resulted in a substantial increase in their spending over their previous approach of spending a natural income only.

Since spending stability also mattered to them, they agreed to use a constant growth rule so their annual distribution would increase with inflation every year. They could adjust their spending level from time to time depending on how they were performing against their target values (see chapter 6). If they had more money than they needed to maintain their capital, they could be more relaxed about spending more (either as a temporary annual uplift or as a lump sum). If they had less, they would be more cautious, ultimately reducing their spending if necessary. It would all depend on how close they were to their overall target value.

Saver: Martello Tower Fund

The Martello Tower Fund (MTF) is the most substantial restricted fund of the fundraising charity Preserving Our Nautical Past. At the moment the MTF does not have any significant spending requirements (other than investment fees and occasional updates on the likely cost of the work of building its sea wall), so its policy is to spend on an ad hoc basis. When it reaches the point when it will start its building work, it will become a spend-out fund and have a spending policy appropriate for that sort of model.

Spend-outer: Butterworth Music Festivals

Butterworth Music Festivals must spend its entire £10 million on bringing music to communities that otherwise might not enjoy any live performances. Its governing document requires that this is done within ten years of making its first grant, or any balance left will be sent to the government as a donation. In theory, there is nothing complicated about its spending policy. The trustees just take out the money when they need it in line with their spending plan.

But nothing in life is ever that simple. The trustees originally made a schedule of their expected payments for the next ten years and gave it to their investment manager to implement. These projections are now in some disarray because their investment manager has earned more money than they expected, and it turns out to be more difficult to spend the money than they had expected because of the time it takes to make assessments and find projects of sufficient quality to fund. As a result, they have been working closely with their investment manager to model their latest future budgets and how to invest the money appropriately. As much as the trustees want to speed up their spending, they still want to spend wisely.

They considered using a fixed rate of spending but rejected that in favour of something more flexible. They have decided that, when they get near the end of the ten-year spending term, they will grant any remaining investments to one or two of their preferred beneficiaries to make sure the £10 million (together with any additional income) has been fully spent, but without them having to spend out to an exact zero balance. This will give the trustees the greatest flexibility in closing down in an orderly way.

Conclusion

Spending levels should be kept as high as possible and only adjusted downwards if you do not have enough in your reserves to maintain their target values. Although in many ways there is nothing wrong with using natural income as the basis of your spending decisions, you are likely to find total return more rewarding in terms of both spending and investing. The next chapter looks at the investing part of this equation.

Notes

1 James Tobin, 'What Is Permanent Endowment Income?', *American Economic Review*, 427, no. 2, 1974, pp. 427–32.

2 'Total return investment for permanently endowed charities' [web page], Charity Commission for England and Wales, 2023, www.gov.uk/government/publications/total-return-investment-for-permanently-endowed-charities/total-return-investment-for-permanently-endowed-charities, accessed 20 January 2024.

3 *Charity Reserves* [PDF], Charity Commission for England and Wales, 2003, https://assets.publishing.service.gov.uk/government/uploads/system/uploads/attachment_data/file/284727/rs3text.pdf, p. 24, accessed 20 January 2024.

4 'Total return investment for permanently endowed charities' [web page], Charity Commission for England and Wales, 2023, www.gov.uk/government/publications/total-return-investment-for-permanently-endowed-charities/total-return-investment-for-permanently-endowed-charities, accessed 20 January 2024.

5 Caroline Banton, 'Total return: Definition, formula to calculate it, examples' [web article], Investopedia, www.investopedia.com/terms/t/totalreturn.asp, 28 April 2021.

6 Elroy Dimson, Paul Marsh and Mike Staunton, *Global Investment Returns Yearbook 2024*, London, London Business School, 2024.

7 'Shortcomings of the Retail Prices Index as a measure of inflation' [web article], Office for National Statistics, www.ons.gov.uk/economy/inflationandpriceindices/articles/shortcomingsoftheretailpricesindexasameasureofinflation/2018-03-08, 8 March 2018.

8 The CPI can be consulted at 'UK statistics' [web page], WTW, www.wtwco.com/en-GB/Insights/campaigns/uk-statistics, accessed 20 January 2024.

9 The latest edition of the Average Weekly Earnings data can be consulted at 'EARN01: Average Weekly Earnings' [web page], Office for National Statistics, www.ons.gov.uk/employmentandlabourmarket/peopleinwork/earningsandworkinghours/datasets/averageweeklyearningsearn01, accessed 20 January 2024.

Chapter five

Investment strategy

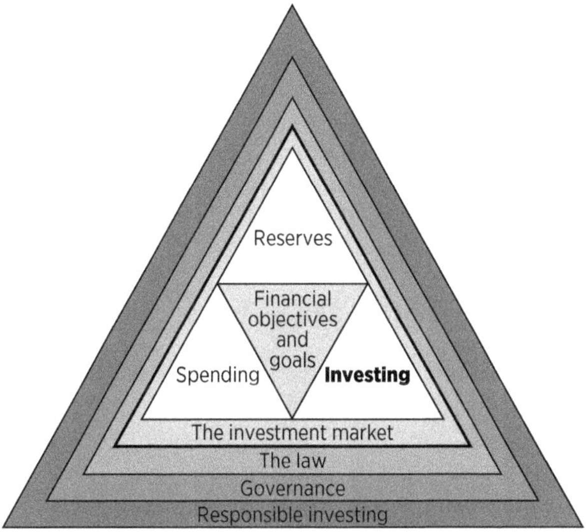

The purpose of this chapter

For charities, successful investing is about making as much money as you can – so you can spend more of it on your charitable purpose. The constraint is not your ambition but how much unpredictability, uncertainty, complexity and even immorality (the topic of chapter 9) you wish to tolerate in how you earn your return. Good investing is focused on understanding your limits well and managing effectively in accordance with them.

This chapter is focused on understanding what these limits are and, importantly, how to know whether you have set them at the right level to help you meet your financial objectives and goals. In investment parlance, this is usually (and misleadingly) referred to as your 'risk appetite'. In fact, it is as much about your appetite for opportunity as it is about your aversion to danger, so better phrases than 'risk appetite' would be your 'tolerance of uncertainty' or your 'tolerance of unpredictability' (this book uses these phrases interchangeably). Where the word 'risk' is used, it should be regarded equally as an opportunity and a potential hazard unless the context dictates otherwise, such as a permanent loss of capital. And as markets go up more than they go down, it would probably be better to substitute the word 'opportunity' for 'risk'.

This chapter starts by addressing the important question of whether investing is the right choice for your charity and how it might relate to the other options available to you. It then thoroughly explores the central concept of risk and unpredictability before moving on to how this feeds into your investment strategy and how you can use diversification to reduce the unpredictability of your portfolio's outcomes. The next, crucial section introduces the concept of having different attitudes to this unpredictability about future returns for different time horizons so as to ensure your investment decisions are appropriate for how you plan to use different pots of money. Finally, the chapter looks at the choices our three fictional charities have made in their financial strategies.

Is investing the right choice for your charity?

Before you start to think about *how* to invest, the first thing to do is to step back and consider *whether* you should be investing at all. Even charities with well-established investment activities will benefit from occasionally reassessing their assumptions about why and how they are investing. For example, your charity might be struggling to find money to help its cause, perhaps because of the impacts of a serious event (such as the COVID-19 pandemic or war). On a strictly investment basis, you are likely to achieve more by investing in your purpose than you are by earning money from future returns. The same applies to fundraising opportunities. If you were confident that a fundraising push would deliver a step change in your income, then it would make financial sense to invest in fundraising, not in stock markets.

When deciding whether investing is right for your charity, a good place to begin would be to ask yourself: if you were starting out with a pile of cash, would your first decision be to create an investment portfolio? Data from *Charity Finance* magazine suggests that there could be better approaches to investing in markets. For over 25 years, *Charity Finance* has tracked the growth in different sources of income of the largest UK charities. For the top 100 charities (measured by income), all other forms of income have grown more (see figure 5.1), and the same is true of the next 250 too.

Figure 5.1 Charity Finance 250 Index, 1996–2022

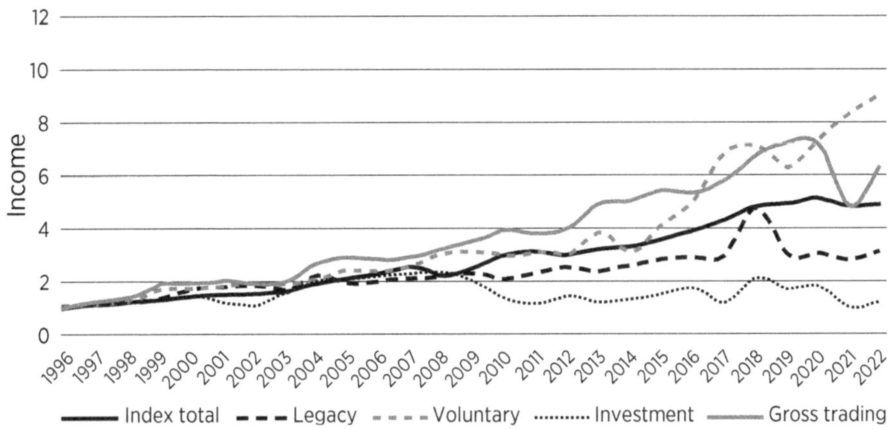

Note: The numbers represented by the Y axis are simply the index's way of portraying the growth of income and have no external meaning.

Source: Charity Finance 250 Index, published in *Charity Finance* by Civil Society Media.

This is not a reason to hastily liquidate your entire portfolio or breathe a sigh of relief if you have not yet dipped a toe into the investment world. Just because the top 100 or next 250 charities have seen more growth in their income from fundraising and other non-investment sources does not mean that all charities will have enjoyed such success. For the right charity, investing in fundraising or trading can be better than investing in stock markets, but for many – and all those without a fundraising or trading infrastructure – an investment portfolio will play an essential role in generating income to fund spending.

The point is that you should not automatically assume that investing is right or wrong, but instead think carefully and realistically about the best way to earn a return for your charity to spend based on your own unique circumstances. There are two major areas that you might want to consider beyond investing in the stock markets: fundraising and social investments.

Fundraising

Could you use some (or all) of your capital (i.e. the money you are considering investing) to generate a better, faster-growing and more relevant source of income by investing in a fundraising initiative instead of investing in financial markets? For example, if your charity supports a new and suddenly popular cause, it may make more sense to invest in your fundraising capacity so as to meet the immediate demand (and then later invest any surplus in the financial markets), as fundraising will give you higher short-term returns. This is the domain of fundraisers and if you are considering this route, you should get their expert advice on what results would be possible (and likely) and whether or not your charity would be able to achieve similar fundraising results to a well-known, top 250 charity name such as those shown in figure 5.1. DSC's book *Fundraising Strategy* is also a useful source of information on fundraising approaches.[1]

Imagine you have two sources of income, both of which give you £100,000 of income a year. One is an investment portfolio that is worth £2.5 million, and the other is your fundraising programme. Although your fundraising programme has no value on your balance sheet, it can make sense to think of it as also being worth £2.5 million, because it also gives you £100,000 a year. It is just as valuable to you as your investment portfolio. It might even be that your fundraising income is more reliable than your investment income, in which case it will provide you with a better balance between risk and reward. And, even if your fundraising income is no more reliable than your investment income, it is unlikely to behave in the same way as financial markets so it may well complement your investment income by providing a source of diversification (see page 91). But if you're starting from scratch, an investment portfolio may well offer an easier ride because it generally works from day one.

Social investments

Investing in a financial portfolio is only a means to an end, not an end in itself. Sometimes it can be much simpler, cheaper and more effective to invest directly yourself. For example, some charities have decided to provide discounted workspaces for artists or fund laboratories for scientists. These social investments, also called 'impact investments', can maintain their value, create an income and generate opportunities that might not otherwise have existed.

Social investments are increasingly considered to be a type of investing in their own right. See chapters 7 and 9 for more information.

Making the decision for your charity

The point is that when thinking about your investment strategy, you should see it as part of your whole financial package and allocate capital to the best-returning assets. So your first task as an investor is to determine what kind of return each activity – investments and fundraising – is likely to provide after costs and then reflect on the best balance between them for your charity. If you don't yet have either an established fundraising programme or a mature investment portfolio, your conclusions may initially be provisional, but it is important to at least consider the options you may have, based on some realistic estimates.

Assuming that you have decided investments should make up some portion of your charity's investing activities, the next step is to understand a key concept in investing: risk.

All about risk

The most important decision in investing is how to allocate your investment portfolio between the different asset classes (cash, bonds, equities, etc.; see chapter 3). It is this process, called asset allocation, that translates your tolerance for unpredictability and uncertainty (your risk appetite) into an investment strategy. This in turn will determine how much you can earn and therefore how much you can spend. Your tolerance of this unpredictability is informed by what you are trying to do (your financial objectives and goals; see chapter 2), how much latitude you have in achieving those goals over time (your reserves policy; see chapter 6) and what you are hoping to spend every year (your spending policy; see chapter 4).

Risk versus unpredictability and uncertainty

For most people, a financial risk is a risk of losing money permanently. However, to an investment professional, risk means unpredictability, uncertainty or volatility – or, more specifically, that you cannot know precisely what a given asset will be worth at a future point because the market might have gone up, gone down or stayed the same. The point is that the value of a risky asset in the days and years ahead cannot be predicted or relied upon. 'Risky' doesn't mean that a company in which you have invested is more likely to go bust; it just means that the company's value is more likely to change (either up or down). This can be illustrated by way of a riddle:

> **Question:** Two people separately jump out of a plane flying high in the air. One is wearing a parachute and one is not. Which person is at greater risk?
>
> **Answer:** The fate of the person who jumps from the plane without a parachute is certain: they will die. There is no uncertainty, so that person is not exposed to any risk. In contrast, the person who jumps out of the plane with a parachute is at greater risk because there is more uncertainty about their fate: they might survive, or their parachute might malfunction and send them to their death.

Based on this understanding of risk, for most spender and saver charities, a risky asset is as much an opportunity to buy cheaply as it is to lose money. For spend-out charities (and other bodies that need predictability, such as pension funds; see page 58), volatile assets will be a much less enticing prospect. The key thing is therefore to understand your tolerance for uncertainty and unpredictability based on your financial objectives and goals. To understand this, consider another riddle:

> **Question:** A potato rolls into a chip shop. To what risk is the potato exposed?
>
> **Answer:** It is a potato and it has no conception of the future, so it does not care what happens to it in the chip shop. It is at no risk of being disappointed. The potato's owner might be exposed to some risk. To be at risk, the outcome must matter to you.

The point here is that you need to understand *why* you are investing (i.e. your financial objectives and goals) before you can gauge whether unpredictable assets are right for you and in what circumstances. The key skill in investing lies in buying assets only when you understand (a) where the uncertainty is and (b) whether this uncertainty is tolerable for you. This means that what is a risk (according to the common understanding of this word) for others may not be a risk for you. You may still be rewarded for taking what others consider to be a risk (because riskier assets commonly provide higher returns), even though the risk doesn't really matter to you.

Avoiding 'proper' risks

Following is a list of what would be considered 'proper' risks according to the day-to-day understanding of the word. If things go wrong in these areas, bad things happen, unlike in the case of investment unpredictability, where good things are as likely to happen as bad things.

Counterparty: A counterparty is the person sitting on the other side of a contract that you rely on to do what they have committed to do (see page 33 for more information). If the counterparty gets into trouble, you may face either a delay in recovering your funds or a significant loss. Firms that are regulated by the Financial Conduct Authority are less likely to present counterparty risk, but it exists everywhere. Diversification (see page 91) is an important way of mitigating this risk.

Liquidity: This refers to your capacity to raise cash from an asset. Chapter 3 goes into detail about the liquidity of different asset types. The key point is that an illiquid asset can be difficult to sell quickly. Another common trap lies in single funds that contain a mixture of liquid and illiquid assets. If such a fund gets into trouble, the early sellers will use up the liquidity and the fund will have to delay repaying the remaining investors.

Donor stock: Some charities are founded with a gift of shares in a particular company. This automatically creates a conflict between loyalty to the donor and the duty of a charity to consider diversification (see page 138). Obviously, a portfolio of only one stock means that you are wholly exposed to the company's fortunes, but equally it means that you will be more engaged in how the business is doing (and how responsibly it is being managed). In the end, all portfolios made up entirely of donor stock will either diversify or go bust. The important question is which comes first.

Poor advice (business risk): While it's absolutely true that no manager wants to lose their client's money, the other thing that matters greatly is not losing the client. Clients take a long time to land and are very valuable once on a manager's books, so some managers have little conviction and often invest in companies simply because other people do, not because they think they are any good (see chapter 10 on finding a suitable investment manager).

Service levels: Poor client service from your manager is more trouble than it is worth. Two key safety measures are to never use a manager who is not regulated and always get references from other clients focusing on client service, timeliness, and accuracy (and sometimes cost) of reports. For example, an inability to provide you with accurate and up-to-date figures for your accounts can have serious consequences for how your organisation is perceived in terms of financial competence, as well as hindering your ability to monitor the manager.

Fraud: Always maintain clear segregation of duties between those who can authorise your instructions and those who can execute (see page 144 for information on conflicts of interest). Always remember that if something sounds too good to be true, it usually is.

Why taking risks matters

You get paid for taking risks (i.e. accepting unpredictable or uncertain returns). This is so fundamental to the investment process that it is worth dwelling upon. Following is an example of how it works.

Let's say that two people want to borrow money from you. Abi has a steady income from her business, but Philip's business has been more erratic. You have £5,000 to invest. Abi's business looks like a much safer bet, so what would Philip have to do to get you to lend to him rather than to Abi? The answer is that Philip would have to make his offer much more attractive, so he would tempt you by offering you a larger share of the profits or a higher interest payment than Abi. Consequently, as sure as night follows day, investors expect to be paid more for being exposed to more uncertainty. If this didn't happen, people would only invest in safe ventures because there would be no reason to invest anywhere else (and the markets would grind to a halt).

This does not mean that just because something is more risky you are more certain to receive a higher return. Some investments are simply bad. In other words, be careful to distinguish between 'risk-free return' (possibly Abi) and 'return-free risk' (possibly Philip).

Living with uncertainty

If your investment strategy is aligned to a spending policy that delivers the cash you need and your reserves policy gives you latitude in how you meet your financial objectives and goals, you will have a much higher chance of tolerating any uncertainty about the value of your investments and you will be paid for that. This uncertainty might be more than you expect or it might be less, but understanding the difference between the commonplace definition of risk and the investing definition (i.e. unpredictability) is vital to being a successful charity investor. As such, if an investment manager suggests to you that your financial objectives and goals might best be served by adopting a risky strategy, it is important to remember that they don't mean they want to increase the chance of permanently losing your capital. Instead, they are simply saying you could manage to live with a higher level of unpredictability.

Unpredictability and uncertainty are also closely tied up with timescales. As explored in chapter 2, the longer your time horizon, the more uncertainty you will be able to tolerate (see page 24). For example, if you have a long-term horizon (say, over five years), you may be willing to live with more unpredictability than an equivalent charity with a short-term horizon because you have more time to recover from any period of low or negative returns. This commonly applies to spender and saver charities. For those charities, risk is a quality that it is necessary to respect and even love, but not fear.

The efficient frontier

Based on the understanding of risk above, investment strategy translates the historical uncertainty of asset returns into a graphical representation called the 'efficient frontier'. In this model, unpredictability is measured by the volatility of the assets' total return (i.e. their income and capital gain or loss; see page 64). The model was created by Harry Markowitz in 1952 and has become a central component of modern investment approaches.[2] It says that the more volatile a return, the higher the compensation should be to the owner (so the asset continues to attract investors), as in the example of Abi and Philip above.

The idea of the efficient frontier can be used to plot asset types on a graph to show their relative volatilities and returns, as shown in figure 5.2 (see chapter 3 for information on long-term expected returns). The figure shows that cash is the least volatile and lowest-returning asset. Its price is the most certain and it is therefore considered the least 'risky'. Bonds are considered to be one step up from cash in both returns and volatility. Further up the scale, equities have much more unpredictable total returns so they should be rewarded more highly than cash. Property tends to lie between equities and bonds.

Figure 5.2 The relative volatilities and returns of four common asset types

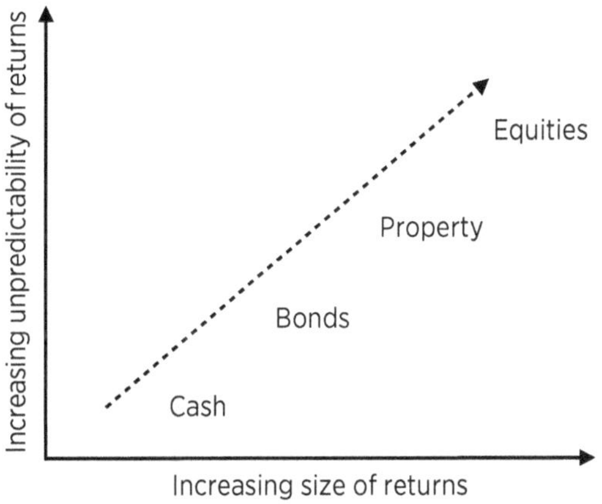

Although the efficient frontier model is a good way to think about volatility and return over the very long term (i.e. decades), it can still fail woefully over quite long multi-year periods (where bonds may outperform equities, for example – see the box below). Nevertheless, the model is useful because it describes a way to think about unpredictability, risk and return.

Incorporating inflation into the efficient frontier

Efficient frontier charts of the type shown in figure 5.2 tend to depict the same thing – annual volatility against returns. A weakness is that they often do not include the effect of inflation and can measure volatility in different ways. These different versions show that over longer time horizons, equities can be less volatile than bonds because of the way inflation reduces long-term returns. This reverses the conventional wisdom that bonds are less risky than equities over the long term, instead demonstrating that they will be more risky and unpredictable. A tolerance for uncertainty, unpredictability and volatility therefore remains under-recognised as a source of advantage for those charity investors who are not alarmed by short-term price fluctuations (usually saver and spender charities).

Building your investment strategy

Now that we have established how important the concept of risk or uncertainty is in investing, we can move on to consider the actual components of an investment strategy. There is a potentially bewildering array of options available to you as an investor, so it can be helpful to think of these options as a sliding scale of unpredictability, where you pick a point on the scale that is right for your charity. You can then use the scale to communicate your risk appetite to your investment manager, which will help them to choose a suitable combination of assets for your charity.

Deciding on risk or reward

You do not choose what level of return you can have by saying 'high', 'medium' or 'low'. Everyone always wants the highest level they can have, so in reality what you earn is simply a by-product of your tolerance for uncertainty and loss. Figure 5.3 shows how this balance between unpredictability and return works; it presents the same information as in figure 5.2 but more simply, with just two extremes: cash/bonds or equities/property. This is because whatever your appetite for unpredictability, you will always want the greatest return from your investment. The left-hand end represents a more predictable outcome and the right-hand end represents a much higher degree of unpredictability. In the middle would be different blends of the various asset types. The implication is that at any point along the line you will always want the maximum return that is available given your appetite for unpredictability and uncertainty. This is the basic version of the sliding scale of risk and uncertainty, and it shows the essential choice that you face when it comes to investing: it is not possible to have both high returns and stable (i.e. not volatile) asset values.

Figure 5.3 Simple risk (unpredictability) and returns

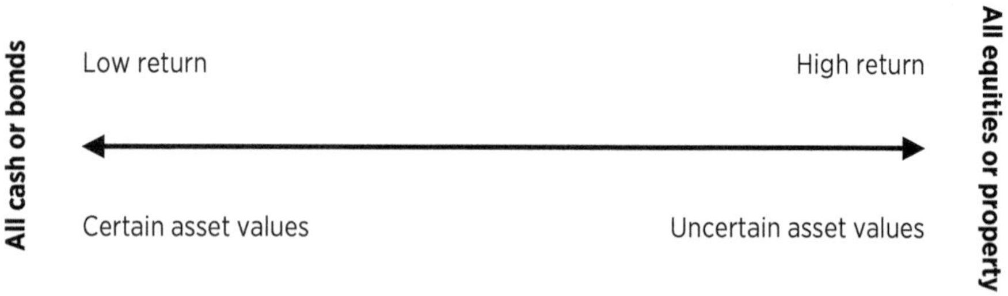

As this chapter has established, the amount of uncertainty and unpredictability that you can tolerate is key to determining your future returns and investment strategy. It follows that being able to maximise how much uncertainty you can tolerate will enable you to achieve the largest returns. The importance of this cannot be overestimated because it is too easy to simply opt for a low- or medium-risk portfolio when a more unpredictable one might be sufficiently reliable for your charity's needs and would return commensurately more. Opting for a too-safe portfolio would be like instructing your fundraising director that it was okay to be unambitious – some money would be fine, but the director needn't worry about getting the most out of your fundraising investment. No one would give an instruction on that basis, so why would you ask an investment manager to do that?

Ultimately, deciding between risk and reward is a simple matter of time. The shorter your time horizon and the more your need for certainty, the further to the left of the scale in figure 5.3 that you must sit. Likewise, if you have a longer time horizon, you will be more tolerant of uncertainty and so can sit further to the right on the scale.

Incorporating inflation

The scale can be modified to incorporate the impact of inflation on assets, as shown in figure 5.4. Inflation matters because if you ignore it, the number of things that your assets can purchase (or the amount you can afford to pay your staff) will diminish over time.

Figure 5.4 Risk (unpredictability) and returns after inflation

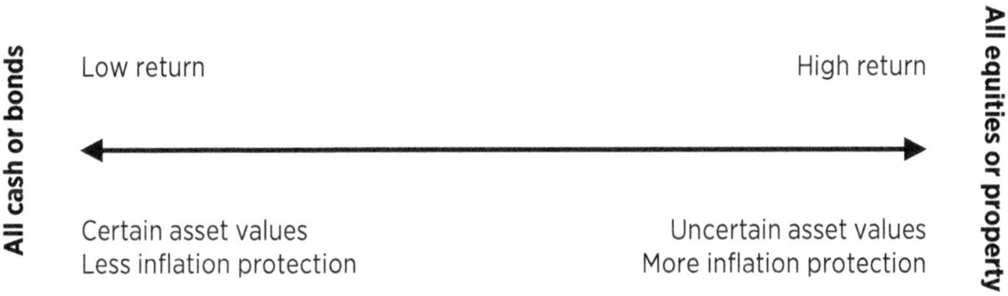

Some assets provide better protection against inflation than others (see chapter 3). The best way to think about this is that assets that generate a fixed income will not fare well in an inflationary environment because if your income is fixed (e.g. as in a bond paying a fixed income), it stays the same while inflation pushes up your costs. Over time, what you can purchase with your fixed income is slowly eroded.

Unlike bonds, equities (and to a lesser extent property) have 'pricing power'. This means that as inflation increases, the company can increase the cost of what it sells to its customers, thereby maintaining its dividends in line with inflation. How this happens is covered in chapter 4.

Again, deciding where you are on this scale is a matter of time. If your charity intends to be around for a long time, you have little choice other than to start at the right-hand side of the scale. Your portfolio will be unpredictable, but you will also have something more important – better inflation protection.

Incorporating spending demands

As we know from the efficient frontier model, the more volatile a portfolio, the higher its long-term returns will be, so the higher the spending it will be able to support (as long as it is combined with a good spending policy that can smooth returns where required; see page 63).

Figure 5.5 Risk (unpredictability) and returns after inflation with spending level incorporated

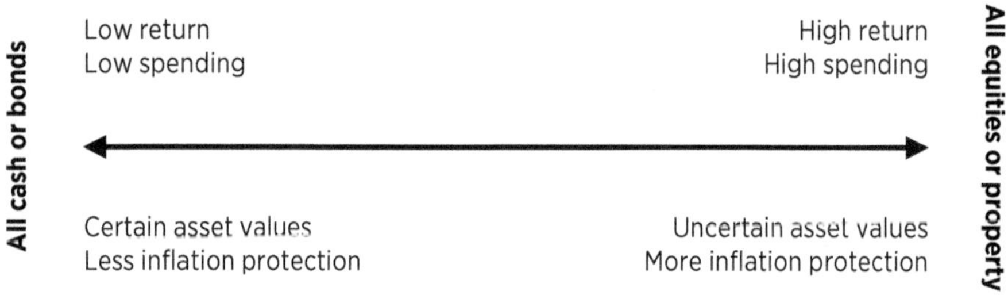

If you are going to be ambitious about what you can do for your beneficiaries, you will want to be able to spend as much as possible. That will move you to the right-hand side of the scale in figure 5.5, unless of course you are expecting to spend everything in the near future (when you would need to be on the left-hand side in order to preserve the value of the money you are about to spend).

Adding in liquidity

If we add in some tolerance for assets that can't easily be sold in times of financial distress (such as private equity), then it is possible to increase returns further since illiquid assets are less attractive than liquid ones – this is an option that spender and saver charities may wish to take. You should always keep enough cash or liquid assets on hand to meet your short-term commitments (wages, grants, etc.) and needs, which means that spend-out charities will want to avoid these illiquid assets in their portfolios.

Figure 5.6 Risk (unpredictability) and returns after inflation with spending level and liquidity incorporated

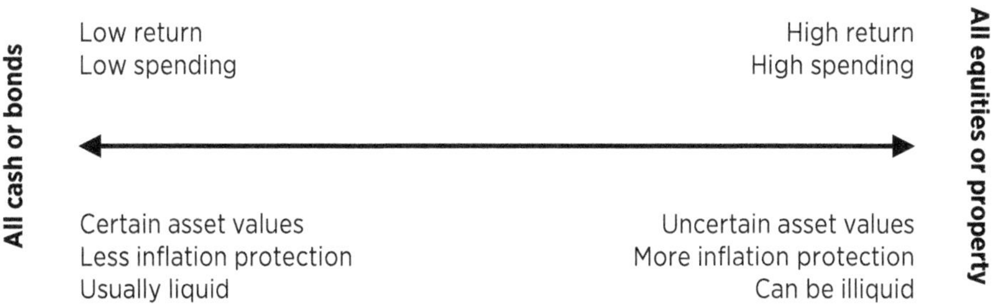

As shown in figure 5.6, adding in illiquid assets has the potential to increase your returns (assuming it is done skilfully), but it is not an option that is available to all investors. If you need the cash soon, you shouldn't invest in illiquid assets, regardless of the extra return that could be available.

Incorporating governance

The balance between risk and reward, inflation, spending demands and liquidity is a question of portfolio construction. The most important attribute of a well-run charity is steadfast governance, whose key component is well-laid plans developed to tolerate all of the uncertainties above. Without it, there may be times, such as a stock market rout, when you will be tempted to sell everything to save what you can before running to the hills. Strong governance is what will enable you to stand fast against this temptation. Therefore, the final part of the jigsaw is the governance characteristics of your organisation (see figure 5.7).

Figure 5.7 Risk (unpredictability) and returns after inflation with spending level, liquidity and governance incorporated

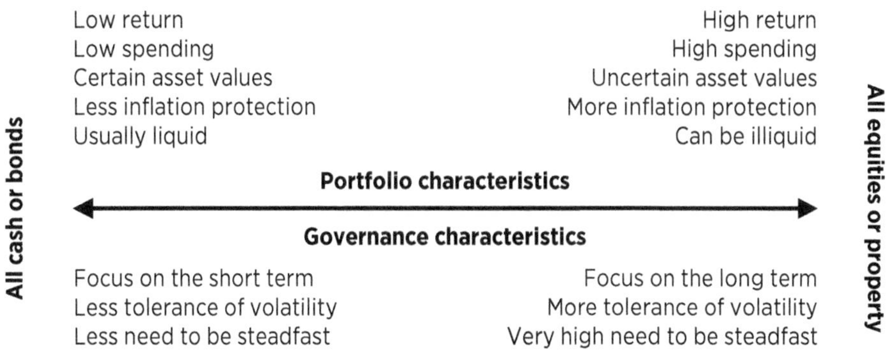

In short, a better-governed organisation can tolerate more uncertainty and volatility, which will over the long term give it higher returns, better inflation protection and larger long-term spending budgets. This does not mean that organisations that invest in non-volatile assets (and therefore choose to accept lower returns) have poor governance: non-volatile assets might be the right choice for your financial objectives and goals. It simply means that if your governance is unreliable, you will be an unsuccessful investor – and that the consequences are likely to be far worse if you choose to invest in volatile assets.

Good governance is therefore the 'asset' of choice and this is dealt with further in chapter 8. It is quite possible to spend hours agonising about risk appetites and asset allocation while completely ignoring the importance of good governance. If there is a solid underpinning to your governance, you will be able to access much higher returns because of your better tolerance of the associated unpredictability.

Investment strategy overview

Another approach to thinking about this balance between risk and reward is that you have to choose only two out of the following three items:

- a stable and certain value for your capital;
- protection for your assets and spending against inflation;
- a larger amount to spend.

For instance, if you want to protect your capital from inflation, but also want to have a stable value for your assets, having a larger amount to spend will not be an option that you can choose. Deciding which of these three items you can most painlessly do without is helpful in highlighting your priorities.

Table 5.1 illustrates how you might think about your priorities, depending on your overarching financial objective. Your financial objective will determine whether you prioritise a certain capital value, inflation protection or having a larger amount to spend.

Table 5.1 Choosing between risk and reward

Financial objective	Certain capital value	Inflation protection	Larger amount to spend
Spender or saver	✗	✓	✓
Spend-outer	✓	✓	✗

Diversification

The principle of diversification sits at the heart of how an investment strategy is translated into choices about which assets to buy. In reality, your investment manager will likely make most of the detailed decisions on your behalf on the basis of your ability to live with uncertainty and unpredictability (covered later in this chapter). However, it is important to have at least a basic understanding of the role that diversification plays so that you can appreciate the choices being made on your behalf.

Simple diversification

Diversification is often said to be the only free lunch in the world of investment management. If an asset's value is volatile, choosing another asset to pair it with will reduce that volatility – so long as it moves in the opposite direction (known as being 'negatively correlated').

Figure 5.8 shows the impact on annual returns of owning two companies, one making winter coats and the other swimwear. In the winter one company does well while the other does badly, and vice versa in the summer. If you put all of your money in one company or the other, you would make the same amount of money, but half the year would be very profitable and the other half very sparse. By holding half your money in each company, you can earn the same return but with greater consistency.

Figure 5.8 An example of simple diversification

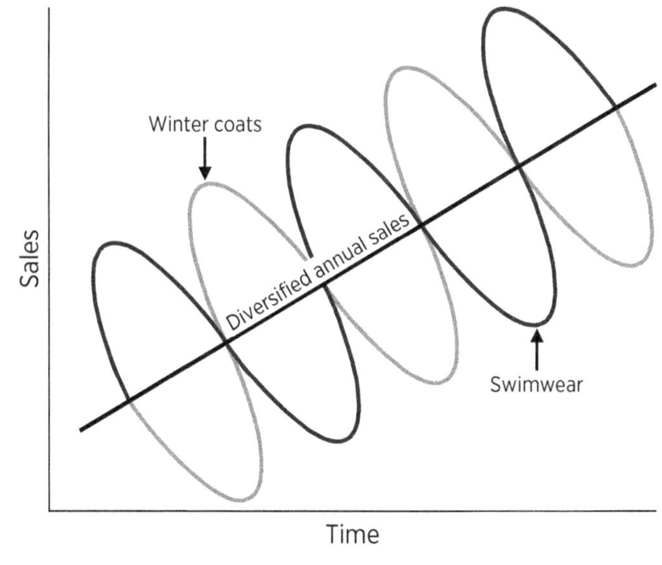

Diversification is said to be a 'free lunch' because your return is unaffected, but you make the money with more stability and less uncertainty (or, in investment terms, lower risk). The alternative is to try and read the weather well and sell swimwear when it is sunny and winter coats when it is not. This requires you to get two decisions right every time (what to own and what not to own), and to do so consistently and repeatedly. That's just not feasible.

Problems also arise when assets that you think are diversified turn out not to be. An example is that in times of acute financial stress (such as the 2007–8 global financial crisis or the onset of COVID-19), everything tends to go down together (usually except for gold and cash). In those circumstances, you might find that supposedly diversified assets (such as equities and bonds) all fall in value at once. This is why understanding how your portfolio is likely to behave in a crisis is an essential part of being a good investor.

Implications of diversification

Bonds and equities are generally regarded as being negatively correlated, which is to say that they move in opposite directions to each other, like swimwear and winter coat sales. Figure 5.9 shows the effects of mixing together different quantities of equities and bonds, and how the return and volatility change as the mix changes.

Figure 5.9 Examples of equity and bond diversification

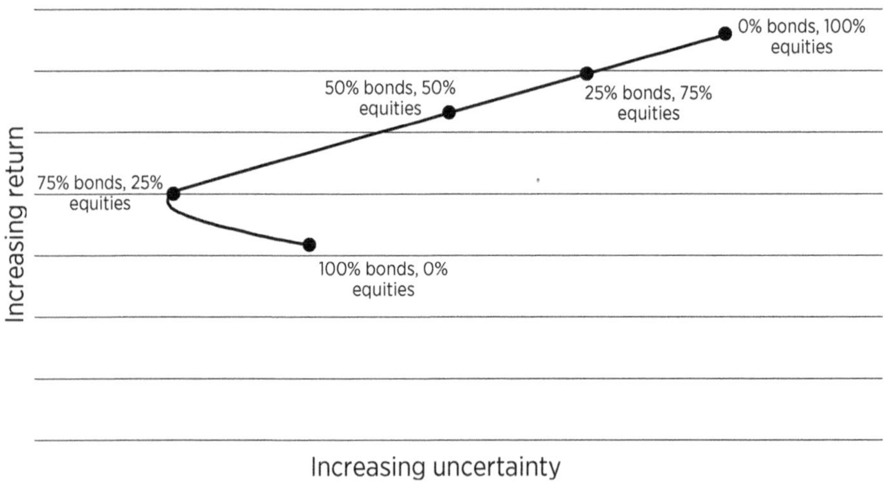

What is most interesting in figure 5.9 is that adding only a small amount of equities to a bond portfolio improves the return and reduces the uncertainty. This is because the extra diversification improves the return without introducing much additional volatility. However, this only works in small proportions before the equity volatility overwhelms the uncorrelated volatility of the other assets and becomes dominant.

Figure 5.9 shows the theoretical limit of what can be achieved with just two asset types (bonds and equities) based on historical data.[3] However, there are of course more assets to invest in than just bonds and equities. As more and more diversifying assets are added to the model, it becomes more and more stable, since each piece becomes less and less significant, but the overall principal (or shape) doesn't change. An example of a realistic portfolio for a spender charity might be mostly equities (65%), a little property (15%), some bonds (15%) and the remainder cash (5%). Such a portfolio would be likely to weather most financial storms over the long term as its assets' characteristics would complement each other.

Over-diversification

There always comes a point where a cake can no longer be usefully divided into smaller segments and remain easy to eat. The same is true of investments. A danger lies in holding so many assets or stocks that any winners (and losers) will make such a tiny impact overall as to be insignificant. Very generally speaking, and depending on the approach, much more than 50 stocks starts to add pointless diversification. For example, putting 2% (i.e. one-fiftieth of the money you have available to invest) in a music royalty or gold fund isn't going to move any performance needle because it's so small.

There are basically three types of asset to think about – equities and property, cash and bonds, and everything else. Each can be subdivided into innumerable parts, but with each subdivision more complexity and opacity are added. It is easy to become too clever when diversifying within these asset classes. If you demand a very detailed level of diversification within an asset class (such as the amount in UK equities compared to US equities), you must be confident that you have some extra insight into the asset class that your investment manager does not have. It is best to leave diversification choices to your manager, but to keep an eye on whether your portfolio is becoming more diversified than necessary. A more complicated portfolio will be more confusing for you to understand and more expensive to manage.

It is also worth remembering that diversification can often be the enemy of engagement, which is a key component of responsible investment (see chapter 9). After all, if you are really committed to something, you will take a particular interest in its well-being. This is difficult or impossible to achieve if you have many small holdings in a long list of companies.

Never take diversification at face value. It is always best to understand why something is a diversifier. For example, property is considered to be less volatile than equities, but that is because equities are traded daily, which makes it possible to have good information about their daily market value. On the other hand, property is traded much less often and is usually valued by a surveyor, not a sale. This will make the reported changes in value smoother and therefore the asset class appear less volatile. Sometimes assets appear diversified just because they are valued less frequently and differently.

Different risk appetites over different time horizons

Often charities think of themselves as having a single long-term horizon with one risk appetite (such as 'medium'). In fact, many charities – especially spenders – have two:

- **Spender charities** might have one time horizon for what they plan to spend in the near future (a short-term horizon with a low-risk appetite) and one for the long term (with a much higher risk appetite). This is a bit like having a bank account and an investment account – they do different things for different pots of money.
- **Saver charities** will usually have an overall long-term horizon, but they might have a smaller pot of money with a shorter-time horizon for spending.
- **Spend-out charities** with a short-term horizon (up to around five years) might have only one time horizon, but anything longer and they will likely need a long-term horizon as well.

This section draws on the information above about uncertainty, portfolio construction and diversification to explore how you might use different investment strategies for different pots of money, depending on when you expect to need to spend them.

Why have multiple time horizons?

As we have seen, one of the problems you will face as an investor is the uncertainty of knowing what your investments will be worth when you need them. The nearer that date is, the less room you have for manoeuvre, so there is a significant difference between investing for the long term and investing for the short term. A portfolio designed around a short-term horizon has little time to recover from market falls, whereas a portfolio designed around a long-term horizon could have its assets locked away and inaccessible at short notice.

A great failing of charity investments is that too often trustees confuse their short- and long-term horizons, as described in this lovely quote:

> They change their minds very easily. On the one hand they say they want an extremely safe option because they've got to start building work in September, but at the same time they feel they should have their money in Chinese equities because they read it in the *Daily Mail*.[4]

The advice is always clear: if you need certainty, you will have to surrender some of your return. A poorly specified approach to time horizons can lead to inappropriate investing and financial problems.

Reserves versus liquidity

Chapter 6 explains that reserves exist both for accounting purposes (how are you doing against your objectives?) and for liquidity purposes (can you pay your bills on time?). That chapter focuses on reserves as an accounting (and accountability) function. In contrast, this chapter focuses on investments, and having a pool of liquid, safe assets that you can draw on at any time regardless of the prevailing market conditions. So, how much money you decide to keep is an accounting decision whereas the form in which you hold that money is an investing one.

Chapter 6 suggests having two types of reserve:

- a **spending reserve**, to identify money you have already earmarked for spending;
- a **long-term reserve**, which acts as the engine room for your future returns.

Once you have set aside the money you know you will need to spend (usually in the near future), you know that the remainder can be invested for a higher, less certain return.

This section concentrates on ensuring that you have sufficient liquidity for your immediate needs (and covers cash investing). It therefore answers a different question to the one considered in chapter 6, which is not about liquidity but about accountability.

Introducing the short-term portfolio

The short-term portfolio is where you will keep most of your working capital and emergency money. It will be invested in safe or liquid assets because they are most likely to maintain their nominal value (i.e. the value before they are eroded by inflation) in uncertain times. As we have seen, the safest assets for a short-term investor are the ones that are the most unsafe for a long-term one, and vice versa (see table 5.2).

Table 5.2 Examples of when the same assets can be either safe or unsafe

	Short-term portfolio	**Long-term portfolio**
Safe assets	Cash and bonds	Equities and property
Unsafe assets	Equities and property	Cash and bonds

How long does the short term last?

There is no definitive rule about how long the 'short term' lasts or what constitutes the 'long term', and indeed this will vary from charity to charity. In practice, the investment industry tends to think of up to five years as a short-term horizon (as a rule, more than seven years is certainly long term). This is based on the widely held assumption that, in most cases, it will take more volatile assets at least five years to recover their original value after a fall. This means that if you needed to liquidate your assets within the next five years, you could not be as certain about their values as you would want, so you could not rely on being able to liquidate them at the value you needed. Everything beyond the short term is considered to be long term. If your time horizon is between five and seven years (not definitively short term or long term), you will probably need to develop an especially nuanced understanding of your particular appetite for uncertainty and risk taking.

What's in your short-term portfolio?

Your priority for your short-term portfolio will be a certain capital value. The capital will be invested in low-returning assets, such as cash and bonds, that will produce little income (after inflation); any return that they do create will be used to offset the impacts of inflation. The focus of investing for a short-term portfolio should always be on security, liquidity and return (in that order), as explained in chapter 3 (see page 32). For example, you might invest in government bonds and high-quality corporate bonds for your very near-term needs but accept marginally more risk for the money that you will need in four or five years, such as by investing a small amount in equities. Remember to avoid the common error of short-term investors of reversing the order of the priorities and investing for return first, then liquidity and security last!

Sizing your short-term portfolio

Not all charities spend in the same way and so they will have different needs for working capital and liquidity. For example, some charities make commitments that they settle almost immediately – say, within 30 days. If this applies to your charity, your short-term portfolio will need to have enough working capital to settle those immediate liabilities when required. You probably won't need much more liquidity than what is required to cover your foreseeable cash flow, so your short-term portfolio may simply consist of your bank account. Some smaller charities may want money on hand in case they have to wind up. If this applies to you, the amount of liquidity you require should be enough to settle all of your existing liabilities together with any new ones, such as redundancy costs.

A useful approach to understanding how much money you need to keep in your short-term portfolio is based on how reliable your cash flow is likely to be. Whether you are an investment-led charity or your investments make up a smaller proportion of your income, if you work out the sensitivity of your income and expenditure to uncertainty, it will help you to consider the size of buffer you may want to hold in low-risk assets.

When thinking about cash flow coming in (whether from investment income, fundraising or a mixture of sources), you might use these three criteria:

- predictability;
- depth and diversity of the sources;
- current trends in the flows.

On the other side of the equation, you should consider the flexibility of your cash outflow by reference to:

- the damage to your reputation if your expenditure were to be reduced or cut;
- your ability to rebuild that activity quickly and without damage, if cut;
- how replaceable the income stream (such as trading) is, if at all;
- whether or not the cash outflow can be delayed;
- the likelihood of unexpected outflow (i.e. the need for contingencies).

You can then decide which of the four scenarios in figure 5.10 best describes your need for working capital, which in turn will help you identify how much money you need to keep in your short-term portfolio:

- **Reliable income and flexible expenditure (top right):** So long as your expenditure can be kept within your plans, then you can spend whatever is available and keep only a minimal amount of working capital in your short-term portfolio. It is likely your primary concern will be not with liquidity but with accountability (i.e. demonstrating that you are spending enough).

- **Reliable income and fixed expenditure (top left):** In this scenario there are few surprises to catch you off guard. A good spending policy will help to smooth out any investment volatility, allowing you to keep a minimal amount in your short-term portfolio.
- **Flexible expenditure and unreliable income (bottom right):** This is the most dynamic scenario, where changes to your costs can be made quickly in response to changing income levels. If that is acceptable, then, again, you will require only a small short-term portfolio because you can reduce your expenditure when your income is low. However, if it is not acceptable, you might decide to have a higher level of liquidity for additional protection.
- **Fixed expenditure and unreliable income (bottom left):** If you have a high level of fixed costs where it is difficult to quickly make changes combined with an unreliable income, you will want to focus on liquidity all the time. You will likely hold most of your money in your short-term portfolio in case your income disappoints (or your expenditure surprises).

Figure 5.10 Quantifying your appetite for uncertainty

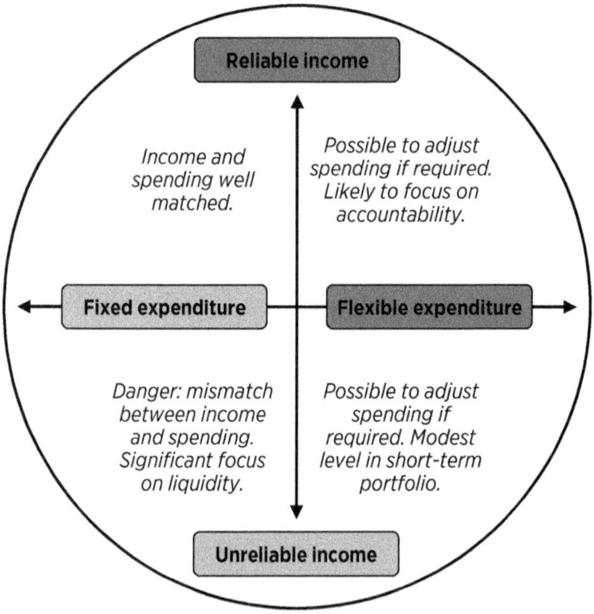

Source: Adapted from *Reserves Policies Made Simple* [PDF], Sayer Vincent, 2015, www.sayervincent.co.uk/wp-content/uploads/2021/08/SV-MS-ReservesPolicies-July2015.pdf, accessed 20 January 2024.

It might seem odd to have room for contingencies in your short-term portfolio when (at least if you are a spender charity) you will have a much larger sum of money that you could access in your long-term portfolio. This is certainly true, but, in terms of clear management, it is much more helpful to keep the sums separate given their time horizons, their different appetites for uncertainty and volatility, and their different investment strategies. The point about a contingency is that you never know when it might be needed, and therefore you should assume it may be needed tomorrow, hence the need to invest it for the short term. Even if you never use it, it enables you to do everything else.

When your spending reserve and short-term portfolio will be the same size

Often, a charity's spending reserve and liquidity needs will be the same or very similar, in which case it will hold its spending reserve entirely in assets with certain values (such as cash). For example, if you are a grant-making charity, you might receive your quarterly income into your bank account and spend it all by the end of the year. In this case, your bank account would be the same as your spending reserve. Your spending would be predictable and controllable.

When your spending reserve and short-term portfolio will be different sizes

More complex charities, such as those with staged grant payments (or other liabilities) that are paid out over several years, might have very different liquidity needs from those that, for example, make a grant and send a cheque immediately. If you have longer-term commitments, you are unlikely to need to keep all these future commitments in entirely safe assets. Instead, you might want to have most of your spending reserve invested in your short-term (safe) portfolio and the remainder in your long-term one, where you can tolerate more uncertainty and earn a higher return.

Introducing the long-term portfolio

A long-term portfolio is usually volatility-tolerant and return-seeking. It gives the lowest priority to certain capital values and therefore can afford the unpredictability of investing in assets that are more likely to give a higher return over time.

What's in your long-term portfolio?

The key feature of investments in a long-term portfolio is that they are selected for being return-seeking. They include assets such as equities, property and more esoteric things like private equity and perhaps commodities (see chapter 3). None of these have reliable values, but all of them offer, to some degree, inflation protection and the possibility of spending more. Remember that because you have already separated out your liquidity needs in your short-term portfolio, you do not need to make an allowance again for them in your long-term portfolio – that would be double counting (and deprive you of potential returns).

Sizing your long-term portfolio

The sections above stepped through the process of sizing your short-term portfolio. Your long-term portfolio is simply the remainder of all your investable assets, which will be everything that you have not defined as being required for your short-term portfolio. For charities with few assets or liabilities other than their portfolio, the long-term portfolio will usually be similar in size to the long-term reserve. More complex charities (with more assets and liabilities) will find that this relationship breaks down as the complexity increases. The focus for the short-term portfolio will always be liquidity, and that for the spending reserve will always be accountability.

Ensuring balance between your short-term and long-term portfolios

It is vital to get the balance between your short-term and long-term portfolios right, because in a crisis (such as a market collapse) it will be too late to top up your short-term portfolio by selling volatile assets in your long-term portfolio, as those assets' value will have plummeted. Once you have settled on an appropriate split, you should stick to it unless your income, liabilities or commitments change. 'Sticking to it' means moving money from one portfolio to the other every year as required as part of a process called 'rebalancing'.

The basic tenet of investing is that the more you can tolerate uncertainty, the more money you are likely to earn. However, from time to time you will face steep losses, although you should eventually recover from these so long as your policy is well designed, diversified and competently executed. Because this won't be a smooth or comfortable ride, one question all charities should ask themselves is what their beneficiaries would want: more cash to spend or more comfortable trustees?

The point is of course that the more money you keep in your short-term portfolio (where you might feel more comfortable), the less you can put to work to generate higher levels of long-term spending. Reckless caution is an expensive business.

Fictional case studies

Spender: Warden's Philanthropy

The investment strategy of Warden's Philanthropy is to earn as much as it can to spend on its charitable purpose, and consequently the trustees have accepted that they will have to be tolerant of a volatile investment portfolio. In order to deal with this, and to give the trustees some reassurance, the charity has created two different investment strategies:

- The charity's **long-term portfolio** will be almost entirely invested in property and equities to ensure inflation protection and a reasonable amount to spend. Asset price volatility is less important than these two issues.
- The charity's **short-term portfolio** is needed for working capital and emergencies. This portfolio must be available to provide liquidity to maintain spending for a foreseeable period if everything else is going wrong. This portfolio will be the same size as the spending reserve. This means that this strategy must put safety first. After all, the trustees are taking all their risk in the main (long-term) portfolio and do not need to take any more risk in the spending reserve. Returns will be low, which is why this portfolio is kept as small as possible.

As shown in table 5.3, the trustees' investing preferences will therefore be different for their long-term and short-term portfolios, and they will be quite comfortable with that situation because they understand it. Their long-term and spending reserves will be the same as these two portfolios.

Table 5.3 Warden's Philanthropy investment preferences

	High return	Low volatility	Some inflation protection
Long-term reserve	✓	✗	✓
Short-term reserve	✗	✓	✓

Saver: Martello Tower Fund

The Martello Tower Fund (MTF) is the most substantial restricted fund of the fundraising charity Preserving Our Nautical Past. At the moment, the MTF does not have any significant spending requirements (other than investment fees and occasional updates on the likely cost of the project when it is begun), so its policy is to maximise what it can earn.

At the outset of the MTF, its investment committee asked for investment advice from a range of providers. They adopted an all-equity strategy based on the advice that if they stayed invested for 30 years and earned annual returns of 5% above inflation, they could end up with almost £4.3 million in today's prices.

While the fund has well over five years left to run, it will remain invested in its long-term portfolio, which is allocated entirely to passively managed equities. Were the fund larger, the committee would have considered investing in more esoteric and illiquid assets, such as private equity, too.

As the time approaches when the fund might start spending and its need for certain asset values begins to become much clearer, the committee will establish a short-term portfolio and start to move money into it.

Spend-outer: Butterworth Music Festivals

Butterworth Music Festivals must spend its entire £10 million within ten years. However, as related in chapter 4, the trustees' initial projections are now up in the air because they have more money than they expected, due to better-than-anticipated performance by their investment manager, and they are also struggling to find suitable opportunities to spend the money.

They thought carefully about their time horizon. Ten years was too long to not earn anything to spend, but too short to put everything at risk while they were busy making spending commitments. In the end, they discussed this with their investment manager and decided to keep all their money in a short-term portfolio but with a slightly higher risk appetite than a regular short-term approach. As their final years came closer, they expected to move more towards the safer end of the short-term risk spectrum.

As a result, they have been working closely with their investment manager to make sure their future budgets and investment portfolio are aligned. This means that when the cash is required, enough will be available and the remainder will be earning a little more than it could if it remained as cash.

Conclusion

In essence, this chapter has been all about the tension between greed and fear – in other words, about finding a balance between the desire to make as much money as you can to spend on your charitable purpose and the desire to lose as little of it as possible. If you understand when and how much money you will need to deliver your financial objectives and goals, you can work out an approach that will maximise your returns and limit your risk. This is the heart of your investment strategy. The next chapter looks at reserves, whose value is the main way you will be able to tell whether you're getting this balance right.

Notes

1 Claire Routley and Richard Sved, *Fundraising Strategy*, London, Directory of Social Change, 2021.
2 H. M. Markowitz, 'Portfolio Selection', *Journal of Finance*, vol. 7, no. 1, 1972, pp. 77–91.
3 The figure is based on widely acknowledged trends as reported in, for example, Elroy Dimson, Paul Marsh and Mike Staunton, *Global Investment Returns Yearbook 2024*, London, London Business School, 2024.
4 'What Investment Managers Really Think about Trustees', *Third Sector*, 20 April 2010.

Chapter six

Reserves policy

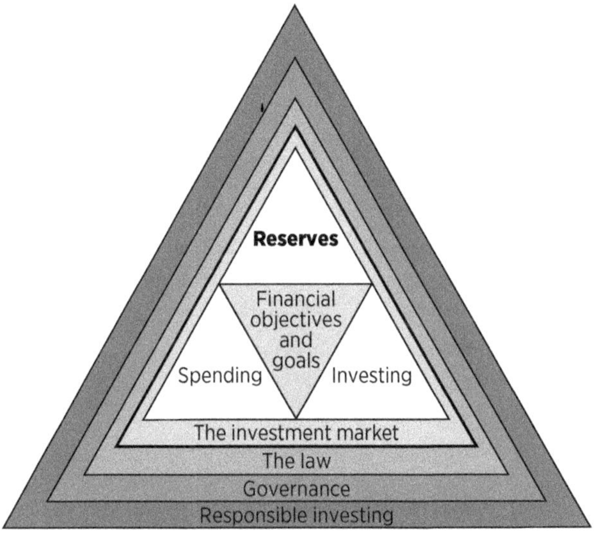

The purpose of this chapter

Reserves are the basis of how charities monitor their progress against their financial objectives and goals. Central to this are the concepts of what is kept back to provide for future spending and what can be spent now. If you don't separate these two time frames, you can easily, and accidentally, undermine your financial objectives and goals and end up saving or spending more than you intend. After all, if you have a goal, such as maintaining your capital against inflation, why would you not measure it to see how you're getting on? If you don't want to know, why set one in the first place?

This chapter comes in four parts. The first part discusses reserves generally in terms of the moral requirement to explain why you intend to keep money back from your beneficiaries. The second part illustrates the need to work to two quite different time horizons – the near and the far – at the same time, and the third describes a mechanism – target values – that will help you do this. The final part puts all of this in the context of the more formal and legal requirements for reserves used by the Charities

Statement of Recommended Practice (SORP) and the Charity Commission's guidance. The three case studies illustrate how the three example charities have applied these principles to their own unique circumstances.

What are reserves?

'Reserves' has a wide variety of meanings for charities, some formal and some informal, but it should always mean something which is kept for use later. In this book the word 'reserves' is used with this general meaning and includes all of a charity's assets, be they money, buildings or special funds. Reserves also have a formal, more technical meaning, set out in the Charity Commission's guidance (i.e. not a legal requirement) *Charity Reserves: Building resilience* (CC19)[1] and in the Charities SORP, which contains the accounting regulations that govern charities.[2]

It is important to understand that some of the ideas in this chapter differ from the Charity Commission's guidance, mainly concerning what is – or is not – included in a reserve. The formal sense – and the reasons for the divergence – are covered towards the end of the chapter (see page 119). For the time being, just think of a reserve as something that is held back and where beneficiaries deserve some explanation about why it cannot be spent now on your charity's purpose.

Understanding reserves better

A helpful way to think about reserves is by imagining a dam and a reservoir. The charity trustees act as the dam and the reserves as the reservoir. It is the trustees who decide how much to keep in the reservoir and how much to release for the beneficiaries in the valley below. Trustees should always be able to justify why they are keeping the reservoir at its current level. Usually this will be to help them manage expected and unexpected events but also to balance the needs of beneficiaries now and into the future as they consider best.

Reserves are what you use to ensure you have sufficient money for a rainy day and can deliver your financial strategy without interruption. But it is important to distinguish at the outset what you are trying to do with your reserves. Broadly, you will need to consider two different functions that reserves can have:

- Reserves are used to **account** for balances in charitable funds and record how much is left so there is accountability to stakeholders for what has been retained (and why). This is an accounting function because trustees have to explain what is left in the reserve, and why. In effect its purpose is to test the present position against your financial objectives and goals for that reserve. This is a backward-looking test.

- Another meaning of the word 'reserve' is to make sure you have enough money in **liquid assets**, such as cash, to allow you to pay your bills as they fall due (and perhaps have enough money for emergencies). This is about liquidity and is therefore an investment question. This is a forward-looking test.

As you can see, these two functions are distinct and rely on quite different considerations, especially in terms of whether they relate to the past or the future. They must be treated separately to be at all useful and you will only get confused if you try to look both to the future and to the past in the same policy. This chapter is about the first function: reserves that are used for accountability and accounting. Reserves for liquidity are covered in chapter 5 (see especially page 95), on investment strategy, because liquidity is an investment issue.

Using reserves to monitor performance against your financial objectives and goals

Chapter 2 looked at setting an overarching financial objective and financial goals, and chapters 4 and 5 respectively examined how to determine a sensible level of spending and how your investments can support that spending most effectively. Reserves are ultimately how you determine whether your spending and investment decisions are supporting the achievement of your overarching financial objective and goals. Your investment returns will increase the size of the reservoir (in the dam analogy above), but equally your spending will reduce its level. Reserves are how you track these changes over time. The two activities of investing and spending will determine how your reserves change in size, and that in turn will determine whether you are meeting your overarching financial objective and goals – or not (see figure 6.1).

Figure 6.1 The relationships between financial objectives and goals, spending policy, investment strategy and reserves

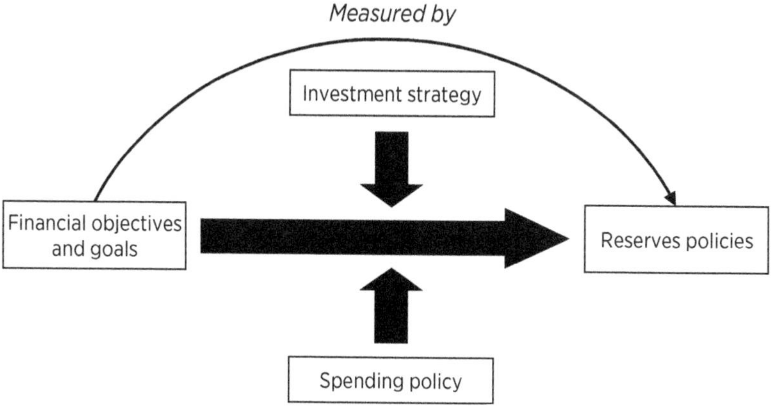

Your reserves show the values of your fund (or funds if you have more than one) and form part of your charity's balance sheet. They help you recognise your moral obligations to your beneficiaries as well as recording your legal obligations.

Managing time through reserves

Some charities have so much money in reserve that it dwarfs their operational expenditure many times over. Consequently, they have to be careful to separate what they plan to spend now from what they intend to keep for the future. If they don't do this, sums allocated for imminent spending will simply get lost in the larger sum they are keeping for the long term. It is therefore helpful to think in terms of having two reserves:

- The **long-term reserve** can be patient, flexible and tolerant of uncertainty. For a saver or spender charity, it will normally be a considerably larger reserve than the spending one.
- The **spending reserve** is where you keep the amount you have decided to spend in the near future (through your spending policy), so it is earmarked for spending and not mislaid within a long-term strategy.

Although this way of looking at reserves diverges from the Charity Commission's conceptualisation, it is not a new way of thinking. Traditionally these two separate reserves were called 'capital' (long term) and 'income' (short term), but these names no longer work because the Charities SORP is focused on legal structures, not time horizons. For example, 'capital' only relates to endowments (rather than any money being held for the long term) and there is no such phrase as 'income reserve' to describe money held for the short term (just 'restricted funds' and 'unrestricted funds'). So, instead of using the terms 'capital' and 'income', this chapter uses 'long-term reserve' and 'spending reserve' to reflect this broader way of thinking about reserves. The remainder of this chapter focuses on reserves as an accounting and accountability device, because decisions about what to spend and what to retain are reflected in your accounts.

Table 6.1 summarises the relationships between the two reserves (for accountability) discussed in this chapter, the two portfolios (for liquidity) discussed in chapter 5, and the traditional concepts of capital and income. See chapter 5 (especially pages 96 and (100) for information on the relative sizes of your reserves and portfolios.

Table 6.1 The relationships between short- and long-term investment portfolios, the long-term and spending accounting reserves, and the traditional concepts of capital and income

Time horizon	Investments (chapter 5)	Reserves (this chapter)	Similar to
Long term	Long-term portfolio	Long-term reserve	Capital
Short term	Short-term portfolio	Spending reserve	Income

As noted in chapter 5, the more assets and liabilities a charity has, the more likely the long-term and short-term portfolios and reserves are to have different values.

Most charities are free to decide what they spend and what they keep (the exception is permanent endowments; see the box below), and those charities' trustees should publicly explain how they have made that choice, not least in their accounts. By separating their funds into these two types of reserve, they will achieve that.

Reserves in charities with permanent endowments

Permanent endowments are a type of reserve where the donor has specified that only the income can be spent, with the capital being reinvested. This is a legal requirement which affects how money can be earned and spent. This can be ameliorated by using a total return resolution, but either way you will still have to account separately for the long-term and spending parts of the fund (see appendix 2 for more information). In addition, some assets outside a permanent endowment, such as a painting or a property, might be covered by a legal requirement that they cannot be sold (such as at some museums).

Managing different reserves differently

Effective financial management is difficult to do if you do not separate your long-term and short-term time horizons because the impact of a sudden and unexpected fall in value will feel very different for the two reserves. A long-term reserve might see huge gyrations in its value within a single year, reflecting its tolerance for volatility. Unless you separate that money from your spending reserve, those gyrations will swamp your spending plans, to the extent that in a large market fall (or market gain) you will become confused about how much your spending policy allows you to spend.

Another way of thinking about this is in terms of management accounting. You will want to monitor your spending reserve much more often than your long-term reserve, just as someone might look at their bank account every week but only look at their investments every six months. You will want to frequently see management accounts that report on your regular income and expenditure (in your spending reserve) as the year progresses. However, seeing a report once or twice a year on progress in your long-term reserve will probably be sufficient given its much longer time frame. The two reserves work on different time frames and so should be treated differently.

A spend-out charity will normally have a single (spending) reserve so it is clear what there is left to spend because there is no long term and it is not trying to balance two time horizons. If your overarching financial objective is to spend out within five years, you may therefore wish to skip ahead to the section 'Introducing target values' (page 113). However, if your spend-out horizon is more distant or you aim to exist in perpetuity, you may want to read on.

Spending reserve and restricted, designated and general funds

In charity accounting parlance a spending reserve might be called a restricted fund, a designated fund or a general fund. However, any of these funds could also be held for a long-term purpose. This book's use of the terms 'spending reserve' and 'long-term reserve' avoids this potential confusion, but you should be alert to other possible terminology in your annual accounts and other reports.

Dividing up your spending and long-term reserves

The spending reserve

As explained, investment-led charities need an approach where they can separate what they have agreed can be spent from what they plan to keep for the future. One of the advantages of spending your natural income (see page 59) is that it deals perfectly with this separation in time because the income (i.e. what you can spend) goes into your spending reserve and is clearly marked as available for spending. If your spending policy is to spend all your natural income, you can skip ahead to the section 'Introducing target values' (page 113).

Charities that spend a total return don't have the same advantage as spenders of natural income because their capital and income returns are mixed up. Their solution is to transfer from their long-term reserve what their spending policy says is to be spent next month, next quarter or next year – in full. In this way, any accumulated underspend or overspend is visible in their spending reserve.

Spending what you intend

If you are spending based on a total return spending rule instead of your natural income, you might only transfer from your investments what you need to meet your current spending commitments. This means, for example, that if you had planned to spend £10,000 but ended up spending £8,000, you would only need to transfer £8,000 to balance your account and the remaining £2,000 would stay in your long-term reserve. In all likelihood, everyone would then forget that they were meant to have spent the extra £2,000, and that would deprive your current beneficiaries unnecessarily. This is especially important if you habitually underspend your budgets and want to carry that spending capacity forward into the following year.

This is illustrated in table 6.2, which contains two options for how to show a transfer from the long-term reserve to the spending reserve. In the 'part transfer' option, only what is needed to fund the actual spending commitments is transferred. In contrast, in the 'whole transfer' option, everything that is available for spending is transferred. Even if it is not completely spent, it will be identified as available for spending in the future.

Table 6.2 The importance of capturing commitments to spend: comparison of options

	Option 1: part transfer	**Option 2: whole transfer**
Transferred to spending reserve	+£8,000	+£10,000
Actually spent	–£8,000	–£8,000
Total reduction in long-term fund	£8,000	£10,000
Balance left in short-term spending reserve	**-**	**£2,000**

This example shows how easy it is with the part-transfer method to lose track of what your spending policy allows you to spend. Using the whole-transfer method increases accountability by clearly showing what was (and still is) available for spending.

Anything that isn't held in a short-term reserve will be held in a long-term one.

The long-term reserve

As mentioned, an important job of charity trustees is to decide how much should be kept for beneficiaries' future needs and how much can be spent on them now. The long-term reserve measures this – specifically, it answers the question, 'How much of our assets do we want to keep for the long term?' If you rely on your accumulating capital gains to answer this question, you will soon find that there is no relationship between how much your capital increases and how much you need your long-term reserve to grow to achieve your financial objective and goals. Capital growth and your financial objectives and goals are completely different things: if you want to know whether you are delivering against your financial objective and goals, you cannot just assume accumulating capital will do it for you.

Here's how our three types of charity use the long-term reserve:

- **Spender charities** use long-term reserves to monitor the amount being maintained against inflation.
- **Saver charities** use long-term reserves to monitor a sum to see if it is growing fast enough to meet a specified spending goal by a target date.
- **Spend-out charities** might have no long-term reserve and instead only have a spending reserve (unless the spend-out point was very extended).

This measurement is only reliable, however, if you have separate long-term and spending reserves. For example, many spender charities set an investment goal, often referred to as a 'benchmark' (see chapter 11), of matching the Consumer Prices Index (CPI) (see page 68) plus 4%, and their investment manager will report on progress against that goal. Spender charities often choose this target because it looks like a good way to show that they are protecting their capital against inflation while earning enough to spend 4% on top of that. However, the reality doesn't necessarily work in this way. First of all, the charity may have other assets that aren't managed by an investment manager and which won't be monitored by them. Even if that's not the case, the investment manager probably won't send it exactly 4% each year (as explained on page 65), nor are those assets likely to increase by exactly the same amount as CPI. And all this assumes the charity spends exactly what it was given to spend – no more, no less. Last, an investment manager will only measure the growth in the sum of money they manage, and from when they began to manage it when they took over the mandate rather than from the point the charity wishes to measure the growth from. In short, conventional investment benchmarks don't answer the question of 'how are we doing against our financial objectives?'

Separating your long-term and spending reserves solves this problem. Unlike an investment goal, such as matching the CPI plus 4%, your long-term reserve will measure whether or not your long-term assets have kept up with their target after accounting for what you have earned and what you have spent. For example, if a spender charity planned to spend 4% it would set an investment benchmark of CPI plus 4% but would only need its long-term reserve to increase by CPI (to keep up with inflation). Everything else should be spent. In other words, the long-term reserve will be measured against the value you need it to have to meet your financial objectives and goals. This is your target value.

Introducing target values

It is all very well having financial objectives and goals, but if you don't specify what value you are trying to maintain or by when, you will never know whether you have succeeded. When you set any sort of objective, it should always be possible to recognise when you have achieved it, otherwise what would be the point of the objective? Therefore, knowing the actual number you are trying to maintain or reach is essential.

Your long-term and spending reserves will have different target values because they have different objectives.

Target values for your long-term reserve

Some pension funds define themselves by how much money they need to pay out the pensions they have promised to their members (see page 58). Saver charities will have obligations a bit like that, but spender and spend-out charities won't:

- If you are a **spender charity**, your reference point will be historical. Instead of asking whether you have enough money to meet your future obligations, you will monitor whether you still have as much money as when you started, after inflation and spending.
- If you are a **saver charity**, the focus is on whether you have more than you started with. You will have a future value that you need to achieve, a bit like a pension fund does (but one that you can vary), and that will be your target value.
- If you are a **spend-out charity**, you will have a target value of nil. What will be important is to measure the rate of your spending to ensure that it will end as planned. This measurement is normally done through some sort of budget.

The benefits of setting a target value to measure the health of your long-term reserve are considerable:

- It is a good way to express what you are trying to achieve.
- It will be the reference point to enable you to recognise your success against your financial objectives and goals.
- It gives you a framework to help you understand differences between the value of your portfolio and your target value.
- It enables you to increase or decrease your spending levels with more confidence.
- It helps trustees to hold their nerve if markets are falling by providing a level to which assets can recover, so they know that the assets are back to normal. Without a target value, it is very difficult to know this.
- Similarly, without a target value, you might assume that the highest value your portfolio has ever achieved is the one you always have to get back to, which is nonsense (see chapter 8 for more on this topic).

The key point about setting a target value is that it allows you to see everything you need to understand whether or not you are achieving your financial objectives and goals. Not only does this include the impact of your investment returns but also, importantly, it includes the effects of your spending (which, as mentioned earlier in this chapter, your investment manager won't know about and so can't report to you on).

Determining the target value for your long-term reserve

If your charity's objective is to spend out, determining your target value is relatively simple. There are two options, both equally valid. The first is to fix the amount you can wisely spend every year, and when you finally close will depend on the investment returns you make over that period. The alternative is to have a fixed end date and adjust your spending to have nothing left by the right date. Either way, your target value is nil and you can skip the rest of this section.

If you are a spender or saver charity, your objective will probably be to maintain or grow your capital against a measure of inflation on an ongoing basis (or pursue another specific goal, as in the fictional example of the Martello Tower Fund). To determine your target value, you will need to know:

- what you mean by inflation;
- when you should start measuring from;
- how to compare your starting value to your current value.

The following subsections look at each of these topics in turn and then consider the question of how to know whether your start date and target value are realistic.

Choosing the type of inflation to use

The inflation rate you choose to aim to match should be appropriate for how you spend your money. As explained in chapter 4, there are various indices of inflation, each of which measures different segments of the economy. If you fund a wide range of items, you may find a general form of inflation is best, such as the CPI. If you mainly fund salaries, an index such as Average Weekly Earnings will be more suitable. There are more esoteric indices that can be found on the website of the Office for National Statistics (see www.ons.gov.uk/economy/inflationandpriceindices). See page 68 for more information to help you choose between the various types of inflation.

Choosing your start date

Choosing a start date gives you a sensible reference point from which to track your target value and thus see whether you have indeed protected your original capital against inflation. The most obvious time to pick is when your charity first received any money, but sometimes this is too long ago for there to be any data available. The point is to identify a value that is meaningful to you and that will make sense as a reference point. If you are a long-established charity, it might be 100 or more years ago, but equally you can choose yesterday if that seems more suitable.

A good approach is to look for a relevant moment when you have some indication of the market value of your assets at the time. You might find this in your first annual report, or another report from a relevant but more recent time, or perhaps even an old valuation of some sort (possibly from a valuer, an insurance company or an investment manager). If you are struggling to know where to look, your investment manager or lawyer might be able to help. Unless you have a permanent endowment (see the box on page 109), the choice of what you want to keep for the future is yours so it makes sense to be pragmatic about it and to choose a start date that will make sense for you.

Comparing your starting value to your current value, after inflation

Once you have chosen a provisional start date, you can compare the value of your assets at that time with what their value would have been if they had kept up with inflation. An online tool such as Measuring Worth[3] or the Bank of England's inflation calculator[4] will tell you what any value is in today's money from the thirteenth century onwards. For example, according to Measuring Worth, if you had assets worth £20,000 in 1970, they would have been worth approximately £262,500 in 2023 (the latest year the calculator offers at the time of writing).

You can then use this information to see whether the money you have now is more or less than it would have been if you had grown that original sum from your start date in line with inflation. This will tell you if you have been saving money you could have otherwise spent, or if you have perhaps been spending too much. If it is the former, you could consider spending more, but if it is the latter, you might want to consider spending less. Or you could just start from now and apply a spending rule from chapter 4.

For example, a saver charity will have been given a sum of money on a specific date and it will want to watch that sum grow towards its target, as well as being able to see that it is keeping up with inflation. Figure 6.2 shows an example of how this might look in practice. You can see that this charity's assets have kept up with inflation, although sometimes they have been behind and at other times ahead of the target due to the volatility of the invested assets.

Figure 6.2 Using inflation as a target value, 2002–23

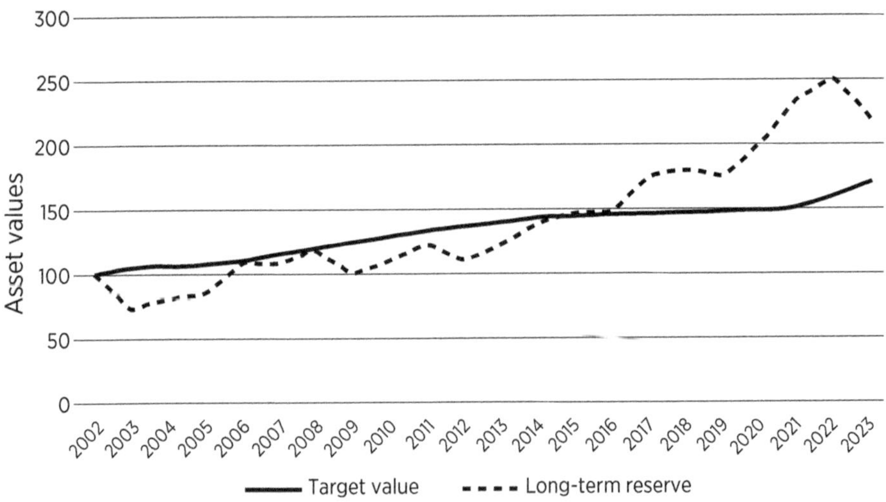

Source: Legal & General Investment Management (LGIM). Data taken from a portfolio based on 70% in LGIM's Global Equity fund and 30% in LGIM's UK Conventional Government Bond fund, after spending its natural income. Consumer Prices Index data from the Office for National Statistics. The numbers represented by the Y axis are simply the index's way of portraying the growth of asset values and have no external meaning.

If you are a spender charity, the same principle applies. If you were given a sum of money on a particular date then you can see whether, after your spending, it is continuing to grow in line with inflation. If you are ahead of target, that's good, because you have more elbow room to spend more; however, if you're behind, it's something to watch in case you are spending more than you are earning. In chapter 11 there is more detail on setting up ranges to help you recognise when things are going wrong (or right) (see page 232).

Ensuring your start date and target value are realistic

To determine whether your start date and target value are realistic, the approach depends on whether you are working with a permanent endowment. If so, the guiding principle must always be to attempt to achieve intergenerational equity (see page 57). This means that the original gift, or a recognisable and justifiable updated value of it, has to be identified so it can be protected from inflation in the future. For other types of long-term reserve, you should aim to achieve what you see as the right balance between the past, the present and the future.

Normally, when a start date is unrealistic, it means that your current value is so far below the value it would need to be to have kept up with inflation that you would have to stop spending for years before you had made up the shortfall (in the case of a permanent endowment) or that the discrepancy is so high as to make the exercise pointless (for other long-term funds). Sometimes it is better just to accept that there has been a permanent loss of value which can never be recovered and choose a more realistic start date, perhaps one that begins after the losses were incurred. This is a much more complicated problem (often with legal dimensions) for permanent endowments.

Sometimes the reverse is true and you find you have a substantial cushion between your current value and your inflation-linked target value. If that is the case, you have a choice between spending this cushion (quickly or slowly) or using a start date with a higher value. To illustrate the difference a start date can make, figure 6.3 shows exactly the same data as figure 6.2, but with a start date ten years later. It results in the portfolio value always being ahead of inflation.

Figure 6.3 Using inflation as a target value, 2012–2023

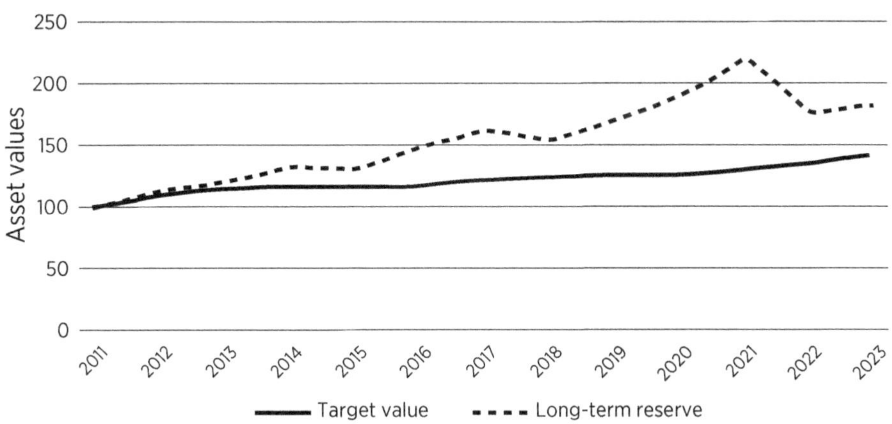

Source: Legal & General Investment Management (LGIM). Data taken from a portfolio based on 70% in LGIM's Global Equity fund and 30% in LGIM's UK Conventional Government Bond fund, after spending its natural income. Consumer Prices Index data from the Office for National Statistics. The numbers represented by the Y axis are simply the index's way of portraying the growth of asset values and have no external meaning.

If you do not have an obvious date from which to begin your calculations, it is easy to think that this process is too difficult or uncertain to get exactly right, and to proceed without any target value. However, this would deprive you of all the advantages that the framework provides, such as knowing you can spend more when your investments perform well, or being confident about how far you have to go to recover from a market fall.

As with so many ideas in investing, it is important to avoid the best being the enemy of the good. If you are struggling to decide on a target value, it can be simplest to decide on a value that will give you a similar level of spending to your current amount, or perhaps a little more. If you can arrive at a target value that has durable relevance for you, it will serve you well, regardless of the precise accuracy (or otherwise) of your starting point. However, if you change it too frequently, or just for convenience, then your target value will lose all meaning and you will forfeit its benefits as a robust, effective tool for financial management. Nevertheless, there are situations where changing it is sensible: for example, if you made a one-off decision to spend half of your long-term reserve on a special project, you would want to recalibrate your target value accordingly to reflect what is left.

Target values for your spending reserve

In the same way that you can use target values in your long-term reserve to tell whether you are progressing as you hope, you can also use them in your spending reserve to tell whether you are spending as much as your spending policy allows you to, or whether perhaps you are spending more than you should (if the reserve slips into the negative). However, this is much simpler because the only changes will be caused by what you put in and what you take out. There should not normally be volatility in the underlying assets to confuse the situation, and because it is short term, you won't need to worry about inflation so much. In some years you might spend more and other years you might spend less, but the spending reserve will always contain what is left to spend.

As in the case of the long-term reserve, having a target range to say what you think is a 'normal' amount for your spending reserve is how you become accountable for what is retained in the fund. If you have too much money in your spending reserve, then you will be failing to spend everything your spending policy allows, and therefore spending less than you could on your charitable purpose.

Legal structures and guidance on charity reserves

This section first outlines the various legal structures for charity reserves. It then explores how this chapter's broader concept of reserves can usefully and useably be mapped onto the formal guidance published by the Charity Commission and the Charities SORP.

Structure of charity reserves

Figure 6.4 shows that charities have two basic types of reserve: those that can only be used in law for specific purposes set out by the donor (special reserves) and those that can be used as the trustees, and only the trustees, decide (unrestricted reserves). Each type of reserve has its own family of sub-reserves, which are technically known as 'funds' (and are described here as such). All charities will analyse their assets according to these fund types in their statutory accounts. Both the Charities SORP[5] and *Charity Reserves: Building resilience*[6] have helpful glossaries that cover these various types of reserve.

Figure 6.4 The types of funds (reserves) used by charities according to the Charities SORP

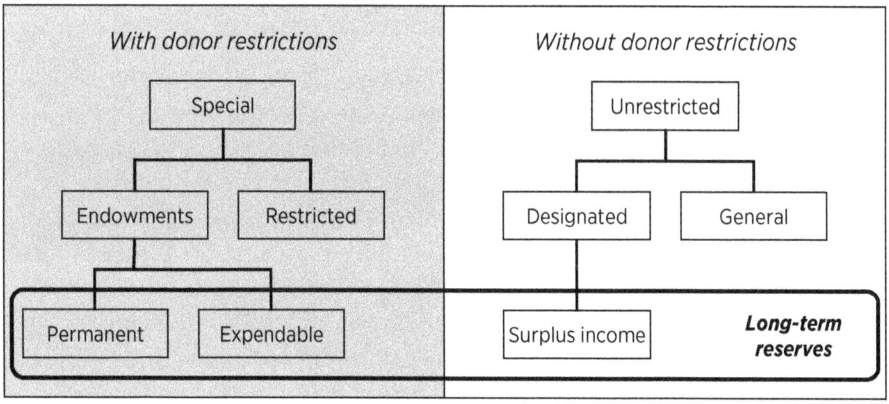

Special funds

Special funds are governed by specific legal restrictions imposed by a donor on how the money can be used. The most common restrictions are what the money can be spent on and, less often, whether the capital and income can be spent equally freely. It usually requires a legal process to change these rules, but for sums smaller than £25,000 this can sometimes be done through a trustees' resolution.[7]

There are two types of special funds: endowments and restricted funds.

Endowment

An endowment is a restricted form of capital. The donor will have made it clear by donating an endowment that their intention was that their gift would be invested for the long term. There may or may not be documentary evidence supporting the decision to classify the gift in this way. If there is no written evidence, you could take legal advice to establish that the money is in fact an endowment rather than just surplus income and, if so, whether its income is restricted or unrestricted. Sometimes trustees have simply retained a substantial amount of surplus income (perhaps from a large, one-off donation) which they have incorrectly treated as an endowment. These are really only designated funds (see below) arising from unspent, surplus income.

Endowments have two simple subdivisions:

- **Permanent** means that the donor specified that the asset must be used to further the charity's purpose (e.g. in the case of a building) or that only the income may be spent and the capital cannot (although the capital might grow or shrink through normal investment gains and losses). Sometimes these endowments are very old, but not always. They can give rise to either unrestricted or restricted income.
- **Expendable** means that both the capital and the income can be spent as the trustees wish. By implication, it must be assumed that if the donor made the gift as an endowment rather than simply donating income, their expectation would be that the charity should have a bias towards keeping the capital for the long term, but without the trustees' hands being tied about spending it all at some future point. In other words, if a donor does not donate their gift as a permanent endowment, you can draw the conclusion that it is a deliberate instruction that you can spend the capital if you want. Many modern endowments are in this form and periodically trustees do decide to spend them out.

Restricted funds

Restricted funds are another type of special fund that must be spent on the purpose specified by the donor. Only the donor can place these restrictions, not the recipient charity. A restricted fund will only exist where its terms are narrower than the charity's objects (e.g. one particular strand of the work of the charity).

Unrestricted funds

Unrestricted funds or reserves cover everything else and are much less complicated. Their charitable purposes are as wide as the charity's own purposes. They are made up of general income that is yet to be spent and that can be expended on any purpose within the charity's objects, at any time. These funds can also be subdivided into designated funds, but any subdivision can be changed by a board resolution and will not require a legal process.

There are two types of unrestricted funds: designated funds and general funds.

Designated funds

Designated funds are allocations made by trustees for particular projects, such as saving for a future building purchase. This is a way of earmarking reserves to show how your charity intends to use some of its funds on a particular purpose that the trustees have chosen. As mentioned above, a long-term fund of surplus income (i.e. a designated fund) is not legally an endowment, but, if designated, it can be treated in many ways as though it were one by using appropriate target values, spending policies and so forth.

General funds

General funds are the most desirable type of charity money because they can be applied to any of a charity's purposes without restriction. This money can be saved, spent or designated as trustees see fit, but it cannot be used to create an endowment or restricted funds.

Fitting the long-term and spending reserves into the Charity Commission's guidance

There is an enormous range of charities in terms of size, structure and scope of activities. The needs of complex charities with multiple sources of income and types of expenditure will be very different from those of simpler charities led primarily by their investments, and these different types of charity will think differently about their reserves, accountability and spending plans. This section illustrates how investment-led charities in particular can use long-term and spending reserves within the formal reserves frameworks recommended in *Charity Reserves: Building resilience* and the Charities SORP. More complex charities can also apply the principles to any investment funds that they manage.

Charity Reserves: Building resilience explains that 'reserves are that part of a charity's unrestricted funds that is freely available to spend on any of the charity's purposes'.[8] Therefore, this definition excludes all special funds from the need for accountability about what is kept or spent, and the guidance goes on to list further items (such as some properties) that could be excluded from the general reserves too. But trustees can liquidate and sell all their assets if they choose to do so (except for any permanent endowments and any assets you are not allowed to sell, such as museum exhibits) and spend everything on their beneficiaries. Therefore, there is no reason why investment-led charities should not seek to include assets such as endowments and restricted funds when setting target values for their long-term reserves. Table 6.3 summarises the difference between the approach suggested by the Charity Commission's formal reserves guidance and this chapter's broader conception of long-term and spending reserves.

Table 6.3 Suggested exclusions from reserves policies

<table>
<tr><th>Exclusions in the Charity Commission guidance</th><th>Exclusions in this chapter</th></tr>
<tr><td>Permanent endowments</td><td rowspan="5">None – the trustees should explain why they keep any of their reserves. Reserves should have target values to record this decision about what is kept but not spent.</td></tr>
<tr><td>Expendable endowments</td></tr>
<tr><td>Restricted funds</td></tr>
<tr><td>Designated funds</td></tr>
<tr><td>Land/building uses for charitable purposes</td></tr>
</table>

This section describes how to align with the Charity Commission's suggested approach to reporting on your fund balances while following the broader guidance in this chapter. When it comes to reporting, the Charities SORP does not distinguish between long-term and short-term reserves.[9] Instead, it analyses funds according to their legal basis, which results in separate lines for endowments, restricted funds, designated funds and unrestricted funds. Table 6.4 (the likes of which you might include in the 'Financial Review' section of your trustees' annual report) is a simplified illustration of how you can separate your long-term and spending reserves (and time horizons) and still be consistent with the Charities SORP guidance on formal reporting (it will be helpful to read this section in conjunction with the appendix on total return accounting, which contains a more comprehensive example).

Table 6.4 Example of how to bring your long-term and spending reserves in line with the Charities SORP guidance on reporting reserves

Reserve/fund	Closing balance (£000s)	Target value (£000s)	Notes on target values
Long-term reserve			
Permanent endowment	1,220	1,200	Maintain value of fund vs inflation (spending)
Expendable endowment	4,883	4,800	Maintain value of fund vs inflation (spending)
Restricted fund 1	988	1,000	Maintain value of fund vs inflation (spending)
Designated fund	500	1,000	In the process of building up a fund (saving)
	7,591	8,000	
Spending reserve			
Restricted fund 1	22	5	Available for spending (spending out)
Restricted fund 2	6	0	Aim to spend balance shortly (spending out)
Unrestricted fund	590	300	Six months' running costs (spending)
	618	305	
Total funds	8,209	8,305	

The table shows the different types of fund that you can have on your balance sheet, except that they are spread between long-term and spending reserves:

- **Endowments** (both permanent and expendable) are, by definition, long-term funds.

- **Restricted funds** can be either long term or spending, or both. In the example there are two funds:
  - Restricted fund 1 (which comes from fundraising for a scholarship fund) is split into a long-term fund and a spending fund. This keeps the fund's capital separate from what has been identified as spendable.
  - Restricted fund 2 is a donation that hasn't been fully spent in the year it was given so it is shown in the spending reserve in the expectation that it will be spent in the following year.
- Here, the **designated fund** shows that the trustees have decided to build up a long-term fund and are in the process of doing so. It is designated to show that it is not available for other purposes (or for spending).
- Here, the **unrestricted fund** is kept for unexpected spending, such as projects going over budget.

An important thing to notice in table 6.4 is how the target values are used. Each fund has its own target value and the notes indicate how each is being used – as a spender, saver or spending-down reserve (remember that, as explained in chapter 2, you can have different financial objectives for different funds as well as one overall financial objective for your charity; see page 17). Including the target values next to the closing balances shows whether the charity's finances are ahead or behind where they are meant to be (based on the charity's financial objectives and goals).

While this format can be adapted to fit in with the formal Charities SORP reporting requirements (see appendix 2), it also works very well as part of your management reporting and as part of the 'Financial Review' section of your trustees' annual report. In these contexts, it shows a simplified but complete illustration of how you are planning to use all of your long-term and spending reserves (and over what time horizons), rather than just parts of them.

Fictional case studies

Spender: Warden's Philanthropy

The original endowment of Warden's Philanthropy was left as a permanent endowment, and the trustees have now adopted a total return resolution (as described in chapter 4). They used the Bank of England inflation calculator to work out that the original gift of £200,000 (made in 1860) would have been worth £18 million in 2021 if it had grown in line with inflation. The fact that it was actually worth £40 million made the trustees realise how unfair the treatment of the money had been to earlier generations because they could have spent an additional £22 million while still maintaining the value of their original endowment in real terms, had total return been available as an option. After passing their resolution to move to total return accounting, the trustees of Warden's Philanthropy had £35 million in their long-term reserve and the balance of £5 million in their spending reserve.

They set target values for their two reserves:

- Although the trustees put £35 million into their **long-term reserve**, they decided to give it a target value of £32 million in case the markets slipped back and they sunk below the target value they aimed to maintain into the future against CPI inflation (which could affect their spending – see chapter 7). They wanted to make the target value lower than £35 million because they thought that the market values seemed unusually high at the time they made their decision and they wanted some form of cushion to rely on should the markets fall.
- They put £5 million into their **spending reserve**. Its target value was set at £1 million because that was the level the trustees felt they needed to keep to cover unexpected opportunities and emergencies. As part of that decision, the trustees decided that they should spend the remaining £4 million to try to ease some of the effects of the recent austerity in their community. They would also use some of the £4 million for a series of extra-large awards in their prize fund.

More detail is given in the appendix on total return accounting.

Saver: Martello Tower Fund

The Martello Tower Fund's investment committee has a known target of how much money it needs to deliver the building work to save the fort in today's prices. This seems relatively straightforward, so the question that is exercising the trustees is whether or not they could actually make a surplus.

The charity has done very well against its objectives, notwithstanding a worrying dip in years 12 and 13. Now, after 18 years, it has more than enough money to start work immediately. As a result, the committee members are asking themselves whether to change how the fund is invested so there is less uncertainty and risk in the current approach, or whether to continue to try and make more money. In other words, when should they stop being a saver and become a spend-out fund? The discussion is ongoing.

Spend-outer: Butterworth Music Festivals

The trustees of Butterworth Music Festivals have a seemingly simple task – just give away all the money they have within ten years of their first grant. All the money is in their spending reserve and their target value is nil, with a carefully planned smooth path to get there. But things are never that simple, not least because the trustees are obliged by law to give away the money responsibly and not just throw it away, and that requires planning.

The trustees produced a plan showing how much they would have left by what stage, which went off course early on. This was caused by surprisingly successful investment returns accompanied by difficulties spending the money. As a result they are some way behind their plans and are having to adjust fast. In response, they have rethought their future budgets and recalculated when cash is likely to flow out of their account. They can now move forward more confidently armed with clear numbers about what they need to spend and by when to avoid handing money over to the government because it hasn't been spent in time.

Conclusion

If you go to the trouble of setting an objective, you should take just as much trouble (or more) about measuring whether or not you have been successful and thereby demonstrating accountability to your stakeholders. This is where clear and sustainable reserves policies are indispensable. In a world where you will inevitably need to deal with uncertain asset values, only your reserves can give you the confidence that you are on track with your plans.

Notes

1 'Charity reserves: Building resilience (CC19)' [web page], Charity Commission for England and Wales, 2023, www.gov.uk/government/publications/charities-and-reserves-cc19/charities-and-reserves, accessed 20 January 2024.
2 *Charities SORP (FRS 102)* [PDF], 2nd edition, Chartered Institute of Public Finance and Accounting, 2019, www.gov.uk/government/publications/charities-sorp-2005, accessed 20 January 2024.
3 See www.measuringworth.com/calculators/ppoweruk.
4 See www.bankofengland.co.uk/monetary-policy/inflation/inflation-calculator.
5 *Charities SORP (FRS 102)* [PDF], 2nd edition, Chartered Institute of Public Finance and Accounting, 2019, www.gov.uk/government/publications/charities-sorp-2005, accessed 20 January 2024.

6 'Charity reserves: Building resilience (CC19)' [web page], Charity Commission for England and Wales, 2023, www.gov.uk/government/publications/charities-and-reserves-cc19/charities-and-reserves, s. 6, accessed 20 January 2024.
7 Charities Act 2011, s. 282 (as amended).
8 'Charity reserves: Building resilience (CC19)' [web page], Charity Commission for England and Wales, 2023, www.gov.uk/government/publications/charities-and-reserves-cc19/charities-and-reserves, s. 3.1, accessed 20 January 2024.
9 *Charities SORP (FRS 102)* [PDF], 2nd edition, Chartered Institute of Public Finance and Accounting, 2019, www.gov.uk/government/publications/charities-sorp-2005, accessed 20 January 2024.

PART II
Context

Chapter seven
The law

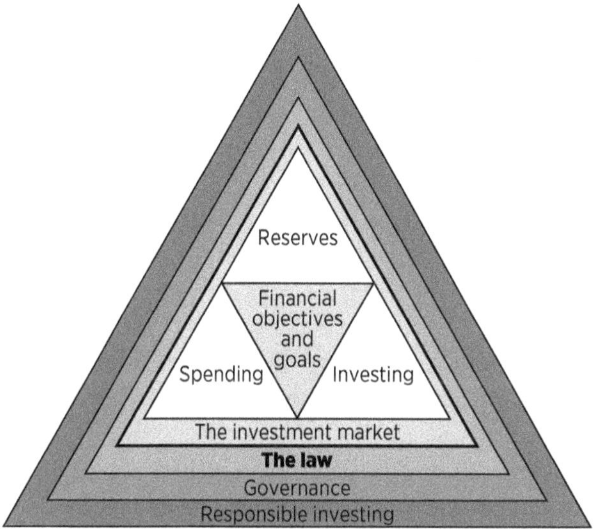

The purpose of this chapter

Trustees must act within the law, and if they do, the law will protect them. Sometimes trustees are hesitant about their duties or their risk appetite based on a misunderstanding of the law, and that can lead to them achieving less than might be possible. Although a wise trustee facing a significant decision will always want to obtain specific advice on the problem from a charity-specialist legal adviser, the fundamentals of the law around charity investment are easily understood and simple to enact.

After a brief summary of the legal context, this chapter first considers the three principal ways a charity can invest and how they sit within the law and the Charity Commission's guidance. It then moves on to consider the major pieces of legislation and case law and the related guidance, summarising the key points that charity trustees (and those around them) need to be aware of. Next, it debunks some of the myths that can hold back trustees' ambitions for their charity. Finally, the case studies consider some of the law-related decisions made by the three fictional charities.

The legal context

Before we begin, some context: this chapter is based on English and Welsh law. As mentioned in the introduction to this book, some parts of Scottish and Northern Irish law are different, and charities in those countries should take their own advice in this area. For English and Welsh charities, this chapter should be used as a guide and not authoritative advice. That is the preserve of lawyers. Different charities can be set up in different ways, and not all provisions regarding charity investment apply to all charities equally.

Figure 7.1 provides an overview of how the law flows through the process of investing. The starting points are your charity's governing document and the English and Welsh legislation applicable to your charity (mainly the Trustee Act 2000 and the various Charities Acts), which give you permission to invest and sometimes tell you how to invest. This legislation in turn underpins the Charity Commission's guidance. Bear in mind that unincorporated charities' investing activities (see box below) are governed by the Trustee Act 2000, whereas other charities' investing activities are governed by their governing documents, but the Charity Commission applies the same principles to all charities in its guidance.

A third element is common law (i.e. the judgments of the courts over time). This mostly relates to deliberations about the meanings of words, such as what is or isn't an 'investment' (in contrast to trading or inappropriate speculation).

Investment managers are subject to their own legislation (including the Financial Services Act 2000). This legislation governs their behaviour in relation to their clients, whether charities or not (the legislation specific to investment managers is not covered in this book but the Financial Conduct Authority's website – www.fca.org.uk – is a good starting point for those who want to learn more about this topic). Together, all of these elements form the context in which you make your investment decisions.

There is an infinite number of portfolio variations, but at their heart all will follow this basic cascade of authority and guidance. Remember that the law determines what you *must* do, and the guidance reflects the Charity Commission's *recommendations* as to how to interpret the law and your governing documents. Occasionally, the guidance can go further than the law; in such cases, where you might want to depart from the guidance, it is wise to take legal advice.

Figure 7.1 The cascading authority of charity law

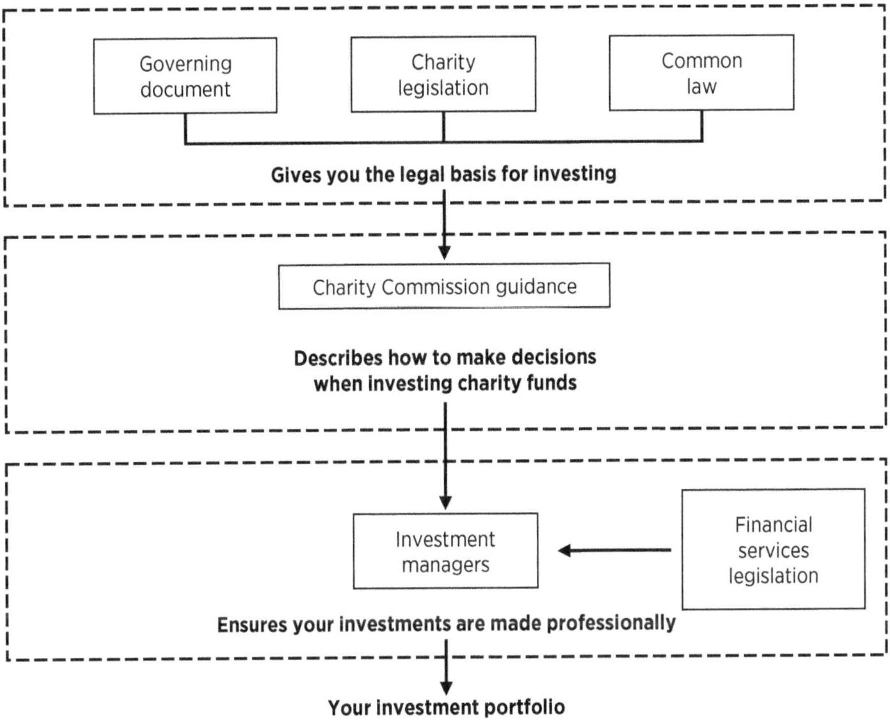

Incorporation

Incorporation is a legal process that creates a perpetual legal person to act in the place of a set of individuals. This legal person can do things in its own right. Small charities are often unincorporated (but can still be registered charities), which means that the trustees own any assets on behalf of the beneficiaries. In contrast, when a charity is incorporated, it owns the assets in its own right. This avoids hassle when trustees join or leave, because the ownership of the assets doesn't need to change. Some charities accomplish the same thing by using a firm called a 'nominee' to hold their assets for them.

Charities can be incorporated in various ways, including by Act of Parliament, but the most common forms are:

- as a **company** limited by guarantee;
- as a **corporation**, such as a charitable incorporated organisation (CIO);[1]

- as an **incorporated body of trustees,** where the trustees can own assets collectively but without the charity becoming a company or a CIO – this is simple to achieve (by applying to the Charity Commission under part 12 of the Charities Act 2011) and effective in avoiding the need to change who owns things on behalf of the charity as trustees come and go.

Problems can crop up when charities that have endowments (especially permanent ones) and that are also charitable companies want to reorganise themselves, such as in a merger. If this applies to you, you will need to seek legal advice.

What is an investment?

The Charity Commission currently recognises two types of investment: financial investments and social investments.[2] To these might be added a third – investing in a charity's purpose or fundraising (see figure 7.2) to seek a return (either social or financial). The third type is not an investment in the context of this chapter, but (just like the first two) it represents choices trustees make with their capital.

Figure 7.2 The three types of charity investment

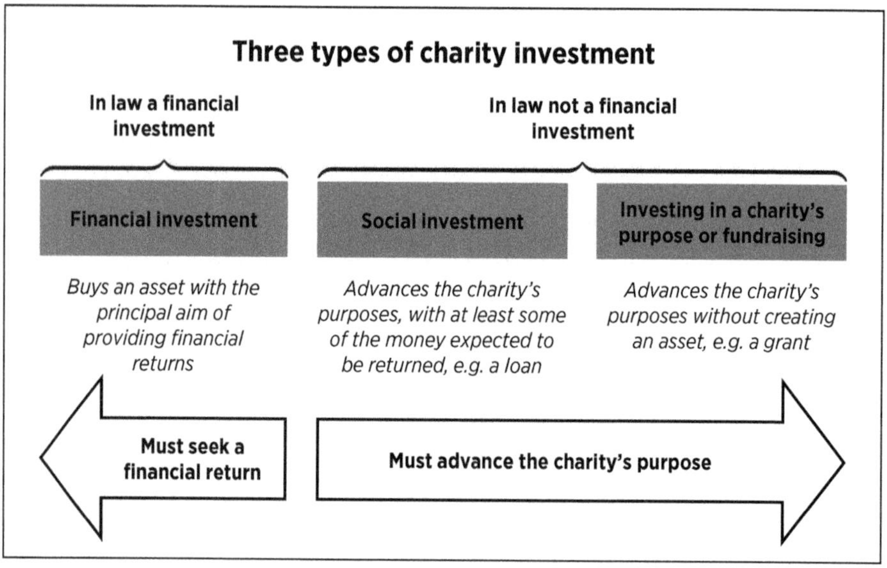

The more traditional view of an investment is therefore now described in the guidance as a 'financial investment' and it seeks to create an income or growth in an underlying asset. This distinction between financial investments and other types of investment (however defined) is important because the special rules flowing from the Trustee Act 2000 are only relevant to financial investments. As such, where an investment is made for a financial return, it will always be subject to the Act's explicit legal requirements. The law also incorporates some of the principles of financial investment into social investment (see page 136). Note that managing cash is considered an investment decision in the Charity Commission's guidance.

The following subsections provide brief summaries of these types of investment based on the descriptions in the Charity Commission's guidance *Investing Charity Money: A guide for trustees* (CC14).[3] It is important to note that all three types of investment are also covered by the general duties of trustees in *The Essential Trustee: What you need to know, what you need to do* (CC3) (see page 142).[4]

Investment 'sins'

In law, whether something is a sin in financial investment doesn't so much turn on profit or loss but on whether making the investment was within the charity's powers, or whether the trustees acted improperly (and irresponsibly). Good returns matter but they are not the first consideration. Similarly, it is easy to sin when making a social investment if the social good is not within your charity's purposes, or if it was for the public benefit but the private benefit was not justifiable. Bear in mind that poor financial investments can show up much more clearly than poor social investments or poor spending decisions – even if the sums are the same. This is because it is easy to see poor financial returns but less easy to identify whether you have made a poor social investment or spending decision because the value of a social outcome is much harder to judge than the value of a financial one. However, just because your investments have not performed well does not necessarily mean that you have made a mistake.

Financial investment

The purpose of financial investment is normally to yield the best financial return possible within the level of risk and values that you consider to be acceptable according to your financial objectives and goals (see page 23). This means that you can think beyond just maximising your financial returns and consider the more nuanced guidance throughout this book about choosing the right investment approach for your financial objectives and goals. You also have discretion to prefer or exclude investments that might advance or conflict with your charity's purpose, even if that means you might earn less or be less diversified (as clarified in the important case *Butler-Sloss v. Charity Commission* in 2022; see page 141).

Social investment

Sometimes you might want to spend money on something because it will directly further your charity's purpose because you may be more interested in doing good and less concerned about how much money you get back. Until recently these types of investment were known as 'mixed motive investments' or 'programme-related investments', but importantly they still required you to make some sort of financial return (even if this would have been less than you would have received if you had treated the same asset as a financial investment). The Charity Commission's revised presentation of the law is much simpler because you need only to expect *some* of the money to come back to you (unlike with a gift, where you don't expect anything to come back to you). Where an investment cannot be wholly justified as a financial investment, it may be possible to justify it as a social investment, so long as it advances the purposes of your charity. Loans and guarantees to advance your purpose are now clearly allowed as social investments (rather than having to be justified as financial investments).

In legal terms, this type of investment is not a financial investment and is covered by legislation other than the Trustee Act (see below). As such, the Trustee Act's strict rules applying to financial investments do not apply to social investments, although similar principles are applied in CC14 (see page 143). Keeping a careful record of your intentions when making such decisions is therefore important.

If your investment is partly financial and partly social, it will be a social investment.

Investing in your charity or its fundraising

Investing in your charity or its fundraising isn't usually considered an investment in any legal sense or in the Charity Commission's guidance because it does not create an asset on your balance sheet. Nevertheless, it remains an important way that charities can and do invest to earn a return or deliver their purpose on a day-to-day basis. For some charities this can be more rewarding than investing in financial assets such as stocks and shares. Charities will treat this as expenditure instead.

Trustee Act 2000

The Trustee Act 2000 is the primary legislation relating to the trustees of any unincorporated body that holds its assets for the benefit of a charitable trust, be it a charity or not. It does not apply to charities that are also companies or corporate bodies (unless the company holds property on trust, such as a permanent endowment), but the Charity Commission has absorbed the relevant principles of the Act into CC14.[5] An investing activity that seeks the best financial return is always governed by those principles. If you are just transferring money, such as giving a guarantee without seeking a financial return (see page 140), then the activity is not a financial investment and not covered by the principles, even though you might get your money back. The following subsections look at the core principles of the Act in turn.

Duty of care

The Trustee Act imposes a 'duty of care' on trustees.[6] This means that if a trustee has particular knowledge or experience (such as being a surveyor or an accountant), they must apply that expertise when making decisions for their charity. They must also exercise such care and skill as is reasonable in the circumstances. It is not acceptable to think that their knowledge or experience does not apply just because they are working pro bono or not acting in a professional capacity.

General power of investment

The Trustee Act gives all unincorporated charities wide powers of investment.[7] As a result, charities are no longer restricted to old-fashioned limits such as holding a majority of their assets in bonds (a requirement in the now defunct Trustee Investment Act 1961). Charities that are also companies or corporate bodies will usually have this general power to invest in their constitution, and if so, the Charity Commission still expects them to apply the Trustee Act principles when making decisions. However, you must still check your governing document in case there are specific restrictions that apply to your charity. If so, you will need to take legal advice if you want to follow a different path to that set out in your governing document.

Standard investment criteria

The Trustee Act sets out standard investment criteria that sit at the heart of all trustees' investment duties, and they are clear and straightforward. They concern suitability and diversification.[8]

Suitability

You must make sure any investments that you authorise are suitable for your charity.[9] Examples of unsuitable investments can include those that:

- **offer too low a return**, or too little income for the level of risk being taken;
- **are too esoteric** to be properly understood, such as cryptocurrency and blockchain assets, classic cars and wine collections;

- **are too illiquid** in relation to your charity's specific cash-flow needs, meaning you might not be able to turn the asset into cash when you need to;
- **are legally too complex** for the charity to manage.

However, these are only examples – any other of a whole range of considerations can make an investment unsuitable. What is suitable for one charity may not be suitable for another; your financial objectives and goals (see chapter 2) will help you to determine what is suitable for your charity.

Diversification

You must consider whether your investments are sufficiently diversified for the needs of your charity.[10] Diversification is a central theme in investing (see page 91) and it can be done in many different ways, such as by asset class, by time frame, by how assets are valued or by type of activity. It is possible, in some circumstances, not to have a very diversified portfolio – for example, if your charity's wealth comes from a family company left to the charity on the basis that the donor stock must not be sold. Another example would be investing everything in one building with a single tenant. Neither is considered best practice and where possible both should be avoided.

Advice

The Trustee Act requires that before making an investment or when reviewing one, trustees must 'obtain and consider proper advice about the way in which, having regard to the standard investment criteria, the power [to invest] should be exercised', except if the trustees 'reasonably conclude' that 'it is unnecessary or inappropriate to do so'.[11] In other words, you must get advice unless you do not consider it necessary – for example, where you have sufficient expertise within your charity or the values involved are what the guidance calls 'small'.[12] If you decide that you don't need third-party advice, it is best to carefully document why this is the case.

This is important because sometimes potential advisers insist that you use their services, claiming that you 'must' always get advice (and, by implication, follow it). This is simply not legally accurate, and you should avoid using any investment 'expert' who perpetuates this falsehood. Bear in mind, though, that the newer, updated Charity Commission guidance CC14 (see page 143) is firmer on the requirement to take impartial, professional advice 'unless you have a good reason not to'.[13]

The Act then goes on to say that 'proper advice is the advice of a person who is reasonably believed by the trustee to be qualified to give it by his ability in and practical experience of financial and other matters relating to the proposed investment'.[14] Interestingly, 'qualification' relates to ability and experience, rather than any specific professional qualifications.[15]

Where the issue is complex or especially uncertain, or there is a potential conflict of interest (see page 144), it is wise to get expert independent advice. An investment manager will usually not be able to give independent advice because they will advise only on their own products, but they may be able to suggest an appropriate firm, as will networks such as the Charity Finance Group (www.cfg.org.uk).

Written agreements

The Trustee Act is clear that if trustees delegate their powers of investment to anyone else, they must put in writing both the policy they want to be implemented and the terms of the delegation.[16] In other words, you must have a written agreement with your investment manager and a written investment policy statement (see page 166).

Property

In addition to these principles in the Trustee Act, there are separate laws specifically governing the disposal of property. These requirements relate to valuations, advice and certificates, and they are contained in the Charity Commission's guidance *Sales Leases Transfers or Mortgages: What trustees need to know about disposing of charity land* (CC28).[17] These are mandatory and more detailed than the requirements for other forms of investment.

You will likely need to take legal advice if you wish to invest directly in or dispose of property – but then this is usually necessary for any property transaction. Note that the Charities Act 2022 makes provisions (not all yet in force) to relax some of these requirements, but the Charity Commission's guidance is yet to be updated at the time of writing.

Charities Act 2011

The Charities (Protection and Social Investment) Act 2016 established the power for unincorporated and most incorporated charities to make 'social investments' (see page 136) by inserting provisions into the Charities Act 2011.[18] However, not all incorporated charities automatically have this power. In particular, charities established by Act of Parliament or Royal Charter are not covered by this Act (although, if this applies to your charity, you may still be able to make such investments if your governing document allows it).

Requirements for making a social investment

Before making a social investment, you must consider whether you need to seek advice that is relevant to the social investment.[19] Although this is still advice, it is different from the advice relating to a financial investment (see page 138) because it is not focused solely on financial returns. It can incorporate advice on a wide range of factors, such as the likely success of the proposed social investment or its legal, financial or accounting aspects. Additionally, CC14 says that you should be satisfied that the social investment is in the interests of your charity, taking into account what you expect from helping to achieve your charity's purposes and making a financial return.[20] Obviously it is essential to make a record of this decision internally, and the reasons for it.

Once you have made a social investment, you must review it from time to time, just as you would any financial investment. When reviewing it, you should again consider whether you need any external advice.

Guarantees

A guarantee is a commitment to take on someone else's obligation in certain circumstances. For example, an arts charity might want to underwrite the production of a new play in case ticket sales are lower than expected. A guarantee can be given with or without the requirement of a financial return, so long as it will advance the charity's purpose. The Charities Act clarifies that, as a social investment, a guarantee is considered to have made a financial return if it is not called on, or only partially called on, because it is made with the intention of advancing the charity's purpose. If the whole sum is lost, it is considered a gift rather than an investment, and the trustees must consider the gift to be one they would have made under other circumstances (i.e. if they had not made the guarantee).[21] In other words, before you make a guarantee, you must be certain that however the guarantee turns out, it will further the purposes of your charity.

Permanent endowments

The Charities Act 2011 has special provisions (summarised in CC14[22]) relating to permanent endowments and how they can be used for social investments. In brief, you must be sure that these investments would not contravene any of the existing restrictions that apply to the permanent endowment. If your charity has adopted a total return approach (see page 59) to the investment of its permanent endowment, you can decide to use some of your total return fund to make social investments. However, any losses must be offset (over time) by other gains in your charity's total return investment portfolio. This is to ensure that your charity's permanent endowment keeps its overall value in the long term. If you are operating under the standard rules for permanent endowments then you cannot make a social investment if you anticipate making a financial loss.

Butler-Sloss v. Charity Commission (2022)

The case *Butler-Sloss v. Charity Commission* was decided in 2022 and provides important clarity on the law around charity investment. It explains that 'charity trustees' primary and overarching duty is to further the purposes of the trust' and that a charity's financial investments must be made with a view to supporting its charitable purposes.[23] It goes on to say that normally this is done through obtaining the highest financial return at an appropriate level of risk (under the Trustee Act 2000), but sometimes particular investments can be excluded if, on balance, they might conflict with the charity's purposes. This is especially true of investments that would directly conflict with a charity's purposes. The case clarifies that trustees can prefer some types of investment over others to advance their purpose (subject to the standard investment criteria; see page 137) and can use their financial assets in other ways to advance the charity's purpose, such as by voting at shareholders' meetings.

Trustees can avoid investments that they are satisfied will lose them support among donors or the confidence of their beneficiaries, but they must be careful not to assume that their own moral perspective is representative of the views of their donors or beneficiaries, who might legitimately have differing views.[24] Specifically, the judgment says, 'in considering the financial effect of making or excluding certain investments, the trustees can take into account the risk of losing support from donors and damage to the reputation of the charity generally and in particular among its beneficiaries'.[25]

The judgment also clarifies that where a charity's governing document prohibits it from making specific investments, they cannot be made.[26] It also suggests that the law relating to financial and social investment is quite distinct, but at least some of the attributes of a financial investment must be present in a social investment (otherwise it would just be a grant).[27]

It contains this clear summary:

> Essentially, trustees are required to act honestly, reasonably (with all due care and skill) and responsibly in formulating an appropriate investment policy for the charity that is in the best interests of the

> charity and its purposes. Where there are difficult decisions to be made involving potential conflicts or reputational damage, the trustees need to exercise good judgement by balancing all relevant factors in particular the extent of the potential conflict against the risk of financial detriment.[28]

The implications of this case are fully reflected in the reissued version of CC14: *Investing Charity Money: A guide for trustees*, published in 2023.[29]

Charity Commission guidance

The Charity Commission's guidance covers all parts of the investing landscape shown in figure 7.2, either directly (in the cases of financial and social investments) or indirectly (in the case of investment in a charity's purpose or fundraising). The two most relevant guidance documents (already mentioned above) are *The Essential Trustee: What you need to know, what you need to do* (CC3),[30] which covers the general duties of trustees, and *Investing Charity Money: A guide for trustees* (CC14),[31] which covers investing for charities.

You should also be aware of the Charity Commission's guidance on conflicts of interest in *Conflicts of Interest: A guide for charity trustees* (CC29).[32] No investment (of whatever kind) should offend the rule against trustees benefitting from their trusteeship, save to the extent this is permitted by their constitution.

This caution about private gain is separate from the care needed when making social investments, which, of course, need to be for the public benefit. This is covered in *Public Benefit: running a charity* (PB2).[33]

The following subsections explore each of these four publications in more detail.

CC3 – The Essential Trustee: What you need to know, what you need to do

The Essential Trustee covers the general duties of trustees. These duties apply to any activity that charity trustees undertake, whether it involves an investment or not.[34] However, some have particular relevance to investing:

- **Time horizon:** 'with your co-trustees, make balanced and adequately informed decisions, thinking about the long term as well as the short term'.[35]
- **Appropriate use of resources:** 'make sure the charity's assets are only used to support or carry out its purposes'.[36]

- **Risk:** 'avoid exposing the charity's assets, beneficiaries or reputation to undue risk' and do not 'over-commit the charity' (i.e. with future obligations that may be unaffordable).[37]
- **Prudence:** 'take special care when investing or borrowing'.[38]
- **Compliance:** 'comply with any restrictions on spending funds or selling land'.[39]
- **Accountability:** 'ensure accountability within the charity, particularly where you delegate responsibility for particular tasks or decisions' (e.g. to an investment manager).[40]

CC14 – Investing Charity Money: A guide for trustees

Investing Charity Money: A guide for trustees is the principal guide for trustees on what they need to consider when making financial or social investments.[41] These include cash held in a bank account. It is the centrepiece of the Charity Commission's guidance for trustees on investing and was redrafted in 2023 to be simpler and briefer, including incorporating the points made in the *Butler-Sloss* case (see page 141). The main topics of this guidance are as follows:

- **'Your trustee duties'** covers the fact that your investment decisions must be designed to further your charity's purposes.
- **'Financial investment'** covers what financial investments are, specific trustee duties in relation to financial investments, and how to deal with an investment which conflicts with your charity's purpose (including various examples).
- **'Social investment'** covers what social investments are; trustee duties when making social investments; what counts as a financial return from a social investment; making decisions, taking advice about them and reviewing them; and the fact that guarantees are social investments (including various examples).
- **'Setting your charity's investment policy'** covers investment objectives (note that these are not the same as this book's financial objectives and goals), time frames, liquidity, attitudes to risk and writing an investment policy document.
- **'Investment types'** covers the various types of asset that are either financial investments or social investments, the duty to consider suitability and diversification, investing in your charity's trading company or in companies connected to your trustees, and high-risk investments.

- **'Taking advice and delegating'** covers trustee oversight, taking professional advice, using and delegating to an investment manager, and pooled versus collective funds.
- **'Reviewing and reporting on your investments'** covers disclosing your investment policy and performance in your annual report (for registered charities only).
- **'Investing your charity's permanent endowment'** covers how to find out if an endowment is permanent or not, the standard rules, total return, and the relationship between permanent endowments and social investments.
- **'Tax on investments'** refers to the HM Revenue and Customs guidance *Annex III: Approved charitable investments and loans.*[42]
- **'Advice for charities that mainly invest cash'** covers the fact that cash is still an investment so the usual rules apply (i.e. develop a policy, take advice and review regularly).

CC29 – Conflicts of Interest: A guide for charity trustees

The Charity Commission's guidance on conflicts of interest applies when a decision maker is also a beneficiary (directly or indirectly). The guidance outlines three simple steps to follow:

- Identify the potential conflict.
- Try to avoid it.
- Record it.[43]

Potential conflicts of interest often crop up. For example, a member of a charity's finance committee might be involved in the management of its investments through the company they work for. In this case, the committee should first seek to understand the nature of the conflict – for example, is the individual actually involved in providing the investment management service to the charity or does the individual work in an unrelated part of the company? In the former case, the conflict probably should be avoided (and that person not used). However, in the latter case, the firm could be used (although it would be preferable not to), so long as the individual was not involved with the charity's account and any conflict was considered a low risk.

The key is to follow the Charity Commission's guidance and avoid conflicts of interest where possible. Where you do need to manage a conflict of interest, it is important to do so with honesty, integrity and firmness.

PB2 – Public Benefit: Running a charity

In social investment, a problem can arise if your charity's money provides a private benefit. For example, a charity might subsidise a community bakery that is privately owned. The Charity Commission's guidance says that trustees must ensure that any private benefit is necessary in the circumstances and reasonable in amount.[44]

Common misconceptions of the law around charity investing

The law around charity investing is generally clear, with helpful and concise guidance from the Charity Commission. However, misconceptions and myths do still crop up. It is important to be aware of these so as to avoid unnecessarily limiting your ambitions but also to ensure that you don't expose yourself to undue risk.

Trustees must invest cautiously

Investing is about taking risks and managing them well. The Charity Commission refers to the 'duty of prudence' and this is an important point to keep in mind: trustees should be neither cautious nor adventurous, but prudent.[45] A prudent person will take necessary risks in the interests of gaining a better return. In contrast, a cautious person might avoid such risks and forgo the better return, and an adventurous person might take risks without carefully assessing the likely outcome. Accidents will happen, though it is important to make these as infrequent as possible. It can also be helpful to keep in mind that accidents are a natural part of investing; it is in the nature of risk.

Trustees must always take advice

Trustees and staff are often told that they *must* take external, professional advice on investment matters, and indeed this is the expectation in the Charity Commission guidance unless you are dealing with limited, low-value investments. However, as outlined earlier in this chapter and on page 48, this is not what the law says – rather, the Trustee Act 2000 says that you must *consider* taking advice and do so unless you reasonably conclude it is not necessary or appropriate.[46] This advice can come from an independent firm or a 'trustee or other individual with relevant experience and ability' and should be impartial.[47] If you think you already have access to good enough advice from your finance committee, for example, then you will need do no more since you will have taken advice as the law requires. However, you should be sure to ascertain that the advice you are receiving truly is impartial, and then note your decision not to seek external advice somewhere, such as in your meeting minutes. Remember that it is not formal qualifications that are required but experience and knowledge of both investments and charities. Both are critical qualifications for good advice.

Trustees must always treat their beneficiaries equally

Intergenerational equity is the idea that you should treat your current and future beneficiaries equally. As mentioned in chapter 7 (see page 57), the term was first outlined in 1974.[48] The implication is that if you overspend now, there will be less for future generations, but this frequently means that charities spend less than they might out of caution, meaning that their current beneficiaries receive less than they could. In fact, the principle of intergenerational equity only applies explicitly to permanent endowments operating under a total return order, although common law applies it to the standard rules too.[49] All other charity funds can be spent in whatever amounts the trustees decide are in the best interests of the charity and its beneficiaries – unless there are other prohibitions on disposal, such as at a museum or gallery.[50]

If a charity's investments suffer significant loss, its trustees will be prosecuted by the Charity Commission

Over the years there have been a number of charities that have lost many millions from their investments without any trustee going to prison. This isn't because they had good lawyers; it's because when something unexpected goes wrong, the Charity Commission is reluctant to punish people who are doing their best and trying to make sensible decisions, so long as they took due care, behaved reasonably and followed the Commission's guidance. The previous (and longer) version of CC14 contained this useful statement (although the current version no longer includes this wording, the message still applies in practice):

> If trustees can demonstrate that they have considered the relevant issues, taken advice where appropriate and reached a reasonable decision, they are unlikely to be criticised for their decisions, or for adopting a particular policy.[51]

However, if trustees have behaved negligently or improperly, then the Commission will rightly be unforgiving. After all, it's not the trustees' money – it's for someone else.

Incorporation protects you from financial liability

If your charity is incorporated as a company limited by guarantee or a CIO (see box on page 133), individual trustees are generally shielded from financial liability if something goes wrong. However, again, this protection assumes that the trustees have acted properly rather than negligently, and have kept records of their decisions that demonstrate this. If you have been negligent (or have acted unlawfully) and something goes wrong, you are likely to be exposed to personal financial liability.[52]

Fictional case studies

Spender: Warden's Philanthropy

Warden's Philanthropy is a simple trust that has a permanent endowment and some surplus income. The trustees have become a corporate body under part 12 of the Charities Act 2011. This means they can own their investments as a single body, rather than as a series of individuals owning the investments collectively on behalf of the charity. As a result, when a trustee retires, the charity does not have to renew all of its agreements relating to its investments.

A new chair joined the charity and as part of her induction she read the Charity Commission's guidance *Investing Charity Money: A guide for trustees* (CC14) to help her understand her duties better. This prompted a discussion among the trustees about when they had last reviewed their portfolio against the standard investment criteria, and the duties of suitability and diversification. No one could remember doing this previously, not least because 'they didn't do numbers'. The chair suggested this fell short of the duties they had as trustees. She undertook a small review herself by going to meet the charity's investment manager to see whether the portfolio was suitable for the charity and sufficiently diversified.

What she found was that the investment portfolio included a small shop on the high street, a cottage (let to the people who also rented the shop), a share in a Brazilian banana farm, a private equity fund and a mixed portfolio of stocks and shares. It turned out that some of these more unusual assets had been historical gifts that had never been sold. They had all just been looked after by the same investment manager for decades, all based on a very old agreement. The trustees had known what they owned and how this had come about, but they had never thought about their assets in the context of the standard investment criteria. As a result, they decided to thoroughly review their assets to ensure they complied with their duties as trustees.

Saver: Martello Tower Fund

The Martello Tower Fund (MTF) is the most substantial restricted fund of the fundraising charity Preserving Our Nautical Past (PONP), which is established as a CIO. The fund was created from a £1 million gift given with the special purpose of preserving a historic coastal fort against rising sea water by saving enough money to build a sea wall. The donor was keen that as long as this main financial goal was met, the charity could also take advantage of social investment opportunities, such as giving guarantees, should suitable opportunities arise.

Before the charity had accepted the gift, it had checked the governing document of PONP to make sure that, as the host for this fund, PONP had the necessary power to invest the MTF as the donor wanted. It turned out that it hadn't. The trustees discovered that for some reason the charity had unusual clauses governing its investment choices; consequently, it was unable to invest in any assets other than UK gilts or UK historic buildings. This would have meant that this new fund would have suffered from the same investment restrictions, which meant the MTF's investment committee didn't have the option to pursue the wider investment opportunities allowed by the donor of the fund.

The charity quickly decided to change its governing document to give itself wider investment powers, similar to those in the Trustee Act 2000. The trustees took legal advice to effect this change. The charity's lawyer suggested that, for safety's sake, they could include an explicit extra power to make social investments in case they wanted to make some over the coming years. This was formally approved and their governing document updated.

Spend-outer: Butterworth Music Festivals

Butterworth Music Festivals is a young charity established as a charitable trust. It has wide-ranging investment powers that are in line with the Trustee Act 2000, which means it has plenty of flexibility in how it invests its money. Its purpose is simply to spend £10 million on bringing music to communities that otherwise might not enjoy any live performances. It will do this over a ten-year period.

Among their first steps, the trustees had thought about how they wanted to invest the £10 million and whether they needed to take external specialist advice. They had decided that they would need advice because ten years was a little too long to just leave the £10 million in a bank account, and they didn't feel confident enough to manage a more sophisticated approach well enough without specialist support.

One of the trustees owned a regulated investment management firm that advised private clients. He had acknowledged this conflict and recommended that a colleague, Sam, at his business should manage the portfolio for the trustees instead of himself. Although Sam had no charity experience, the trustees were persuaded that without Sam's advice, they could be personally liable if their portfolio lost money. They did not appreciate the conflict of interest that this situation represented (i.e. that the trustee in question still stood to profit from the arrangement and so was not independent) and carried on regardless.

After being appointed, Sam invested the charity's money in a series of esoteric and expensive funds that were ill-suited to the charity's short-term, volatility-intolerant strategy. Some time later, during a discussion with a lawyer about an unrelated matter, this conflict was exposed, and the lawyer suggested resolving the situation in line with the Charity Commission's guidelines. As the returns, luckily, had been reasonable so there was no financial loss overall, the lawyer suggested that it was not necessary for the trustees to report the matter to the Charity Commission under its serious incident reporting regime.[53] Shortly afterwards, the trustee in question resigned, a new trustee was appointed and the investment management position was retendered. The trustees henceforth agreed to always seek charity-specific advice on their reorganised investment mandates from a well-known charity manager.

Conclusion

The law on investing for charities is for the most part extraordinarily simple: take advice if you are not sure about what you are doing, record your decisions, and exercise prudence, not caution. Above all, never trust anyone who suggests that you risk losing your house if you do not take (their) advice. However, the law itself isn't enough, and that is where good governance comes in, as explored in the next chapter.

Notes

1 For more information on CIOs, see Gareth G. Morgan, *Charitable Incorporated Organisations*, 2nd edition, London, Directory of Social Change, 2018.
2 'Investing charity money: A guide for trustees (CC14)' [web page], Charity Commission for England and Wales, 2023, www.gov.uk/government/publications/charities-and-investment-matters-a-guide-for-trustees-cc14, accessed 20 January 2024.
3 Ibid.
4 *The Essential Trustee: What you need to know, what you need to do* (CC3) [PDF], Charity Commission for England and Wales, 2018, https://assets.publishing.service.gov.uk/government/uploads/system/uploads/attachment_data/file/866947/CC3_feb20.pdf, accessed 20 January 2024.
5 Ibid.
6 Trustee Act 2000, s. 1.
7 Trustee Act 2000, s. 3.
8 Trustee Act 2000, s. 4.
9 Trustee Act 2000, s. 4 (3) a.
10 Trustee Act 2000, s. 4 (3) b.

11 Trustee Act 2000, s. 5 (1) and (3).
12 'Investing charity money: A guide for trustees (CC14)' [web page], Charity Commission for England and Wales, 2023, www.gov.uk/government/publications/charities-and-investment-matters-a-guide-for-trustees-cc14, accessed 20 January 2024.
13 Ibid.
14 Trustee Act 2000, s. 5 (5).
15 Trustee Act 2000, s. 5 (4).
16 Trustee Act 2000, s. 14 (4); 'Investing charity money: A guide for trustees (CC14)' [web page], Charity Commission for England and Wales, 2023, www.gov.uk/government/publications/charities-and-investment-matters-a-guide-for-trustees-cc14, accessed 20 January 2024.
17 'Selling, leasing or otherwise disposing of charity land in England and Wales' [web page], Charity Commission for England and Wales, 2023, www.gov.uk/government/publications/sales-leases-transfers-or-mortgages-what-trustees-need-to-know-about-disposing-of-charity-land-cc28/sales-leases-transfers-or-mortgages-what-trustees-need-to-know-about-disposing-of-charity-land, accessed 20 January 2024.
18 Charities Act 2011, pt. 14A, s. 292.
19 Charities Act 2011, pt. 14A, s. 292c, 2b.
20 'Investing charity money: A guide for trustees (CC14)' [web page], Charity Commission for England and Wales, 2023, www.gov.uk/government/publications/charities-and-investment-matters-a-guide-for-trustees-cc14, accessed 20 January 2024.
21 See Charities Act 2011, s. 292A; 'Charities and investment matters: Legal underpinning' [web page], Charity Commission for England and Wales, 2023, www.gov.uk/government/publications/charities-and-investment-matters-a-guide-for-trustees-cc14/charities-and-investment-matters-legal-underpinning, accessed 20 January 2024.
22 Ibid.
23 *Butler-Sloss & Ors v The Charity Commission for England and Wales & Anor* [2022] EWHC 974 (Ch) (29 April 2022), www.bailii.org/ew/cases/EWHC/Ch/2022/974.html, s. 78 (2).
24 Ibid., s. 78 (8).
25 Ibid., s. 78 (7) and (8).
26 Ibid., s. 78 (5).
27 Ibid., s. 78 (4).
28 Ibid., s. 78 (9).
29 'Investing charity money: A guide for trustees (CC14)' [web page], Charity Commission for England and Wales, 2023, www.gov.uk/government/publications/charities-and-investment-matters-a-guide-for-trustees-cc14, accessed 20 January 2024.

30 *The Essential Trustee: What you need to know, what you need to do* (CC3) [PDF], Charity Commission for England and Wales, 2018, https://assets.publishing.service.gov.uk/government/uploads/system/uploads/attachment_data/file/866947/CC3_feb20.pdf, accessed 20 January 2024.
31 'Investing charity money: A guide for trustees (CC14)' [web page], Charity Commission for England and Wales, 2023, www.gov.uk/government/publications/charities-and-investment-matters-a-guide-for-trustees-cc14, accessed 20 January 2024.
32 'Conflicts of interest: A guide for charity trustees (CC29)' [web page], Charity Commission for England and Wales, 2022, www.gov.uk/government/publications/conflicts-of-interest-a-guide-for-charity-trustees-cc29/conflicts-of-interest-a-guide-for-charity-trustees, accessed 20 January 2024.
33 'Public benefit: Running a charity' (PB2) [web page], Charity Commission for England and Wales, 2013, www.gov.uk/government/publications/public-benefit-running-a-charity-pb2/public-benefit-running-a-charity, accessed 20 January 2024.
34 *The Essential Trustee: What you need to know, what you need to do* (CC3) [PDF], Charity Commission for England and Wales, 2018, https://assets.publishing.service.gov.uk/government/uploads/system/uploads/attachment_data/file/866947/CC3_feb20.pdf, s. 2.2–6, accessed 20 January 2024.
35 Ibid., s. 6.
36 Ibid., s. 7.
37 Ibid., s. 7.
38 Ibid., s. 7.
39 Ibid., s. 7.
40 Ibid., s. 9.
41 'Investing charity money: A guide for trustees (CC14)' [web page], Charity Commission for England and Wales, 2023, www.gov.uk/government/publications/charities-and-investment-matters-a-guide-for-trustees-cc14, accessed 20 January 2024.
42 'Annex III: Approved charitable investments and loans' [web page], HM Revenue and Customs, www.gov.uk/government/publications/charities-detailed-guidance-notes/annex-iii-approved-charitable-investments-and-loans, accessed 20 January 2024.
43 'Conflicts of interest: A guide for charity trustees' [web page], Charity Commission for England and Wales, 2022, www.gov.uk/government/publications/conflicts-of-interest-a-guide-for-charity-trustees-cc29/conflicts-of-interest-a-guide-for-charity-trustees, s. 2, accessed 20 January 2024.

44 'Public benefit: Running a charity' (PB2) [web page], Charity Commission for England and Wales, 2013, www.gov.uk/government/publications/public-benefit-running-a-charity-pb2/public-benefit-running-a-charity, accessed 20 January 2024.

45 Ibid., s. 7.

46 Trustee Act 2000, s. 5 (1) and (3).

47 'Investing charity money: A guide for trustees (CC14)' [web page], Charity Commission for England and Wales, 2023, www.gov.uk/government/publications/charities-and-investment-matters-a-guide-for-trustees-cc14, accessed 20 January 2024.

48 James Tobin, 'What Is Permanent Endowment Income?', *American Economic Review*, 427, no. 2, 1974, pp. 427–32.

49 'Total return investment for permanently endowed charities', Charity Commission for England and Wales, 2023, www.gov.uk/government/publications/total-return-investment-for-permanently-endowed-charities/total-return-investment-for-permanently-endowed-charities, accessed 20 January 2024.

50 'Charity reserves: Building resilience (CC19)' [web page], Charity Commission for England and Wales, 2023, www.gov.uk/government/publications/charities-and-reserves-cc19/charities-and-reserves, s. 6, accessed 20 January 2024.

51 'Charities and investment matters: A guide for trustees (CC14)' [web page], Charity Commission for England and Wales, 2016, www.gov.uk/government/publications/charities-and-investment-matters-a-guide-for-trustees-cc14, s. 3.2, no longer available online.

52 For further information see *Trustee Exemption Clauses* [PDF], Law Commission, 2002, www.treasurers.org/ACTmedia/cp171.pdf, s. 2.21, accessed 20 January 2024.

53 See 'How to report a serious incident in your charity' [web page], Charity Commission for England and Wales, 2019, www.gov.uk/guidance/how-to-report-a-serious-incident-in-your-charity, accessed 20 January 2024.

Chapter eight
Governance

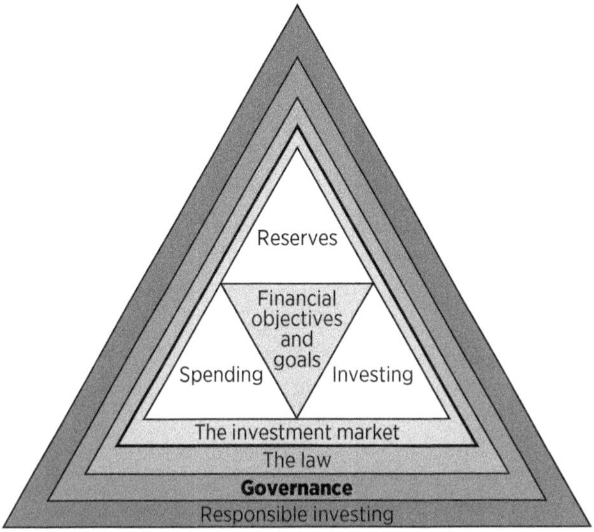

The purpose of this chapter

It's all very well having the most sophisticated investment strategy that can be devised, but this is no good if you pull the plug on it at the first sign of trouble. Being able to manage difficult times successfully – that is, maintaining confidence in your strategy and holding your nerve – is what will enable you to make money over the long term.

This chapter begins by outlining why good governance is so important in supporting good decision-making and monitoring, how little it can cost to achieve, and how much more money it allows you to make. The chapter then suggests a series of principles that you can use to make sure you have the right people to help you implement your investment governance. Next, it lays out one way of writing your investment policy statement, which is a key document that draws together all of your thinking around your investments. Finally, the three case studies examine some knotty governance issues and their potential solutions.

Why does good governance matter?

There is an anecdotal story of a large charity caught in the middle of the terrifying 2008 financial crisis. The trustees were deeply conscious of their obligations to their beneficiaries and were worried about their plummeting asset values. They called an emergency meeting and decided that the best course of action would be to sell half their remaining equities so they could guarantee there being something left if the markets crashed further. But, soon after, the markets recovered strongly – some way beyond their original valuation before the crash. Only half of the charity's assets recovered and the rest remained in cash. A huge amount of spending power was destroyed that day.

It is easy to see why the trustees made that decision, but it was a pivotal event for the charity that permanently restricted its ability to do good. And there are enough similar stories that this kind of chain of events should be recognised as a real risk. Figure 8.1 shows how just such a scenario might play out over a longer time period for two charities with identical portfolios that experience a sharp fall in the market values of their assets. The charity with steadfast trustees experiences a full market recovery while the other experiences only half that recovery because it now has so many more assets in cash. Only trustees have the power to destroy a charity's assets in this way, because they alone have the remit to make such far-reaching and even existential decisions about their charity's money.

Figure 8.1 The potentially powerful effect of sitting out a market fall

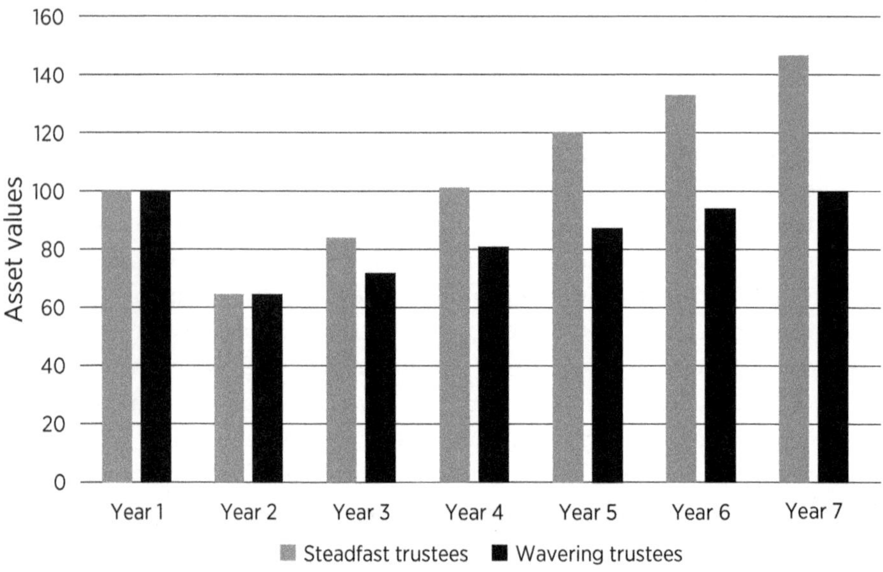

How painful can it get?

When the value of your portfolio sinks suddenly, it is always tempting to sell. But we often forget that markets have many more periods of going up than periods when they fall. That's why markets rise over time. In other words, substantial, long-term market falls where recovery takes decades are very rare. Short-term declines are more common (see table 8.1), however, so if your horizon is short, you need to be alert to the likelihood of these falls – and prepare for them by avoiding assets whose value is known to be uncertain.

Table 8.1 Declines in the S&P Global's 500 (a major index that reflects the top 500 companies in the USA) since 1951

Scale of decline	Average frequency	Average length
–5% or more	About three times a year	44 days
–10% or more	About once a year	114 days
–15% or more	About once every three years	251 days
–20% or more	About once every six years	370 days

Source: 'What past stock market declines can teach us' [web page], Capital Group, www.capitalgroup.com/individual/planning/market-fluctuations/past-market-declines.html, accessed 20 January 2024.

Sometimes people are concerned about really extreme, planet-altering events – nuclear war might be an example, or a meteor strike. With such events, though, the impact would be so serious that whether or not your charity's investment had survived would become insignificant. These are often called 'game over' scenarios. They cannot reasonably be planned for (without disastrous expense) so they are risks that you (along with the rest of the world) would just have to respond to if they arose.

All of this goes to show why good governance is the 'asset' of choice. Nothing is more important. The following subsections go into more detail about the relationship between good governance and investment returns. For more information on trustees' responsibilities and the concept of prudence, see chapter 7.

Good governance helps you to deliver your financial objectives and goals

The decisions that trustees make should always be consistent with their charity's financial objectives and goals (see chapter 2). One key decision-making area is which asset classes to invest in, and you may remember that chapter 3 includes an outline of the classes and their characteristics. Broadly, these range from assets with values that are certain from day to day ('safe') to those with future values that are uncertain ('risky'), with cash at one end and equities at the other. If you want to make more money and you have a long enough time horizon (i.e. if your financial objective is saving or spending), you will likely need to invest in risky assets. Conversely, if you are more focused on spending your existing assets and your time horizon is shorter (i.e. if your overarching financial objective is spending out), you will probably find the asset classes with more predictable day-to-day values are more suitable.

In practical terms, the investment industry tends to place clients into a certain risk profile (low, medium or high) depending on their tolerance for unpredictable returns. Sometimes this grading is broken down further into 'risk buckets', each with an associated asset allocation (see figure 8.2) and a range of potential returns, such as matching the Consumer Prices Index (CPI) or matching the CPI plus 1% for a low-risk portfolio through to matching the CPI plus 5% for the most ambitious (see page 206 for more on return targets). The higher the number, the more adventurous the portfolio.

Figure 8.2 Risk buckets

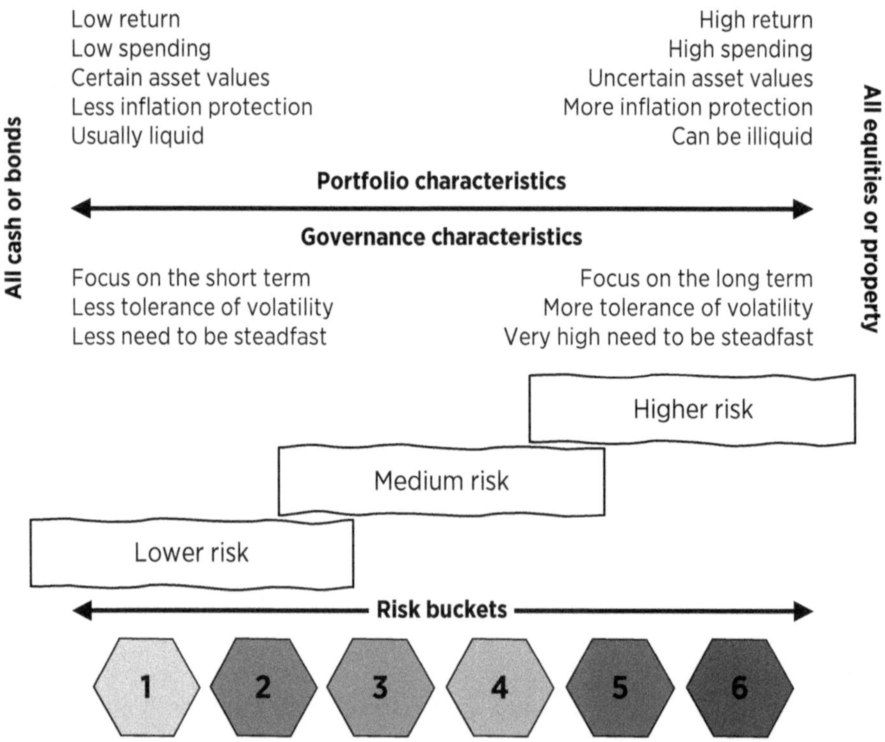

Whatever your risk tolerance, you will need steadfast and resolute trustees because they must stick to the strategy to make it work. However, it can take particular courage to stick to a long-term strategy that requires the use of volatile assets because we are all tempted to buy more assets when we've seen the price go up and sell when it has fallen.

In contrast, as shown in figure 8.3, a charity with good governance will accept the idea of buying when the price of assets has fallen and selling when the price has risen (assuming that these actions wouldn't conflict with its financial objectives and goals). It requires great discipline to do this, but this is what experienced investors tend to do. A common edict is to 'buy cheap, sell high'. All of this is one of the reasons it is so important to develop the right strategy and stick to it through thick and thin, avoiding the twin perils of fear and greed.

Figure 8.3 The relationship between asset prices and decisions to sell or buy

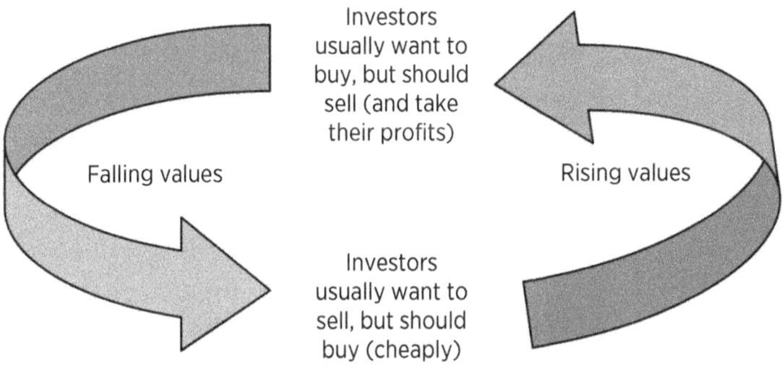

Figure 8.4 builds on the information on asset types in chapter 3 by adding in (at the bottom) the governance characteristics that safer and riskier assets require. If your commitment to your strategy is light, you will be less likely to tolerate a period of intense market volatility where asset values fall suddenly and sharply. The more volatile your assets, the more important it is to expect and even rehearse for such sharp downturns, because they are all but inevitable. One way of rehearsing is to discuss what steps you might take if your assets fell by, say, 10% or 20% and did not recover their loss within the next 12 or 24 months. In this way, you will have explored the sorts of decisions you may be faced with in a calm and rational environment. If you don't exercise good governance by anticipating downturns, your commitment to your financial objectives and goals is more likely to falter.

Figure 8.4 Governance characteristics associated with safer and riskier assets

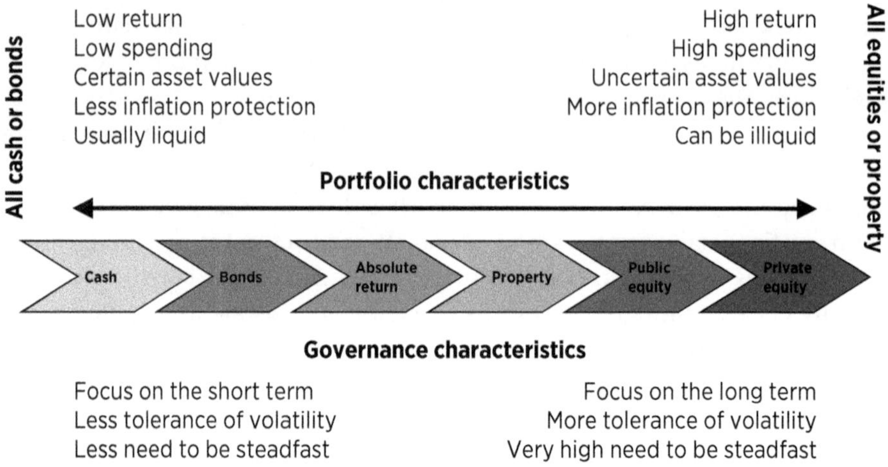

Good governance makes more and costs less

It should be clear by now that having a resilient, steadfast and sensible body of trustees will provide higher long-term returns. It is also cheaper. They do not have to be experts, but they do have to be sensible.

Table 8.2 ranks three important components of investing – manager choice, asset mix and steadfast governance – according to how much each contributes to long-term returns. Steadfast governance is the cheapest to put into place but will make the largest contribution to your returns (think of the example of the trustees who sold at the bottom of the market), whereas your manager will make the least contribution while costing the most. This is not to say that your choice of manager is unimportant; it is just to acknowledge that trustees always have the power to override a manager's good work. If your trustees waver in a crisis and instruct your manager to depart from the agreed strategy, all of your manager's work will be for nought.

Table 8.2 Contribution to return versus cost of three key components of investing (3 = highest)

	Contribution to return	**Cost**
Steadfast governance	3	1
Choice of asset classes	2	2
Choice of manager	1	3

Good governance pays for itself

It can be interesting to calculate how much more money good, well-trained trustees can make your charity (per person) over untrained, nervous trustees who are unwilling to take sensible risks or to stick to the agreed investment strategy in a crisis.

For simplicity, let's imagine that the difference between long-term bond and equity returns is 3% a year. Our imaginary charity has six trustees and a portfolio worth £10 million, and it has a long-term horizon so it can afford to consider volatile assets. As shown in table 8.3, if the trustees were cautious and opted for a portfolio entirely of bonds, the charity might earn £100,000 per year. However, if they instead embraced their long-term horizon and invested entirely in equities, the return might be £400,000 per year. (Again, the scenarios have been simplified for ease of calculation – most charities will have a mix of assets.)

The difference between the two approaches is £300,000, or £50,000 for each of the six trustees. Arguably each of those trustees is adding £50,000 (per year!) to their charity's finances compared to a set of trustees who were unwilling to make a long-term commitment and who would only want to hold the safest of assets.

Table 8.3 Calculating the value of trustees (£10 million portfolio; annual returns after inflation)

Return if 100% of the portfolio were in bonds at 1%	£100,000
Return if 100% of the portfolio were in equities at 4%	£400,000
Benefit of holding equities	£300,000
Number of trustees	6
Value of each trustee	£50,000

Too often, trustees think only about cutting the stationery budget or reducing headcount to find savings. Instead, the first place to start is often to see whether you can earn more money (indeed, this is what a fundraising-led charity would do as a first step in aiming to spend more). Cutting costs is much easier to engage with than looking again at your asset allocation (and appetite for uncertainty), but your asset allocation is likely to have a far greater impact on what you can spend on your purpose than cutting costs at the margin. This is why understanding your tolerance for uncertainty is so important (see page 25). You should never be too cautious but nor should you be wildly overconfident.

The principles of good investment governance

Boards of trustees have overall responsibility for investment matters, but often they delegate financial matters (including investments) to a subcommittee, which might consist of trustees, non-trustees or a mixture of both. Unless your charity is very small, you may find this to be the best approach as it provides space and time for proper scrutiny of your charity's financial affairs. The remainder of this chapter refers to the 'investment committee' as the body that takes primary responsibility for good governance of investment within a charity, but another common name for this group is the 'finance committee'. Note that even where there is a specialist committee looking after investments, the responsibility sits with all trustees, and it is always shared equally even if one is designated as the finance or investment specialist.

However you structure the group(s) that have oversight of your investments, it is important to ensure that your charity adheres to the following seven core principles of good governance.

Choose the members of your investment committee wisely

There is no strict formula for what makes an effective investment committee. Many charities find that having six or seven people works well, but fewer can be plenty (more is unlikely to be successful as too many voices can hamper decision-making). When deciding on the membership of your investment committee, it can be helpful to keep the Charity Commission's basic duties of trustees in mind (see page 142). Additionally, the following attributes can be particularly helpful in this context:

- a diverse range of views, so as to avoid groupthink;
- curiosity and the confidence to question a technical proposal in non-technical terms;
- the ability to ask questions that are relevant to the decision and to hold out for clear and credible answers in simple language;
- if a member cannot persuade their colleagues of the merits of their views, sufficient humility to collectively agree on a common path;
- the strength of character to stick to the strategy in difficult situations without being rigidly dogmatic;
- a level of comfort with risk and uncertainty, and the ability to make pragmatic decisions in the absence of concrete information about the future;

- the ability to communicate rapidly, clearly and simply in an atmosphere of panic (e.g. amid a rapid market fall);
- a sense of humour and the ability to laugh, because this diffuses difficult situations.

Whoever you appoint, you should try to find people who are skilled rather than opinionated – the distinction is not always obvious, but it can have a huge impact on the success of a committee.

Use your governance budget effectively

Boards and committees will have limited time and perhaps appetite for the intricacies of investment management, and this limited capacity is called a 'governance budget'. Just like with a financial budget, it is possible to exhaust it on the wrong things. Too often, the investment industry or individual trustees will overcomplicate things and run down the governance budget without adding much value. As in any well-run meeting, focusing on a few central questions will deliver good information and clarity about what is at stake. As a rule, the most useful topics for a committee to focus on are the two or three issues that could impair the ability of your investment portfolio to meet your charity's financial objectives and goals over the short and long term, and how you are going to deal with those issues.

Think carefully about which issues you want your committee members to be engaged with and what it is not necessary for them to supervise closely. If your investment manager attends your meetings, tell them in advance what the two or three issues are that you want them to address. This will keep the meeting focused on what matters (and avoid you receiving a sermon on the general state of the financial markets). And there is no real need to see your investment manager more than once a year if nothing has changed. Your manager's regular written reports should be more than adequate for monitoring purposes between these annual meetings – anything more often than that risks being just for entertainment unless the trustees need the manager to respond to a specific question.

Choose an appropriate chair

There are two main schools of thought that apply to choosing a chair for your investment committee: some say it is best to have a technically expert chair, whereas others advocate choosing a lay chair. Another consideration is how important your investment portfolio is to the financial success of your charity. If your portfolio is merely a 'nice to have', then the link between your investment committee and the rest of your charity may not be very significant. If, however, your portfolio represents your charity's entire wherewithal, then you will need to ensure you have a chair who can manage this link effectively. Additionally, this link becomes more important the more focus you have on your approach to responsible investing (see chapter 9). After all, your investment committee must be able to recognise an investment that would embarrass or undermine your charity.

If you choose an expert, they may or may not be a trustee. Having an expert chair can be beneficial because the chair will be able to lead the agenda with an easy understanding of investment management issues. However, it is important for an expert chair to be able to bring the other committee members with them on their decisions – your investment strategy must not become the voice of a sole individual. This is even more important when it comes to engaging with those trustees who are not on the committee, whose buy-in and confidence in the strategy – especially at a time of panic – will make all the difference. In other words, a board should always exercise proper scrutiny of the financial advice it receives, even if that advice comes from one of its own members.

An alternative is to appoint a lay trustee to chair your investment committee, but this person must still have sufficient confidence, intelligence and common sense for the task. The right lay chair arguably should be more likely to ensure that any strategy or solution agreed by your investment committee will have credibility with other lay trustees who are not present at the meetings but who need to have confidence in what is going on. Where investments are particularly important for your charity, it can work well if the chair of trustees also chairs the investment committee (or at least is an investment committee member). In that way, the chair should feel an obligation to go the extra mile to ensure any decisions will be palatable to the board as a whole.

It is also possible to appoint a layperson who is not a trustee, such as an accountant who is not an investment expert but who can act as an effective chair and can contribute in other ways.

Delegate clearly

Delegation is a central aspect of good governance. Responsibilities should be clear and decisions should be taken at the right levels and by the right people:

- The trustees should agree the overall strategy.
- The investment committee should manage the strategy's implementation.
- The investment manager should be instructed in writing.

- The person responsible for finance should execute the decisions as instructed, working within clear guidelines where discretion is required.

When it comes to delegation, there are usually two types of decision: those that require ongoing review (such as half yearly) and those that require occasional review (such as every three to five years):

- **Decisions that require ongoing review:** some decisions will need to be periodically reviewed because your instructions might not be being implemented as you expect. For example, you might instruct your investment manager not to invest in tobacco companies, or specify that they should have good diversification globally. In such cases, it is important to ensure that the manager (or whoever you have delegated to) regularly reports back to you to show that they are fulfilling your instructions and to enable you to reassess your decision if needed. This is covered in chapter 11.
- **Decisions that require occasional reviews:** examples include policy decisions about how much money to hold in your bank accounts, what proportion of your assets to place with each manager (if you have more than one), and whether your appetite for uncertainty and unpredictability is still appropriate. Once these policies have been agreed, you will need to know that they are being implemented but you won't want to keep reviewing the actual decision (at least over the short term) because this can lead to the policy being undermined.

Choose and set your own agenda

Although you will likely delegate the implementation of your investment strategy to your investment manager (see chapter 10), your investment strategy belongs to your charity. As such, you should dictate what you want your portfolio to do and therefore also decide what you want to discuss and review at investment-related meetings. In this sense, you should be setting the agenda on two levels: the broader well-being of your portfolio and how it is being managed, and the specific items you wish to discuss at meetings with your investment manager.

Figure 8.5 shows how the various bodies in and around a charity inform how you might set these agendas. As the figure indicates, your manager should not set the agenda but can be an important source of ideas about what might be discussed, as will investment management conferences, publications such as *Charity Finance* (see www.civilsociety.co.uk) and other networks such as the Charity Finance Group. These are forums where investment managers and finance professionals discuss possible scenarios that might develop (such as a threat of increasing inflation or ongoing market instability) and options that charities might want to consider in response to such events (such as adjusting their spending policies).

Figure 8.5 The agenda-setting environment for investment governance in a charity

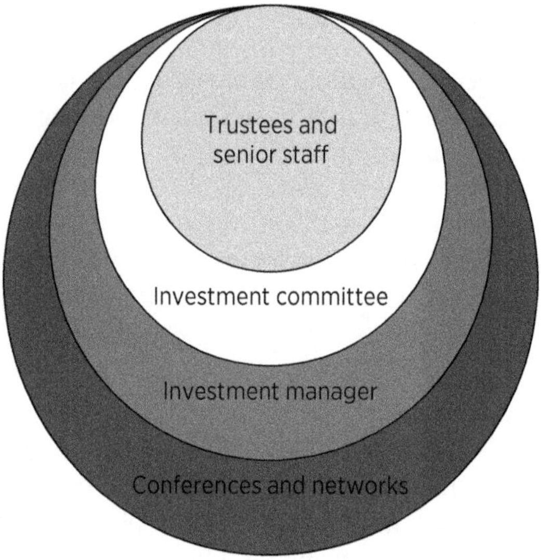

Too often, charities assume that they are not the experts and so look to their managers to tell them how they have performed and what they should be concerned about. Managers should know their investments well, but when it comes to what your charity does and needs, you are the expert, not your manager.

An investment committee meeting is an opportunity to make sure these two worlds are still in touch with each other and that your manager is providing you with a portfolio that will suit you for a range of futures (both in investing terms and in relation to your spending needs). Looking back at historical performance is less important than understanding whether you have the right portfolio for what you are trying to achieve and how it is likely to perform in the future.

A well-run charity should be able to push back against professional advice. For instance, sometimes a manager will suggest that a charity should spend less (normally because future returns are expected to be lower than they have been recently). You should set out your view of the needs of your current beneficiaries and the importance of either maintaining your spending or spending more. Managers will want to be cautious, especially about spending, while trustees will need to be prudent (see page 145). Spender charities should be particularly alert to managers having a bias towards growing the capital value rather than just maintaining it – good managers will encourage you to spend if they think it appropriate.

Codify your investment beliefs and principles

One technique that some committees use is to write down some fundamental principles that underpin their strategy and why they think the strategy will be suitable for the years ahead. For example, you might have decided that you should invest your portfolio largely in property. The belief might be that you think 'local property is a good hedge against inflation, can provide a good income that is reasonably reliable and is an asset class the committee is confident about managing well'. You might also write down a principle about the manager you have chosen and what part of their investing style you regard as attractive (see page 208). Another idea is to write a statement about your approach to managing inflation.

When you decide to review your strategy (see the next subsection), you can refer to these principles and see whether they still hold true. For example, if you decided to invest in local property because it can provide a good return and you are good at managing it but your parade of shops remains empty, you will see there is a case for change.

Balance continuity and change

One of the difficulties of investing is that it is a long-term game, and your efforts will never be rewarded if you continually pull up the plant to check its roots are growing well. Once you have planted it, assuming you have made sensible decisions, you need to give it time to flourish. It is therefore important to avoid frequent strategic reviews. About once every five years is usually sufficient.

Conversely, too much continuity can lead to stagnation, complacency and groupthink, so you should ensure your investment committee has access to fresh ideas to challenge it. For example, your longest-serving member might have been there for nine years and the shortest only one, with the remainder having evenly spread terms that expire in a well-sequenced way. A robust strategy will survive the challenge of new ideas and ideally be improved by it. If you have things right, any challenge will result in no or only modest changes – the default should always be not to change without a good, well-articulated reason that suggests that one of your fundamental beliefs might have been misplaced or out of date.

Charity Commission guidance on good governance

The Charity Commission provides guidance for trustees on making decisions (about anything – not just investments) in *It's Your Decision: Charity trustees and decision making* (CC27).[1] The main points are:

- Act within your powers.
- Act in good faith and only in the interests of your charity.
- Make sure you are sufficiently informed.
- Take account of all relevant factors.
- Ignore any irrelevant factors.
- Manage conflicts of interest (see also the separate guidance *Conflicts of Interest: A guide for charity trustees* (CC29)).[2]
- Make decisions that are within the range that a reasonable trustee body would consider.
- Show how you have followed these principles.

The Charity Governance Code usefully amplifies these points.[3]

Writing your investment policy statement

The purpose of your investment policy statement is to set out the decisions you have made around investing, so that your charity's trustees and staff can clearly understand your policy and why certain decisions have been made. A second – but no less important – function is to communicate to your investment manager(s) what you want them to do on your behalf (see chapter 10).

If you manage your own assets (such as a small property), it is not essential to have an investment policy statement, but it remains best practice. As soon as they begin to delegate any functions to third parties, trustees are required in law to put into writing the terms of what is delegated, to whom and for what purpose (see page 139). Larger charities (with an annual income of over £500,000) are required by the Charities Statement of Recommended Practice to disclose their investment policy.[4]

Given that the trustees have overall responsibility for investment decisions,[5] common sense dictates that they should own the investment policy statement and that it should be consistent with their views.

The information on writing an investment policy statement is included here because it is so closely tied to the area of governance. However, your investment policy statement should draw on your conclusions relating to the information in every chapter of this book.

Relating your investment policy statement to other documents

Remember that your investment policy statement is not the only document that describes what you are delegating and what your expectations are. If you are appointing an investment manager and especially if you will be using several managers, they will each have their own detailed particulars relating to how they will manage your assets for you according to their processes, and these descriptions will be closely governed by the Financial Conduct Authority. Bearing that in mind, a good way to think about your investment policy statement is that it provides the framework for your investing activities, but that the individual manager's agreement with you will describe their mandate in more detail and form the basis for the manager's day-to-day decisions. It will be up to you to make sure the two are aligned as closely as possible.

There are many possible approaches to writing your investment policy statement. One option is to include the subheadings laid out below, although you can exclude headings that are not relevant to your charity. See appendix 1 for actual example investment policy statements for the three fictional charities featured in the case studies. Also note that the sections below refer to a single investment manager, but you may have several.

Introduction

This section should provide a brief overview of your charity, including your legal status (whether you are incorporated as a charitable company or, say, a parochial church council), your purpose, your sources of income, and your financial objectives and goals (see chapter 2). It should explain why you hold investments and state how you intend your investments to be managed (e.g. by an investment manager).

Where applicable, you should mention any legal restrictions, such as a permanent endowment or restricted funds that you are investing. Finally, if your investment powers are unusually constrained in any way (such as an obligation to only invest within the UK), you should state that here.

Financial objectives and goals

Here you should set out your overarching financial objective and goals (as discussed in chapter 2) for your charity or fund. Most importantly, you should specify whether you plan to save (i.e. by growing against inflation – and, if so, by how much), spend (i.e. stay the same size) or spend out.

Your financial objectives and goals will take the effects of both your spending and your investing into account. They are measured by comparing the value of your assets against your target value (see chapter 11).

Spending policy

This section should reflect the decisions you have made about your spending policy (see chapter 4) and how you want to take money out of your portfolio. It should set out whether you plan to spend only your income or use the total return method of spending, and it should state what your spending expectations are, including the year-to-year budget stability that you require. This section might also explain when and how you expect updates to your spending policy to happen, and the role you expect your investment manager to take in this.

Investment policy

Here you should give more detail about what you want from your investment mandates(s) and outline how you want them to fit into your charity's overall financial objectives and goals. You might describe the fact that you have two different risk appetites (if you are a spender), one for the short term and one for the long term, and specify that you plan to manage them separately.

You should state which asset classes you are comfortable with and any restrictions on their use. You might want to state the minimum credit ratings you find acceptable when investing in cash or credit funds (see page 33). Although traditionally an investment policy statement often contained ranges for the weights that could be invested in different types of asset (e.g. 40–60% each in global equities and bonds), the reality is that if you have appointed a manager and explained your risk appetite clearly, they will make these decisions for you, so including specific ranges only undermines their expertise. Of course, if you have specific requirements (such as no investments in cryptocurrencies), then this is the place to mention them. You can also suggest here your expectations for the proportion of high-returning but volatile assets you expect to own in each mandate. These expectations will need to be consistent with your financial objectives and goals and your spending aspirations. Bear in mind, though, that if you specify such requirements, or a specific asset allocation, you are making an investment decision and you should be confident that your view is at least as well informed as your investment manager's would be on the same topic.

Liquidity should be covered too. The key point is to state how quickly you require your reserves (see chapter 6) to be available in cash. For example, depending on your financial objectives and goals, you might require your short-term spending reserves to be available within five days and your long-term reserves to be available within three months. You should also specify your maximum tolerance for funds being locked up for prolonged periods (often called 'gating'; see page 34), which is sometimes a feature of more illiquid assets such as property. Finally, you might indicate how often you expect to receive cash from your portfolio and in what sort of amounts.

Here, you should also specify the base currency of your investment portfolio. This will likely be sterling if your charity spends in the UK; however, if you mainly spend overseas, a US dollar base currency can be appropriate.

Responsible investing

This section should reflect your conclusions on your charity's approach to responsible investing (see chapter 9). You might draw on the responsible investment ladder (see table 9.2) to help you summarise your expectations in relation to exclusions, engagement and impact so you have a clearly recorded minimum threshold for what is acceptable. You should also outline any specific reputational concerns and any industries that you wish to avoid (e.g. fossil fuels if you are an environmental charity).

Investment powers

This is where you will specify any restrictions to be aware of (as much to remind your successors as your investment manager). This includes whether or not you have a permanent endowment.

Governance

This brief section can summarise who is responsible for which decisions and what is delegated to whom. Again, this is principally for your and your successors' benefit, but it will often be of interest to your investment manager too.

Reserves policy and target values

If you have more than one time horizon (see page 94), you should set that out here. For example, if you are a saver charity, you might have one large and growing long-term reserve that you expect to draw upon in 25 years' time and another smaller short-term reserve whose function is to provide immediate liquidity over that period if required. Each reserve will have a separate tolerance for unpredictability in how it is invested (see chapter 5) and different accounting implications (see chapter 6). These should be clearly expressed.

Management, reporting and monitoring

This crucial section should set out the high-level information on how your financial objectives and goals, and also your investment policy, should be implemented and monitored. First, it should outline how you will measure your own progress against your target value as a spender, saver or spend-outer so that you will know, before you do anything else, how you are doing overall. This measuring is something you will likely have to do yourself because your investment manager may not have a complete picture (e.g. they won't know what you've spent or what any other investment managers – if you have more than one – are doing).

If relevant, this section should then state what you are delegating to an investment manager and that you expect your manager to manage your assets in line with your investment policy statement. You can also specify who is authorised to act as a signatory. These are the people who are allowed to instruct the manager to take certain actions on behalf of your charity, either to change the mandate or to add or withdraw money. Sometimes an investment policy statement lists people by name but more normally they list roles (e.g. the chair).

Next, you should state how frequently you want to receive reports from your manager (or whoever will be looking after your assets) and what you want to see in the reports. Finally, you should outline the key metrics you will use to assess performance (see chapter 11).

Approval and review

Here you should state how the authority of your investment policy statement is derived, such as from the trustees or the finance committee. You should then specify how often the policy will be reviewed and whether there are any areas that should be the subject of special attention during reviews. (There may be times when you think your policy should be reviewed outside this cycle – for example, if there has been a significant change in the market or your charity's plans change. In these circumstances, you should refer to your investment beliefs and principles document first; see page 165.) Note that any reviews of your investment manager's appointment will usually be handled separately (see page 222).

Your chair or treasurer should then sign and date the statement.

Fictional case studies

Spender: Warden's Philanthropy

Befitting its focus on people in the Barchester area, the trustees of Warden's Philanthropy are all local. However, care has been taken to involve people from a range of backgrounds and with experience in a variety of fields. As a consequence, the trustees are a diverse, thoughtful group who work well together. This manifests itself not in especially clever systems of governance reviews but in an ambiance of challenge and support, delivered with respect and a sense of fun.

Following the charity's review of its compliance with the standard investment criteria (see chapter 7), it established an investment committee that would hold twice-yearly meetings. The chair of the charity would also chair the investment committee; this was because the trustees had been reminded that investment was such an important part of the charity's wherewithal that the matter should not be entirely delegated to an investment specialist (who may not have had an overview of what the charity was trying to achieve and the views of the trustees as a whole).

The committee members are very conscious of the need to use their governance budget wisely. The first part of their agenda consists of reviewing their progress against their financial objectives and goals and examining their investment performance over the past 12 months (e.g. income levels, liquidity, performance and how the portfolio has dealt with any difficult issues during the year). They then review any individual companies that their investment manager has added to their portfolio to make sure they are properly aware of any emerging reputational risks. Finally, they always end their meetings by reflecting on future expenditure plans, what might happen to the markets, and whether they feel they are still reasonably positioned for those outcomes.

While it seems odd to others, the committee members believe that their role is not to do very much. They value continuity of approach and have satisfied themselves that they have a clear strategy that is working reasonably well: the charity's investments have performed in line with their market-based benchmark and better than their peer group of other, similarly sized charities (see chapter 11). Their view is that there is little to be gained by conducting regular strategic reviews as these might open the door to unnecessary change simply for the sake of change.

Saver: Martello Tower Fund

The trustees of the Martello Tower Fund's parent charity (Preserving Our Nautical Past) do not have significant investments other than this one fund. Consequently, early on they decided to create a small specialist committee to supervise this portfolio and report to the trustees periodically on its management. The committee is made up of a conservationist, a former investment manager and an actuary.

The three members agree that they have sufficient expertise among themselves to manage the fund themselves: they have a good understanding of long-term investing and of the uncertainty associated with high-returning portfolios, and they feel confident monitoring progress against their target by using an ad hoc consultant rather than a long-term appointment. Consequently, they have recommended to the trustees that there is no need to use an external investment adviser or manager until they get closer to starting the actual building work that the fund is intended to support, and the trustees are happy with this recommendation. Where they have recommended that the charity takes independent advice is in the evaluation of potential social investments, since the investment committee members do not feel that they have the necessary experience and understanding of the various risks to act without advice.

There have been occasions when the market value of the fund's portfolio has fallen substantially, and this has caused alarm among the trustees. On one occasion, the trustees asked the committee to attend a meeting with the intention of issuing an instruction to liquidate the portfolio, because the trustees thought that it would be better to guarantee having the cash available to complete at least some of the planned building work rather than risk the value of the portfolio dropping further. However, the committee persuaded the trustees that this would be the wrong time to sell because the portfolio had already lost a large amount and therefore had much less to lose in the future. There was more than enough time left to earn a healthy return before the building work needed to start. The committee explained to the trustees that the fund's target value (i.e. the amount it had been agreed would be necessary to build the sea wall) remained achievable, as did the prospect of a substantial surplus that could be put to good use in the future. The outcome of the discussion was a decision that if the gap between the target value and the portfolio value worsened, the trustees and the investment committee would review the instruction again at their next meeting.

Spend-outer: Butterworth Music Festivals

The first trustee of the charity was an old friend of the donor. She invited three of her acquaintances with a professional interest in music and music education to join her, along with an investment manager friend. As related in chapter 7, there had been an early problem with a conflict of interest relating to the investment manager trustee. However, once this trustee had resigned, the remaining four quite quickly settled into a happy and harmonious way of working together, with meetings characterised by robust discussions and a great deal of laughter. They knew that they still needed expert help in managing their investments, though, especially given the charity's relatively short time horizon, so they recruited another investment manager (where there was no conflict) to help them find a suitable solution for their ten-year investment strategy. They decided against having a specialist investment committee since there were only four of them to begin with and they wanted to remain close to the investments (which they would be drawing on regularly). They had regular calls and meetings with the investment manager as their expenditure plans emerged and developed over the years, enabling everyone to have a clear idea of how much cash would be needed and when.

Conclusion

While governance might seem remarkably uncool, it can be one of the most rewarding assets in which to invest, especially considering how little you need to spend to get it to function properly. It's not so much that good governance is guaranteed to make you a fortune – more that bad governance is very likely to cost you dear. The next chapter looks at a further area of fundamental importance in charity investing: how to invest responsibly.

Notes

1 'It's your decision: Charity trustees and decision making (CC27)' [web page], Charity Commission for England and Wales, 2023, www.gov.uk/government/publications/its-your-decision-charity-trustees-and-decision-making/its-your-decision-charity-trustees-and-decision-making, accessed 20 January 2024.
2 'Conflicts of interest: A guide for charity trustees (CC29)' [web page], Charity Commission for England and Wales, 2022, www.gov.uk/government/publications/conflicts-of-interest-a-guide-for-charity-trustees-cc29/conflicts-of-interest-a-guide-for-charity-trustees, accessed 20 January 2024.
3 'Charity Governance Code' [web page], Charity Governance Code Steering Group, www.charitygovernancecode.org, accessed 20 January 2024.
4 *Charities SORP (FRS 102)* [PDF], 2nd edition, Chartered Institute of Public Finance and Accounting, 2019, www.gov.uk/government/publications/charities-sorp-2005, s. 1.46, accessed 20 January 2024.
5 'Investing charity money: A guide for trustees (CC14)' [web page], Charity Commission for England and Wales, 2023, www.gov.uk/government/publications/charities-and-investment-matters-a-guide-for-trustees-cc14, accessed 20 January 2024.

Chapter nine

Responsible investing

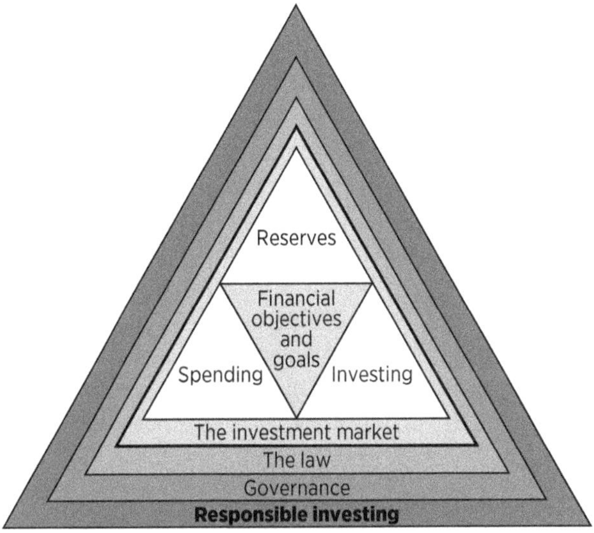

The purpose of this chapter

A charity is nothing without its values and beliefs. They should be central to your charity's discussions about how to spend its valuable resources wisely and effectively. Responsible investing is about investing in line with your charity's purposes and values, in such a way as to safeguard your reputation as well.

The world of responsible investing can seem confusing, but this chapter sets out a series of models that can help you to clearly define what it means to you and how to put it into practice. After looking at what responsible investing means, the chapter outlines how your values and beliefs are linked to your reputation and how this relationship influences your investment returns. Next, it considers the various approaches to responsible investing, examines how you might decide which are appropriate for your charity and in what circumstances, and debunks some of the perceived barriers to responsible investing. Finally, the case studies show a variety of approaches to responsible investing in our three fictional charities.

What is responsible investing?

There are dozens of ways of describing the responsible approach to investing, and many overlap and are confusing. This book broadly considers responsible investing to mean any investment activity where the aim is to go beyond a simple financial return and achieve some sort of moral good.

A related term is 'ethical investing', but this concept tends to be associated solely with excluding undesirable investments. In contrast, the broader definition of responsible investing used here also covers the idea of proactively seeking out ways to advance, or at least not damage, your purposes through investing, rather than just through spending.

Another related term is ESG, meaning 'environmental, social and governance'. Responsible investing and ESG are different concepts but are often used interchangeably. The three pillars of ESG are often allocated equal weights, but you might find that one pillar is more relevant to your charity than another (e.g. if your charity is especially focused on protecting sea turtles, the environmental pillar may be more relevant to you than the social pillar). As such, ESG is simply shorthand for a way of balancing a range of needs that investors are interested in. However, it misses out an important pillar for many investors: 'financial', which captures investors' need to earn a financial return. The acronym should therefore really be 'GFES' (see table 9.1), with governance (see chapter 8) coming first because it is largely a means to an end, be it a financial, environmental or social one (or, more likely, a combination of all three weighted according to your own priorities). As such, whenever you come across the shorthand 'ESG', you should understand it to include a financial component as well, as the majority of investments will aim to earn some sort of financial return on top of their environmental, social and governance benefits.

Table 9.1 The three pillars of the environmental, social and governance (ESG) approach, with the addition of 'financial' (GFES)

Governance	Pushing for businesses to be properly run and treat their stakeholders fairly
Financial	Earning financial returns for investors
Environmental	Encouraging a sustainable future for the planet
Social	Promoting a just and fair society, particularly at work

What does the law say about responsible investing?

The Charities Act 2011, the Charity Commission guidance *Investing Charity Money: A guide for trustees* (CC14) (see page 143) and the *Butler-Sloss v. Charity Commission* (2022) case (see page 141) explicitly recognise the idea of investing to achieve outcomes that go beyond purely financial considerations. This is important because together these sources clarify that it is possible to consider a wide range of non-financial factors when investing. In brief, charities can make two types of investment:

- **Financial investment** is aimed at making a financial return (either from income or capital growth) and is usually a means to an end. There are rigorous standards in law (see chapter 7) for making financial investments which do not apply to making social investments. However, trustees can also use this type of investment to advance their charity's purpose (such as through voting at a company's annual general meeting) and they are allowed to exclude investments that would undermine their charitable purpose or risk the charity losing the support of donors.
- **Social investment** is about more than money, although receiving a financial return remains important, even if it is just some of your original outlay. An example might be a loan to support an activity that a beneficiary cannot afford or risk putting on alone and that, if it goes very well, might result in some (or all) of the loan being returned to your charity. It is the charity's purpose that is important with a social investment. In other words, social investment is an end in itself, not just a means to an end.

Chapter 7 goes into more detail about these concepts and where they sit in relation to the law (beyond investing for a simple financial return). Much of the law is based on your intentions when you make financial or social investments, so it is worth carefully documenting in advance if you consider a specific investment (or portfolio) to be a financial investment or a social investment.

Sometimes you might want to compare a possible financial return against a possible social return. One way to do this is to think about how much income the asset might earn if you were to invest it purely financially, compare this to how much you would expect to earn from investing it socially, and then decide whether the difference is an amount you would want to spend on your charity's purpose. For instance, if you were going to make a social investment of £25,000 and it would pay you 2% per year, you would earn £500 every year. For argument's sake, if you assumed that the same amount invested financially might make you 5% (i.e. £1,250 per year), then the social aspect of the investment would cost you £750 (£1,250 – £500) every year. You can then decide whether this expenditure represents good value in relation to other beneficiaries you might have supported.

Whether or not you can liquidate the investment and get your money back is another, often under-rated factor. CC14 regards the return of at least some of the outlay as an important qualification for a course of action being considered a social investment rather than simply expenditure.

Values and beliefs, reputation, and maximising returns

Each of the various ways of thinking about responsible investing has a place, but collectively they can be disorientating in what is already a confusing landscape. At its core, responsible investing is about a key set of concepts: your values and beliefs, your stakeholders' values and beliefs, and how these two sets of values and beliefs intersect to affect your reputation (see figure 9.1).

Figure 9.1 Values and beliefs, reputation, and the danger zones

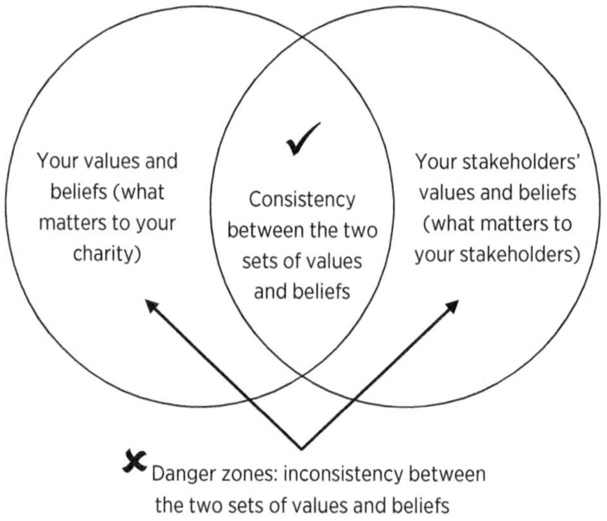

As described in chapter 2, your values and beliefs should be consistent with your charitable purposes and strategy, which in turn will underpin your overarching financial objective and your detailed financial goals (see page 23). All of your charity's activities (financial and otherwise) should be consistent with your values and beliefs.

But your stakeholders have their own values and beliefs too. These stakeholders might include your beneficiaries, the public (e.g. donors and volunteers, or those who might fulfil one of these roles in the future), and charities to which you give grants. Your reputation rests on what matters to these stakeholders and the extent to which they feel that your actions are delivering on those priorities. If they perceive that your values and beliefs are inconsistent with theirs (in other words, if they start to feel like their original reasons for supporting you are no longer valid), you enter one of the danger zones in figure 9.1 and your reputation begins to suffer.

For example, if your purpose were to support recovering alcoholics, your stakeholders might reasonably be unhappy if you were to invest in the alcoholic drinks industry. But, conversely, if your purpose were to support publicans, your stakeholders would likely consider you hypocritical if you excluded alcohol from your portfolio. You must find your own way, but it is a good idea to maintain an up-to-date and well-prepared statement explaining why you believe your responsible investment policy is in the best interests of your charity, should you need to explain this publicly.

It might seem like you have to choose between protecting your reputation and maximising your returns, but there are approaches that combine both. Some investments will both advance your mission and generate an outstanding financial return. This can be true of some firms in the green economy and in venture capital firms, especially those working in drug discovery.

Using your values to determine your approach to responsible investing

The pioneers in the area of responsible investing have often come from religious charities. Such charities are likely to have clear sets of values and beliefs (based on their faith), which can make it simpler for them to agree on what is right and wrong for their specific charity. This approach – of putting the charity's own values at the centre of the discussion – can be helpful when there are many voices within a charity each with their own views on what is 'good' or 'ethical'. A useful example is that Quakers have a mission to end the arms trade.[1] It would therefore be hypocritical for a Quaker trust to own shares in an arms company, and as such Quaker groups commonly prohibit investments connected to the arms trade or the promotion of violence.

The following section goes into detail about the various approaches to responsible investing and suggests some ways of deciding how to apply the concept within your charity.

Components of responsible investing

There are many ways of investing responsibly but they can all be grouped into four main components (as shown in figure 9.2). Generally speaking, the four components sit on a scale from less commitment to more commitment to the issue in question. However, the components can be assembled in different proportions according to what best suits your charity. It is helpful to be able to identify separately which of these components you are using so that you can understand in detail how your responsible investment policy is being delivered.

The following subsections explore the four components in detail. Whichever combination of components you use, it is helpful to detail them in your investment policy statement (see page 166) so you can choose an investment manager who can deliver what you are asking for. You may find table 9.2, which appears later on and draws the components together, particularly helpful in this regard. You might also write a separate policy solely on responsible investing if this area is of particular importance to you.

Figure 9.2 The four main components of responsible investment

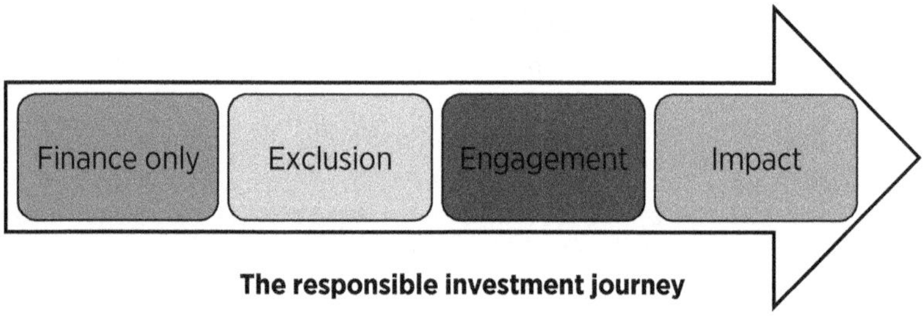

Finance

Traditionally, charities invested only for a financial return, not being especially concerned about how the money was earned. Making money and spending it were considered to be separate activities, with little weight given to aligning the charity's investment practices with its beliefs and values. A hallmark of this approach was an investment committee that was mostly detached from the trustees. Nowadays, while finance remains a consideration in all approaches to responsible investing, it is increasingly rare for charities to approach their investments without thinking beyond it.

Exclusion

The exclusion approach to responsible investing involves choosing not to invest in companies working in certain sectors that are objectionable to your cause – tobacco is a common example. In deciding what to exclude, you will need to exercise a degree of pragmatism. For example, you might deem it impractical to exclude an investment in a paper company that, among other things, provides the packaging for cigarette cartons. However, in reality, your choices are limited by how you choose to invest, whether that is with a segregated mandate or pooled funds (see page 49).

If you are investing with a segregated mandate, you can place restrictions on the proportion of turnover that comes from an objectionable activity. For example, it is common to set a 'hard exclusion' (i.e. investment is banned) where more than 5% of a company's turnover comes from activities that you don't want to support. A lesser, but still meaningful, exclusion would be a 10% threshold. Beyond that level, exclusions begin to lose their meaning because the objectionable earnings start to represent a larger and larger proportion of the total and so make the restriction less effective in the message it conveys to stakeholders.

Where you are investing in a pooled fund, you have to accept the rules of the fund so you cannot dictate what it invests in. Therefore, it is essential to be clear on what the exclusion policy is for a pooled fund because you will not be able to change it. Your only choice is to invest in that fund or not – and, if not, to find another one with more suitable rules for your needs. As such, if you have a set of exclusions that are very specific and that are very important to you, then you may have to use an investment manager who can look after your assets on a segregated basis (which will limit your choice of managers and is usually more expensive).

Common exclusions

Most common (the big six)

- Alcohol production
- Controversial carbon-related industries (such as tar sands and fracking)
- Controversial weapons (such as cluster bombs)
- Gambling
- Pornography
- Tobacco production

Less common

- Alcohol distribution (such as pubs or restaurants)
- Animal testing for cosmetics
- Baby milk substitutes
- Fossil fuels
- High-interest lending
- Human embryological cloning and other similar industries
- Industries that contribute to degradation of the environment
- Intensive farming
- Countries with oppressive regimes
- Tobacco distribution (such as by petrol stations)

Note that many funds that offer exclusions only apply them to equities and not to their bond or property investments. But why would you object to owning the shares in a tobacco manufacturer but not to owning its bonds or to having the manufacturer as a tenant? You may well decide to exclude *all* financial interactions with companies that undertake activities to which you object. If that is important to you, you should find a manager who is able to offer exclusions across all asset classes.

As discussed earlier in this chapter, it is also helpful to consider your stakeholders' views. It can be difficult to foresee all potential objections – as the Sackler Trust found when its beneficiaries started to refuse its offers of grants because of its association with the sale of opium-based medicines[2] – so it can be wise to carry out consultations with significant groups. If you have only a few closely involved stakeholders, you may be able to exercise considerable discretion in your exclusion decisions. However, you should still be mindful of how your investments might be perceived if they were subject to public scrutiny via the media and of the impact that could have on your ability to deliver your charitable purposes.

Engagement

Where you have invested in a specific company, good governance requires that you take an interest in its progress. Most charities delegate this activity to their investment manager and expect them to engage with the company's management to try to promote their interests. This engagement can be towards a financial or social/environmental end, but in the context of responsible investing it is usually social/environmental and aims to encourage companies to adopt more desirable behaviours. Engagement is often done through voting on resolutions at annual general meetings or discussions with management away from the spotlight.

Note that direct engagement principally applies to segregated investments in companies rather than those owned through pooled funds. Because you are unlikely to have a direct relationship with fund managers or any say in how they operate, the options for engagement with pooled funds are limited. The following section largely focuses on engagement by an investment manager with a company in which they invest. Sometimes, smaller charities band together into voting blocs with the aim of making their voices heard at a particular company in which they all have a small stake.

Types of engagement

Engagement occurs on a scale. At the most basic level, your investment manager might engage with a company to make sure that its directors are not awarding themselves unreasonable pay rises or too many share options, or otherwise using your money on ill-advised things. This is still the most common form of engagement, and really it is just an add-on to the basic finance approach to investment. Although it involves holding a company to account for its actions, you aren't doing anything specifically to improve the environment or society.

At the other end of the scale is a deeper, fuller engagement. This type of engagement is about trying to promote change at a company for the better in a way that you could not do if you did not have an investment in that company. As such, it is generally more effective than exclusion. Indeed, many investors now think that a charity should only exclude a company as a potential investment if the company entirely rejects the charity's arguments for change or it makes insufficient progress in changing – in other words, if engagement fails. However, for existing investments, even if a company accepts your arguments, you will need to think carefully about whether you should remain invested or whether the potential reputational damage remains too great. For example, a cancer charity that remained invested in a tobacco company to persuade it to make a safer cigarette would need to be able to justify this decision to its beneficiaries, which might be an uphill struggle.

How to engage

Engagement typically happens through your investment manager, who will act on your behalf in line with your policy on responsible investment (or, if you are invested in a fund, within the fund guidelines). There are three main ways in which investment managers organise their engagement activities:

- Some investment managers do their **own research** on individual companies' practices (but this can be time-consuming, heavy on resources and costly).
- Some use a **blended approach**: they buy this service from a third party – usually called a 'proxy voting adviser' – and combine what they receive with their own research. They might agree with some, but not all, of the recommendations of the third party.
- Others **delegate all their voting** to a proxy voting adviser and carry out little engagement beyond that.

Two commonly used proxy voting advisers in the UK are Institutional Shareholder Services (www.issgovernance.com) and Glass Lewis (www.glasslewis.com). It is a good idea to ask your manager which of the three methods they use and, where relevant, why they have chosen a particular proxy adviser. Similarly, there are agencies such as Sustainalytics (www.sustainalytics.com) that will engage with companies on behalf of investment managers.

The Principles for Responsible Investment and the UK Stewardship Code

There are codes that encourage engagement, such as the United Nations' Principles for Responsible Investment (www.unpri.org) and the UK Stewardship Code (accessible via www.frc.org.uk). Many investment managers (and some charities) sign up to them to demonstrate their credentials as responsible investors. However, it is important to be aware that these codes promote engagement with companies but do not specifically address the *intention* of the engagement. As such, the codes are quite neutral on moral judgements – all they do is express an investor's intention to hold a company's management to account.

That said, these codes remain important because they demonstrate your commitment to the process. After all, it is only through voting and engagement that your investment manager protects your financial interests in a company. A manager that does not do this will appear less credible as a good financial investor, and certainly will not be considered a responsible investor.

Impact

The final component of responsible investing is impact. Some charities invest in assets that they think will positively advance their mission while potentially also providing some income. If you opt for impact investing, instead of choosing what you *don't* want to invest in, you will start by thinking about what you *do* want to invest in. For many charities that choose this approach, usually the aim of doing good with the investment is as important as, or more important than, the financial return.

Impact investing comes in various forms but there is usually an expectation of both a financial return and a social one, so impact investing would usually be considered a social, not financial, investment (see page 136). The proportions of the financial and social returns will vary depending on the investment. For example, a venture capital investment in drug discovery might be primarily a financial investment (but with plenty of social benefits) while providing cheap laboratory space might be primarily a social investment.

Some charities prefer to make their own impact investments (such as buying a property for a specific use) while others prefer to use a specialist fund (which will have its own manager and range of assets). For example, some foundations that promote music have invested their endowments in buying musical instruments, such as Stradivari violins, which they lend to musicians who would otherwise be unable to afford them. These are absolutely investments (because the violins are financial assets of the charity and will ultimately be returned by the musicians and could be sold), but the charity's reward is in impact.

Another example would be investing in a social enterprise whose goals are consistent with your charity's purpose. For example, an environmental charity might invest in preserving and protecting some fields or an area of woodland, which might generate some income while advancing the charity's purpose.

If you are considering investing in this way, you will need to think about whether you require security (collateral) in exchange for the money that you invest, and you might also need insurance. The best security is some form of property or another asset. However, sometimes such investments are not secured against a physical asset (such as a woodland) but a revenue stream (such as payments for supporting refugees by providing housing).

You will also need to think about how to structure the financial return you require in exchange for your investment. Some charities specify variable (performance-related) amounts depending on how successful the service has been against predetermined goals. This is a varied and complicated area, and it is well worth taking specialist advice if you do not already have this expertise within your charity.

What sort of responsible investor do you want to be?

These four approaches – finance, exclusion, engagement and impact – can be thought of as tools in a toolbox that can be used separately or, more likely, in combination depending on your intentions. Broadly speaking, the more responsible an investor you are, the more impact your investments will have and the further along the responsible investment journey you will be (see figure 9.2). This does not necessarily mean your investments will have a lower financial return (think of the returns on successful drug discoveries), but it does mean your focus will be more on impact than on finance. In the best examples of responsible investment, all these tools are present.

The responsible investment ladder (see table 9.2) outlines a simple progression through six levels of responsible investment (with level 1 the lowest and level 6 the highest), showing how these different approaches are commonly combined to achieve closer alignment between investments and purpose. All levels demand a financial return (they are investments, after all) but impact becomes more important the higher you are on the ladder.

Table 9.2 The responsible investment ladder

Level	Exclusion	Engagement	Key features
6	Not necessary (unlikely to own those companies)	Yes, fully run in-house	Full impact investing in such a way as to directly advance the charity's purpose while, if possible, seeking good financial outcomes
5	Potentially still needed	Yes, usually led in-house with some external support	Assets largely chosen for financial outcomes but with good internal engagement on ESG issues; exclusions may be unnecessary at this level
4	Yes, required	Yes, handled partly in-house and partly outsourced	Common exclusions with assets largely chosen for financial outcomes but with internal commitment to ESG engagement
3	Yes, required	Yes, fully outsourced	Common exclusions with engagement focused mainly on financial outcomes with ESG interest delegated elsewhere
2	Yes, required	None, or little	Common exclusions but with little commitment to ESG engagement
1	No interest in exclusion	No engagement at all	Unconcerned about any impact other than financial returns

An important consideration is that the higher up the responsible investing ladder you are, the more work you are likely to need to do yourself. In financial investing, quantitative data is readily available to describe a company's or fund's activities. However, engagement does not lend itself to quantitative processes so easily and therefore you will need to spend more time understanding what the engagement is achieving. Consequently, you will need to be increasingly focused on knowing what you own and why you own it, regardless of whether you use a pooled fund or a segregated mandate. The more layers of funds, the more opaque this becomes.

So, if you have a pooled fund that itself invests in other pooled funds, then it becomes more difficult to know what you own with confidence.

Finally, always remember that investment is a means to an end, whether financial or otherwise. You should always be clear about what you want from an investment and understand the whole package of what it will deliver for your charity in terms of both returns and impact.

The ABC of Impact

An alternative way of thinking about the impact of your investments is Impact Frontiers' ABC of Impact, the key points of which are summarised in table 9.3.[3] This does not easily fit with the narrative of high and low returns associated with responsible and irresponsible investment. It is also complicated to execute because all companies engage in a mixture of good and bad activities, and, like many moral issues, these can be difficult and time-consuming to measure. For example, inventing new drugs to reduce animal suffering is good, but not if the purpose is to be able to keep farm animals in a smaller space and generally treat them less well so as to make a higher profit. Nevertheless, the ABC of Impact is another helpful lens through which to think about your investment manager, or individual companies. Just remember that many companies don't even get as far as 'A'!

Table 9.3 The ABC of Impact

Rating	Meaning	Interpretation
A	Avoid harm	Simplest and most common approach, aiming to minimise damage to the environment and society
B	Benefit society	Some effort is made to promote better environmental and/or social outcomes, such as paying a living wage
C	Contribute to solutions	Companies try to make specific contributions to the environment or society

Barriers to responsible investing

On the whole, charities have often been slow in moving towards responsible investing. There have been a number of reasons for this, including charities' reluctance to accept what might be seen as lower returns for higher principles, legal uncertainty, and a previously limited number of responsible investment offerings coming from the fund management industry. As the following subsections show, however, there are few remaining barriers to responsible investing that cannot be circumvented or entirely dismissed.

Lack of agreement on what to promote at board level

The law is clear that trustees must act in the best interests of their charity (see page 142), but this can be easier said than done. Trustees may struggle to agree on the best way to organise their approach to responsible investing for a variety of reasons.

One reason is that trustees' personal views on what is right and wrong can often cloud the discussion. Boards that have a dominant trustee (such as the founder or a descendant) or a common belief system (such as in faith-based charities; see page 179) can find developing a policy easier because there will already be clear moral leadership. Nevertheless, the guidance is clear that trustees should act collectively.[4]

The most important thing is to make a start on these discussions and to be pragmatic. It is very easy to get bogged down in fine discussions about the merits of a set of activities – or how a particular activity might sit within a responsible investment policy – and thereby use up so much of the board's valuable time that the whole process becomes counterproductive. An effective approach is to take some simple, unambitious steps (such as excluding the most common sectors – see page 181), get used to how they work, and then add another level of activity. An incremental journey is often best.

Concerns about financial implications

Many trustees are anxious about the financial loss that could arise from adopting a responsible investing approach. However, it is becoming increasingly clear that investing using a responsible approach appears not to reduce returns.[5] This may be because responsible companies are likely to pay fewer fines and be better run. They may also be less likely to own 'stranded' assets, which slowly become worthless (e.g. oil in a world that is moving towards lower oil dependency, as eventually nobody will want to buy the oil). Investment managers are often interested in ESG from the perspective of its effect on long-term shareholder value, while charities may view the same issue from a social justice perspective. As with the oil example, these two intentions can coincide.

You may also be concerned that adopting a responsible investing approach will reduce the diversification in your investment portfolio. This is valid to a point, as the key to all investing is an appropriately diversified approach (see page 91). As the discussion of exclusions (see page 180) implies, an inadvertent feature of responsible investing is that there can be a skew towards some companies and away from others. For example, you are less likely to see oil, gas or mining companies in lists of responsible investments and more likely to see companies focused on technology, education and healthcare. The result is that if you choose to invest with a greater emphasis on moral questions, your performance is likely to differ from the performance of standard indices (such as the MSCI World Index), which do not take account of moral issues. Generally speaking, this is not something to worry about: you would not want to invest in unacceptable companies just for the sake of maintaining portfolio diversification. However, you should be alert to the possibility of introducing a skew (compared to common indices) into your investments when instructing your investment manager.

Concerns about what counts as responsible

There is also very little evidence that ESG ratings are related to global stock market returns, suggesting that the way something is counted as responsible is still quite muddled.[6] It can therefore be difficult to know whether an intended investment is really as responsible as you'd like it to be.

Not all investment managers have in-house teams able to assess and quantify the various moral criteria in sufficient depth, so many outsource decisions about what is 'good' and 'bad' to third parties. These rating agencies are different to proxy voting advisers (see page 183) because instead of advising how to vote, they provide underlying data about how 'good' or 'bad' a company might be based on a number of different metrics, from carbon dioxide usage to employment disputes. It is best to think of them as similar to credit rating agencies (such as Moody's or Fitch Ratings; see page 33).

Some of the more accessible agencies that provide details on how 'sinful' a company is are Morgan Stanley Capital International (MSCI) (www.msci.com), London Stock Exchange Group (LSEG) (www.lseg.com), S&P Global (www.spglobal.com) and Sustainalytics (www.sustainalytics.com). However, these agencies sometimes produce quite different conclusions about the same company (see figure 9.3 for an example). This is because what makes something good or bad is subject to a large degree of judgement, and the methodologies used are unregulated and often opaque. It is also important to keep in mind that these agencies report based on the past, not on a company's plans for the future, so the picture they provide may not always be complete. Nevertheless, they can provide helpful guides as to companies' relative levels of 'goodness'. The more important responsible investing is to your charity, the more confident you should be about how a company measures up in this way.

Figure 9.3 Differences in the ratings of Alphabet (the owner of Google) by three different rating agencies

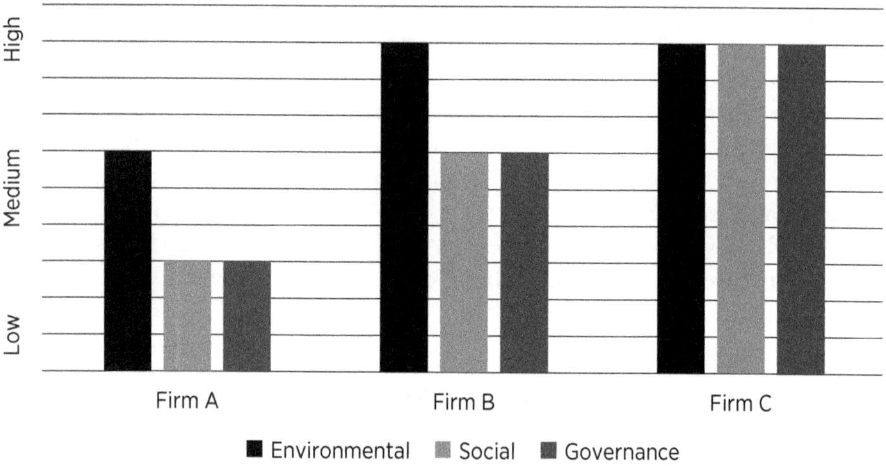

Source: Author's own research as of September 2023.

Greenwashing

Most investment managers are keen to demonstrate their ESG credentials in managing a portfolio. However, sometimes these claims run to little more than a marketing endeavour, also known as 'greenwashing'.

There is no foolproof way of working out which investment managers genuinely engage with companies to make them more effective and which do not. However, as a minimum, managers are now expected to exercise the voting rights on *all* the shares that they own (even if that includes abstaining). You can also check whether a manager is registered with the United Nations' Principles for Responsible Investment or the UK Stewardship Code (see page 184).

Some hallmarks of effective engagement are when an investment manager:

- is able to explain their fund's values to you and demonstrates their alignment with your responsible investing policy without prompting;

- will sometimes vote against recommendations from their proxy voting advisers but can explain why they reached a different conclusion;
- demonstrably collaborates, and occasionally leads, with other investors to achieve a successful outcome through engagement with companies' management or, if necessary, vote on resolutions concerning contentious issues (such as sugar content in foods);
- makes available its full voting record (including abstentions), together with the reasons for its votes if asked.

The Financial Conduct Authority has developed a labelling scheme for sustainable investment products which comes into effect at the end of 2024.[7] The scheme has a general provision against greenwashing. It also contains four labels that can be used to categorise funds that have at least 70% of their assets invested in delivering a 'sustainability objective':

- **Sustainability Impact** funds must directly advance the advertised sustainability objective (e.g. by letting residential units to organisations that support occupants classified as homeless so as to help them progress into self-sufficient living).
- **Sustainability Focus** funds will indirectly advance their advertised sustainability objective (e.g. by investing in climate themes that contribute to the mitigation of climate change and adaptation of society to its negative impacts).
- **Sustainability Improver** funds may meet their advertised sustainability objective over time, but they are not there yet (e.g. an index of companies that are on credible paths to reach net zero by 2050).
- **Sustainability Mixed Goals** funds will both directly and indirectly advance their advertised objective.

From the end of 2024, no UK-based fund will be able to use the words 'impact' or 'sustainable' other than in one of these contexts.

Fictional case studies

Spender: Warden's Philanthropy

The trustees of Warden's Philanthropy have identified responsible investment as a key issue in managing their reputational risk. They only appoint managers who are known to have the highest standards and the lowest tolerance for companies that have questionable behaviours, especially in the field of social justice. This extends across all asset classes and is not limited to public equities. The trustees recognise that these limitations on diversification might reduce the resilience of their portfolio, but they agree that this is a price worth paying to protect their reputation. Their managers are active investors with high levels of engagement with each of their investments.

Warden's Philanthropy offers a prestigious annual prize in the field of social action, and the prize is often in the local news. The trustees realise that the charity's investments are an easy target for journalists so they only use segregated mandates, not pooled funds, even though this is more expensive. This ensures the trustees have good visibility of what the charity owns. In the few cases where the charity owns holdings that might be seen as controversial, it keeps a prepared public statement on why it believes the balance of good and bad in such companies allows their inclusion. It also publishes a list of its top ten holdings annually on its website.

Saver: Martello Tower Fund

The trustees of the Martello Tower Fund's parent charity, Preserving Our Nautical Past, have appointed a committee of experts to advise them on investment and other decisions relating to the fund. The committee has been asked by the trustees to ensure that the investments are responsibly managed. The committee has thought carefully about this and decided that since Martello Tower was closely associated with national defence, it would be wrong to exclude companies that have also been associated with national defence from the portfolio. They have been careful to document the reasons for this decision in case there are press enquiries.

Separately, when the fund was about halfway to reaching the target amount of money required to start building the sea wall, a disused piece of land adjacent to the tower was put up for sale. It was a much-loved local wildlife habitat but it was now likely to be developed commercially. A local charity wanted to buy the land to preserve its future as a community-led wildlife refuge, but it needed time to raise the funds before it could complete the purchase. The Martello Tower Fund's trustees thought that the amenity of the historic tower would be improved by having a wildlife reserve next to it rather than a commercial development, so they decided to help the local charity.

As a precaution, they took financial and legal advice to make sure that the financial return would be adequate for the investment and risk. They asked their financial adviser to calculate the difference in income between the return on the social investment and the return they could expect from their main investment portfolio. The trustees then asked themselves whether they thought this financial cost was worth the social gain, and decided that it was.

They bought the land for the local charity so they could hold it until the charity had raised sufficient funds to buy it from them at the original (modest) price together with a small amount of interest for their trouble. This duly happened two years later, once the local charity had completed its fundraising campaign. This piece of impact investing therefore achieved what is often referred to as the 'double bottom line' of delivering both financial and social benefit.

Spend-outer: Butterworth Music Festivals

Butterworth Music Festivals' trustees had a careful discussion about whether they should have a responsible investment policy of any sort. They considered buying musical instruments to loan free of charge to musicians, but that did not seem in keeping with the transitory nature of the original gift. In the end they decided that they would achieve the most by just spending as much as they could. However, they did decide that they should at least try to avoid harm to the environment in how they invested, just as they tried to avoid damaging the environment when they laid on their festivals.

As a result, they agreed to opt for a broad-spectrum responsible investment fund that fully covered their environmental concerns. The trustees couldn't think of any specific activities that would be contrary to the purpose of the charity, but they did want to avoid putting off any potential audiences that their music festival might reach. Therefore, they wrote a policy that excluded a broad spectrum of 'sin stocks', expecting to be reasonably pragmatic in fitting around the specific offerings of their chosen investment manager. Nevertheless, they were clear that since they were going to invest much of their money in cash and bonds, whatever restrictions they accepted should apply equally to all assets of any excluded company, be they equities, bonds or cash.

Conclusion

At its heart, responsible investing is about finding a balance between your charity's purpose and values and those of your stakeholders, while ensuring that the return you get is consistent with your financial objectives and goals. The next stage is to think about how to implement and monitor the various ideas in parts I and II of this book in a way that is comprehensible, coherent and consistent, and that can be managed effectively within a limited governance budget. The chapters in part III consider these topics.

Notes

1 'Ending the arms trade' [web page], Quakers in Britain, www.quaker.org.uk/our-work/peace/arms-trade, accessed 20 January 2024.
2 Priya Kantaria, 'Arts organisations will not take donations from the Sackler Trust' [web article], Civil Society, www.civilsociety.co.uk/news/tate-says-no-to-the-sackler-trust-s-opiod-tainted-donations.html, 22 March 2019.
3 See 'ABC of enterprise impact' [web page], Impact Frontiers, https://impactfrontiers.org/norms/abc-of-enterprise-impact, accessed 20 January 2024.
4 *The Essential Trustee: What you need to know, what you need to do* (CC3) [PDF], Charity Commission for England and Wales, 2018, https://assets.publishing.service.gov.uk/government/uploads/system/uploads/attachment_data/file/866947/CC3_feb20.pdf, s. 6.3, accessed 20 January 2024.
5 Elroy Dimson, Oğuzhan Karakaş and Xi Li, 'Active Ownership', *Review of Financial Studies*, vol. 28, no. 12, 2015, pp. 3225–68.
6 Elroy Dimson, Paul Marsh and Mike Staunton, *Credit Suisse Global Investment Returns Yearbook 2020*, Credit Suisse Research Institute, 2020, pp. 47–64; Rómulo Alves, Philipp Krueger and Mathijs van Dijk, *Drawing Up the Bill: Are ESG ratings related to stock returns around the world?* [PDF], Rotterdam School of Management Erasmus University, 2024, www.rsm.nl/fileadmin/Faculty-Research/Centres/EPSVC/240223WOR_Drawing_up_the_bill_-_Is_ESG_related_to_stock_returns_around_the_world_.pdf, accessed 4 April 2024.
7 See *Sustainability Disclosure Requirements (SDR) and Investment Labels* (PS23/16) [PDF], Financial Conduct Authority, 2023, www.fca.org.uk/publication/policy/ps23-16.pdf, accessed 20 January 2024.

PART III
In practice

Chapter ten

Appointing a manager

The purpose of this chapter

Once you have assembled all your ideas about spending, risk and responsible investing, you will need to put them into practice. Most commonly, this process begins with a review of your current arrangements. However, if you do not have any existing investment arrangements, it is done by finding one or more investment managers, and this chapter is designed to help you with that task. It covers how to find potential managers, whether to use one or multiple managers, longlisting, shortlisting, interviewing and decision-making, and implementation. Finally, the three fictional case studies look at the appointment process in the context of our example charities.

Finding an investment manager

The whole process of appointing or replacing an investment manager need not be complex. After all, you have done the hard part in setting out your investment needs. All you have to do now is to find the manager(s) who you think will be most likely to help you meet those needs.

From the point of view of an investment manager, the earlier chapters of this book are all about making your charity a better client by helping you to analyse the real-world factors that will influence, and be influenced by, your investment strategy. Being a better client means you will be more successful in getting what you want from your investment manager. Your investment policy statement (see page 166) is the foundation of this relationship. Investment managers will develop their understanding of your needs as their relationship with you develops, but they will always use your investment policy statement as a starting point.

You will get the best results from a new investment manager if they have been properly briefed. If the briefing is missing or incomplete, the manager will have to make assumptions about your needs, and those may well be incorrect. If you don't have all the information, providing a manager with what you do have will be much better than nothing.

Managers versus funds

Throughout this chapter, the concepts 'manager' and 'fund' are sometimes used interchangeably. This is because in some cases (such as pooled funds), the fund 'comes with' the manager, and managers usually have a number of different funds to meet different investment needs. For more detail on how this works in practice, see page 49.

If you are looking to invest with a manager and you have a good idea of what you are looking for, your process for appointing a manager will likely be much less involved than what is outlined in this chapter. For example, you might skip the longlisting process and jump straight to shortlisting. You should adapt the advice in this chapter to suit the complexity of your situation and requirements.

There are two main ways of identifying potential investment managers: using an investment consultant and finding a manager yourself.

Using an investment consultant

There are a number of consultants who can help you deal with your investments, including by finding you a new manager. Investment consultants range from the very large to the very small, and from those with a deep understanding of charity investing to those who think everything looks like a pension fund (see page 58) or a private client. It is best if they are regulated by the Financial Conduct Authority (FCA) if they are going to make recommendations about managers, although some consultants avoid this requirement by only giving their clients a list, not a recommendation.

Investment consultants can be used to outsource the implementation process (and guide you through the key decisions leading up to it). However, they will also have their own business interests, typically including a wish for an ongoing relationship with you. Unless you have a complicated portfolio (i.e. more than one manager), you are unlikely to need this, so you may need to be prepared to communicate (and potentially reiterate) the limits of the service you're seeking.

If you decide to seek advice from a consultant, try to make sure that you use one with good charity knowledge. Only charity specialists will understand the advantages that charity-specific funds bring – such as a charity authorised investment fund (see page 50) – over other types of fund. This is especially true of property funds, where stamp duty introduces considerable extra costs (which UK charity funds do not pay) that can be avoided by investing in specific charity funds.

Managers, consultants and independent financial advisers

One of the many sources of confusion in the financial advice industry is that the terms 'manager', 'consultant' and 'independent adviser' can be used loosely. In brief:

Investment managers decide how to invest your money and can sometimes give advice on which of their own products are suitable. They will be regulated by the Financial Conduct Authority (FCA).

Investment consultants don't manage money but can provide advice on a wide range of products (so long as they are not tied to any particular investment management firm). Investment consultants can be regulated by the FCA, in which case they can recommend specific investments. If they are not, they can only provide a menu of options for you (not them) to choose from. Consultants can be individuals, or firms if regulated. Regardless of whether or not they are regulated, they may (or may not) have any real understanding of the charity sector.

The Money and Pensions Service explains that to be called **independent**, an investment manager or consultant 'must be able to offer a range of products from across the whole market and provide unbiased and unrestricted advice based on a comprehensive and fair analysis of that market'.[1] You may want to consider an independent manager or consultant if you want to be confident that you are receiving impartial advice on which to base your decisions.

Finding a manager yourself

It is quite possible to run a manager selection process yourself and doing so is a perfectly sensible thing to do. It is also in keeping with the Charity Commission's guidance[2] – so long as you document the fact that you have considered taking advice and, on balance, feel at ease with choosing your investment manager yourself.

Staying informed throughout the process

Whichever option you choose, it is wise to be familiar with all of the steps outlined below. That way, even if you choose to use a consultant, you can understand what is happening at each stage of the process.

Deciding between one or multiple managers

One of the first decisions you will need to make is how many managers you want to have, and consequently how much work you want to do yourself to build your portfolio and manage the balance between managers. You have two choices: a single manager or multiple managers.

A single manager

If you give all your assets to a single manager, they will do everything for you by creating a mixed segregated portfolio or using a mixed fund (see page 44), including:

- choosing which shares, bonds or other assets to own;
- deciding the proportions of how your assets should be allocated in order to deliver on your investment goals;
- providing cash, performance reports, audit information and a good client experience.

All you have to do is monitor the results against your expectations. This is the least complicated approach and a sensible one for the vast majority of charities, especially if the manager is experienced in working with charities and understands them well.

Multiple managers

If you do not have a single manager, you will have to decide how your assets are to be allocated between them. Although managers, advisers and your charity's staff might make suggestions, the decision ultimately sits with the trustees.

The decision can be made very simple by appointing duplicate managers with the same brief (such as by dividing your assets equally between two similar mixed funds) or it can be more detailed (involving multiple managers and asset classes). It is important to avoid making things more complicated than necessary, as this can generate four types of problem:

- Having multiple managers can undermine your governance processes because it becomes harder for the trustees to engage with what is going on if the portfolio becomes too fragmented.
- Manager costs will be higher because instead of having one large portfolio at a low fee, you will have several smaller ones at a higher fee.
- Consultant costs will be higher because there is much more money to be made from advising on a complicated portfolio than on a simple one because it has more moving parts to be controlled.

- Having multiple managers reduces the contribution of good (and bad) managers because the more fragmented a portfolio becomes, the less significant the contribution will be from any individual piece. The ultimate outcome is that passive funds (see page 45) become preferable.

When you divide your assets up, each part is said to be a separate mandate or instruction. You might appoint a single manager to hold one overall mandate (such as a mixed fund or your own balanced segregated portfolio), or you might employ multiple managers, each with different mandates according to their specialism (such as US equities or emerging market debt). You can give a manager one or many mandates depending on how specific you want your instructions to be.

Managing multiple mandates

If you appoint a single manager, they will have a single mandate and oversight of your entire portfolio, and will be able to see at any time what is going on within the portfolio. In contrast, if you appoint more than one manager, then only you will have this total oversight of all your mandates. It is important to recognise this and understand the responsibility it brings – only you will be able to check that you have got the correct balance between volatile and stable assets to deliver your overall appetite for risk and uncertainty. Generally, this is not especially difficult to do with tolerable accuracy. However, if you prefer, it is something that investment consultants can help you monitor and adjust.

There are a number of ways of dividing up your portfolio into different mandates. Here are some examples.

Two or more similar mandates

This approach involves simply dividing your assets equally between two or more mixed managers, each of whom can deliver your mandate on their own. The advantage can be that you get a diversity of approaches (so reducing the risk of having a single manager). However, equally, if you appoint too many managers, you may become over-diversified and over-complicate your situation, and so not gain as much from their investment decisions as you might.

Simple fixed-proportion mandates

If you have decided on a simple asset allocation – such as 30% in bonds and 70% in global equities – then it is easy enough to keep an eye on this and automatically move money (without discussion) between the two managers if your mandates get out of balance (say by 10% or more). You might do this once a year (if your asset values have changed) or whenever you need some capital. Unless you appoint one manager for both mandates, you will have to decide on the balance in the first place, though, and this will need to reflect your financial objectives and goals.

You may also have to take advice on the tactical or short-term allocation of assets. A single investment manager with a split of 30% bonds and 70% equities can (if authorised to do so) vary this within certain parameters in the light of prevailing market conditions, and so you might find yourself with a split of 20% bonds and 80% equities if the manager considers that bonds have poor prospects. This is more difficult to manage if you have separate managers for bonds and equities.

Core and satellite mandates

Another option is to have a large, stable and unexciting holding, such as a passive equity fund, that will drive your long-term returns at a low cost (the 'core'). As your 'satellites', you can then choose much more active managers in the hope that they will significantly outperform the core (but in the knowledge that if you choose unwisely, your core will be unaffected).

Geographical or style-based mandates

Apart from investing in different asset classes, some charities also divide up their portfolios by geography or style. For example, one manager might be an expert in the US market, another in European markets and another in niche emerging markets (see page 39). Other charities might divide up their assets to gain exposure to different market styles, such as value or growth (see page 208), or across bonds, government debt and corporate debt.

Deciding whether one or multiple managers is best for you

The point is that if you choose to have more than one manager, you will need to monitor the balances not only between your asset classes (as above for simple fixed-proportion mandates) but also between the different components within your structure (see figure 10.1). If they are out of balance, you will need to rebalance your holdings periodically according to the baseline proportions you decide.

Appointing more than one manager tends to be the preserve of very large investors (say, those with over £50 million), those with a very specific niche investment requirement or those with a particularly engaged board.

Figure 10.1 Trustees' monitoring roles in relation to managers

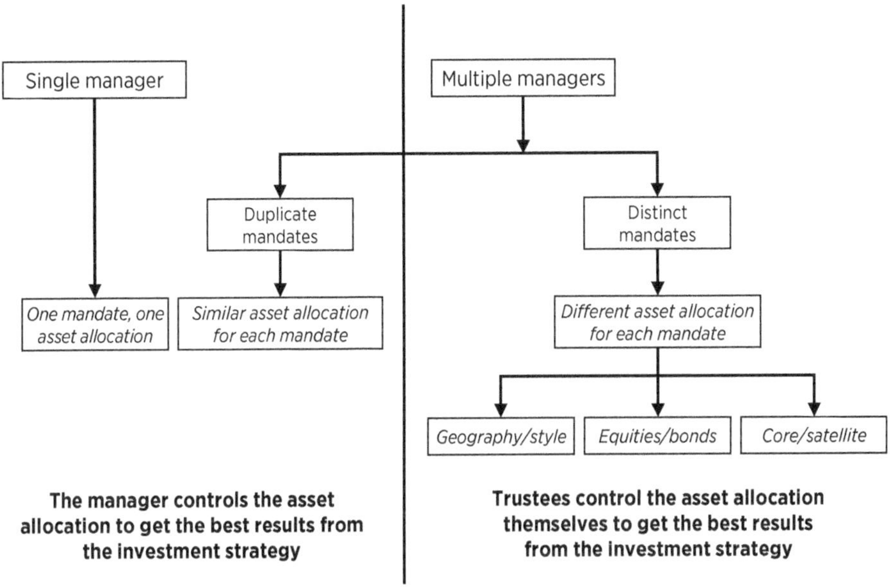

Creating a longlist

Once you have created a plan for how you would like to allocate your assets to one or more managers, you can start to compile a longlist of potential candidates. A longlist normally contains between five and eight names of managers who you are interested in finding out more about (or perhaps between three and seven plus your original manager if you are reviewing them).

Just like when you are choosing any sort of professional firm, there are a number of approaches you can use. For example:

- have a series of informal conversations with a range of managers;
- approach managers you have met through training that they offer (charity investment management firms commonly offer training as it is a good way for them to get in front of potential clients);
- ask your peers for recommendations.

You will also find names of charity-specialist managers in publications such as *Charity Finance* (see www.civilsociety.co.uk) and *Charity Times* (see www.charitytimes.com), and on the Charity Intelligence website (www.charityintelligence.co.uk). However, managers have to pay to appear in these sources, so there may be other managers that are not shown. In addition, most charity magazines are replete with advertisements for charity fund managers that can provide you with ideas. The advantage of this approach is that you will at least find a sample of potential managers who are all interested in the charity sector. If you want to look outside this sector, a site such as Morningstar (www.morningstar.co.uk) will help but it will have a limited charity presence.

At this stage, the most important thing to know is what you are looking for: a mixed fund or something more specialised, such as an equity, property, bond or cash fund. Second-order questions are whether you want an active or passive approach, a firm with a good reputation for responsible investing, or good service if you have rapidly changing requirements. While a recommendation might be what tips the balance in favour of a candidate further down the road (when you have moved on to the shortlist stage – discussed later in this chapter), you should be careful about giving too much weight to this consideration before you have a thorough understanding of the quantitative factors – the purpose of the next stage: sending out a request for particulars (RFP).

Sending out a request for particulars

Once you have a list of managers that broadly meet your longlist criteria, the next thing to do is to create an RFP and send it to them. The main point of this exercise is twofold: to tell the prospective manager about your charity and what you want (including by sharing your investment policy statement) and to ask the potential managers a number of questions that will help you decide whom to shortlist. Asking the same questions of each manager will allow a degree of standardisation, which will make collating and comparing the responses easier.

Do not write to more managers than is necessary to get a good range (no more than the maximum of eight in your longlist) and do give them a strict page limit (probably no more than four or five pages) for their response to avoid you having too much to read. One danger is that you can be so overwhelmed by what you receive that it is impossible to meaningfully process it.

Also, to avoid being overwhelmed, it can be helpful to focus on a small number of specific areas so it is easier to compare results. The replies will later help you to compile your shortlist (covered later on in this chapter). The process of compiling an RFP should examine two areas: data on the manager's approach and historical performance, and an understanding of their investment style (or how they go about making money for you in a sufficiently responsible way). The following subsections cover these two areas in turn.

Investment manager approach and historical performance

What percentage of your assets are charity assets?

Some managers only look after charities and not-for-profit investors, while others look after a wide range of types of investor but have strong charity teams. It can be helpful to know how important the charity business is to the firm overall. A very small percentage of charity assets in a small firm may indicate that the investment firm is not focused on or committed to charity investors. This can have implications for the business's commitment to dealing properly with charity tax, responsible investing, reporting and time horizons, especially for saver and spender charities. However, a small percentage in a large business can still be enough to sustain a highly effective charity team. It is useful to know the total assets that the firm manages, and the charity proportion of that. If a firm looks as if it has a low commitment to the charity sector, ask for examples of charity-specific newsletters it publishes or events that it holds.

Are you owned privately or publicly?

In general, publicly owned businesses (which are listed on a stock exchange) are considered to have a shorter-term focus on profits, which can lead to less operational stability. As such, you may prefer to focus on firms where the ownership is entirely private or has a mix of private and public ownership.

Do you offer pooled funds or segregated portfolios (or both)?

This will tell you if you can tailor the portfolio to your needs, whether it be for the purposes of screening for companies that you wish to avoid owning (see chapter 9) or income generation. Segregated portfolios are bespoke to your needs (but usually only available to larger clients) whereas pooled funds are off-the-shelf products (see page 49 for more information). Some managers offer both. If having a segregated fund matters to you, ask what the minimum investment size is that they will accept.

What proportion of our assets would be invested using third-party funds?

There are arguments both ways for using third-party specialist funds (see page 41). It can be more difficult to know what you own and therefore invest responsibly in these 'fund of funds' structures. It may also reveal a lack of depth in the firm, and potentially another layer of charges. On the other hand, the manager is not limited by having to rely on their own in-house expertise and can buy it in from experts elsewhere.

What asset allocation do you suggest for our charity?

If you are considering off-the-shelf products, you will want to understand what solution the manager is proposing and whether their suggested asset allocation is a suitable match for your investment strategy – for example, in terms of risk appetite, volatility, time horizon and diversification (see chapter 5). They may answer in terms of risk buckets (see page 156).

In brief, what is your investment process?

Managers will want to tell you how they choose the various assets to put in your portfolio and in what proportions, and what systems they have to ensure this process can be used consistently to deliver similar results in the future. This is referred to as their 'investment process' and 'investment style'. Many managers will use elements of different styles, in which case you will want to understand how consistent the manager's approach is over time, again so it can be repeated in the future to achieve similar results. The next section of this chapter (see page 208) describes the major styles that managers might mention when telling you about their approach.

What is your approach to responsible investing and how will it meet our requirements?

This is difficult to assess, but it is up to you to identify where you think the manager lies on the responsible investing ladder (see table 9.2). You should also ensure that the manager's policies on exclusion and engagement reasonably match your expectations (so they are neither much tighter nor much looser). In a pooled fund you will usually have to be prepared to compromise a little.

What is the expected portfolio return?

This will depend on the briefing material that you have supplied to the manager, but expect an answer defined as the Consumer Prices Index plus between 1% and 5% depending on your time horizon and appetite for unpredictability and risk in relation to your returns. The higher the return number the better, but a higher return number also means you will need to reassure yourself that it is achievable, so a fund largely invested in cash is unlikely to give you high returns (see page 32). If your spending policy is to distribute your income only (see page 63), be alert to the difference between the expected portfolio return and income yield.

What levels of income and spending do you propose?

This information will provide a natural starting point for a potential future discussion about what the manager feels they can deliver to you (in your base currency, usually GBP, and per cent).

Do you have a preference for investing in the UK?

It is important to watch out for a preference for investing in the UK (perhaps over 15%) within a global portfolio, because the UK is a small part of the global investment market (about 5%). A high weight can indicate that the manager is a bit old-fashioned in their investment approach.

What are your three- and five-year historical performance figures for your proposed approach?

The next section (on creating your shortlist) looks in more detail at performance. However, for comparison purposes, you will want to ask for performance figures as part of your RFP. This data is straightforward to collect for pooled funds, but if you are looking for a segregated manager, it is much harder. In these circumstances it is best to ask for the data for the manager's standard portfolio for the strategy they are proposing. However, always remember that given a choice, a manager will want to show you their best figures, so you should regard non-pooled fund numbers with a little scepticism.

Always ask for the three- and five-year performance figures to the most recent quarter end, and make sure that they are expressed in GBP (or whatever is your base currency), net of fees and on an annualised (not cumulative) basis. Otherwise, it is easy to end up comparing apples and pears because the data for the different managers will show different things. It is worth taking real care on this. Seek annualised figures from each manager (i.e. figures that have been averaged over a certain number of years) or use a web-based calculator (such as https://everydaycalculation.com/annualized-return.php) to annualise them. Comparative exercises can only be conducted successfully if the figures are prepared on the same basis. One-year returns are much too short to rely on, but three- and five-year figures give a manager time to have periods of weakness while also allowing their strength to shine through over the longer term. Generally speaking, the longer the better.

What is your three-year volatility?

Volatility is a measure of risk and unpredictability (see page 25). The standard unit is three-year volatility. A large number (over 12%) indicates a volatile portfolio and should be associated with higher returns in the long run if the manager is reasonably competent. You would want to avoid a firm that had made a poor return over the long term while having a more volatile portfolio.

Proposed fees

There are many ways fees can be described, and many only reveal part of what you will be paying. For example, if you are told what the annual management charge (AMC) is, you should remember that it only covers the manager's own costs, not those of third-party service providers. It is safer to specifically ask for the ongoing charges figure (OCF), which gives the broadest picture of what you should expect to pay. Even when you have asked for an OCF, you may still be given an AMC figure simply because it is lower. If it doesn't say what it is, check – don't assume.

Fees are discussed further later on in this chapter (see page 215).

What other services do you offer?

The support a client receives from its manager is central to how well the relationship functions. Emblems of good service include regular updates and charity-specific client conferences and events. Everyone you speak to will be extremely personable and you will usually see either a relationship manager or a portfolio manager at your review meetings. Both types of manager have advantages, but remember that at the end of the day it's your money that you want managed, not your relationship.

Investment manager processes and styles

As part of your RFP, you will have asked your potential managers about their investment process or style (see page 206). It is important to ask about this to make sure you understand it and that it makes sense to you (so you can understand better when things go right or wrong). This section therefore outlines the main investment manager processes and styles to help you understand your potential managers' answers to this question in your RFP.

Managers have differing investment styles, and good managers tend to stick to a single style. Different markets suit different styles, which often accounts for under-performance over a period rather than the manager being poor. All managers generally try to do the same thing: work out whether the current price of an asset is significantly lower than what they consider to be its intrinsic value, and, if so, buy more of that asset and less of the ones that they consider to be overvalued. What differentiates one manager from another is that they don't agree on what the intrinsic value is – some might think a specific asset's intrinsic value is low, while others might think it high (and that's what makes a market). The only real exception is the momentum strategy, which follows the current trends in the market (as explained below).

If you are going to choose a manager for a particular style, you will want to be alert that the manager sticks to that style and does not shift towards another style without letting you know. This will be something to address during your ongoing reviews, covered later in this chapter. However, if the manager does change style and chooses not to switch back, ultimately that is their prerogative so you may choose to switch manager.

If you want the manager to be responsive to the market and switch between styles for you, then choose a good all-rounder (see the 'GARP' section below) without a set bias in their approach. The most important characteristics to look for in an investment process are that it is evidence based, has good controls over how assets are allocated, is repeatable and is disciplined enough not to waver in troubled waters.

Following are brief overviews of eight common investment manager styles.

GARP

'Growth at a reasonable price' is the baked beans on toast of the industry. It tends to be the default style for mixed funds and is the most common approach you will encounter. It does not have a particular income bias but looks for companies that can provide a balance between some above-inflation capital growth and a reasonable annual income, all at a fair price.

Income investing

The object of this style is to preserve capital (against inflation) while providing a good level of income. This style must choose assets with high income in preference to similar assets without the high income. However, when it comes to shares, since relatively few have high incomes, this reduces the scope for diversification, especially in technology and growth stocks, which tend to have a low or no income. It also biases managers towards the UK at the expense of other countries because the UK tends to have higher-yielding shares.

Quality

This is a style that is difficult to specify, but you should expect to own well-run companies with good management who allocate capital within their business thoughtfully and who avoid excessive borrowing on their balance sheet. Such businesses may not be large. Quality can be applied to other styles (e.g. quality growth and quality value), and companies with quality shares tend to score more highly on ratings relevant to responsible investing (see chapter 9).

Value

This style might be described as cheap and cheerful. The profits of invested-in companies are stable and well known but the price varies, and a value investor tries to buy a company with this stream of good and fairly certain profits cheaply (i.e. buying them at less than a reasonable price). Value investors tend to invest in capital-intensive businesses (aircraft, mines, oil rigs, etc.) and in more mature industries which are not expected to grow at the same rate as new businesses, such as technology (see 'Growth' below). This style should perform well in periods of higher interest rates, inflation and economic uncertainty.

Growth

This is the opposite to value investing in that you are paying a higher price now for earnings that may or may not appear in the future. If the invested-in company grows as expected and profits increase according to the predictions, your investment will have been a good buy. However, if the projected growth in profits does not materialise, the company price can fall sharply. In other words, growth investing is less predictable than value investing. This style thrives in times of low inflation, low interest rates and market confidence in the future.

Momentum

Momentum does what it says. The manager buys things that are going up and sells things that are going down. This is a style often used in algorithm-based approaches (e.g. 'quantitative' – see below). This approach tends to under-perform when the market changes direction and instead of going up, goes down for a while (until the new direction has been established).

Quantitative

A 'quant' strategy is driven by algorithms that process data from a wide variety of quantitative sources and rank assets in order of their attractiveness. They tend to seek modest out-performance of an index but at a similar or lower level of volatility. To have a robust process, the algorithm should generally be left to do its work uninterrupted without humans intervening to produce what they consider to be a better answer. However, a human might have to intervene to stop the algorithm thinking a newly bankrupt company is just incredibly cheap (for example).

Thematic

With this style, which can be combined with others, companies are chosen for how they fit into the manager's view of the future world – for example, the ageing global population means that certain healthcare companies may become increasingly attractive. The manager will look at potential investments through their chosen themes and then decide which companies are attractively priced in the context of these themes.

Top down versus bottom up

All managers will begin their process either from the top down or the bottom up, so this is not a 'style' so much. This concept relates to the investment process a manager uses to begin to assemble a portfolio. Some start by thinking about global economic trends and then investing in companies that they think will flourish in those environments (top down). Others start by looking at a range of individual companies and then building a portfolio of the ones that they think are the best performers (bottom up). In practice, some firms will either have a process that is mostly bottom up with a bit of top-down analysis, or vice versa.

Creating a shortlist

Once you have sent out your RFP to your chosen five to eight managers, you will likely get calls asking to find out more about your charity. What you want from a candidate firm is their best effort to meet your needs, so it is usually best to be as helpful as possible in answering their questions so they can tailor their pitch to those needs.

You will then need to wait for the managers to formally reply to your RFP (it is fair to allow around three weeks). The next stage is to shrink your longlist down to three or four names that are of particular interest to you (or perhaps two or three plus your original manager if you are conducting a review). This will form your shortlist.

You will have received much useful information in the answers to your RFP and, with luck, no more than 32 to 40 pages from all of the responses. It can be useful to tabulate the quantitative answers to the questions in the previous section (such as on charity asset proportion, performance, volatility and fees) so you can more easily rank the managers. Also try to summarise the investment approach into one of the main types (many are likely to be GARP). You should expect to see clear and thoughtful links between your investment policy statement (which you will have provided along with your RFP) and the firm's replies to your questions.

Once you have done this work, you should go through your longlist and exclude those firms that you do not want to see, probably because they fall into one of the following categories:

- too expensive;
- returns (after costs) less good than others;
- too volatile;
- you don't like the proposed investment solution (too much or too little risk);
- not enough income (unless you are investing for a total return);
- misalignment on responsible investing;
- confusing investment process;
- unable to deliver your specific requirements.

It is best to shortlist managers that are different from each other, rather than ones that are similar (so long as they can all provide the service you require). Choosing managers with different approaches and styles for your shortlist usually makes your final choice much easier. This will take time, particularly if you need to clarify missing data with a manager.

You might also find it helpful to focus on the following few areas when shortlisting based on the replies you have received to your RFP.

Understanding of the charity sector

There are numerous managers that claim to have charity expertise but fewer actually have it. Genuine charity expertise requires an awareness of the legal restrictions on some types of charity funds, an understanding of trustees' responsibilities (including the content of *Investing Charity Money: A guide for trustees* (CC14)), and an awareness of the Charities Statement of Recommended Practice and its reporting requirements (see chapters 7 and 8). Such managers will be visible by producing charity-specific briefings, advertising in the usual charity press and attending relevant events, such as the Charity Finance Group annual conference. You will find that each four-page RFP response usually has a number of annexes containing this sort of information.

Understanding performance and volatility

Clearly you will want to appoint the manager that will make the highest return for you, but not at any price – the size of the return must be compared to the amount of risk taken. A less good manager can get the same return as a better manager simply by having a more volatile portfolio. It is important to think about historical returns in the context of the amount of volatility that the portfolio has been exposed to over the period in question because this will translate into unpredictability in your future returns.

The most common way of looking at this trade-off is shown in figure 10.2, which compares average annual returns (which, as mentioned, should be over three or five years) with how volatile each portfolio was over that period (see page 245 for information on how to calculate volatility). The object of the exercise is to find the manager that is closest to the top left corner of the chart, because this provides the greatest return for the least volatility. A fund in the bottom right would be notable for giving a poor return with significant volatility – in other words, return-free risk (see page 83). Where there is more than one fund to choose from, you will want to look at other factors to inform your decisions.

Figure 10.2 Example of how to compare managers' returns and volatility

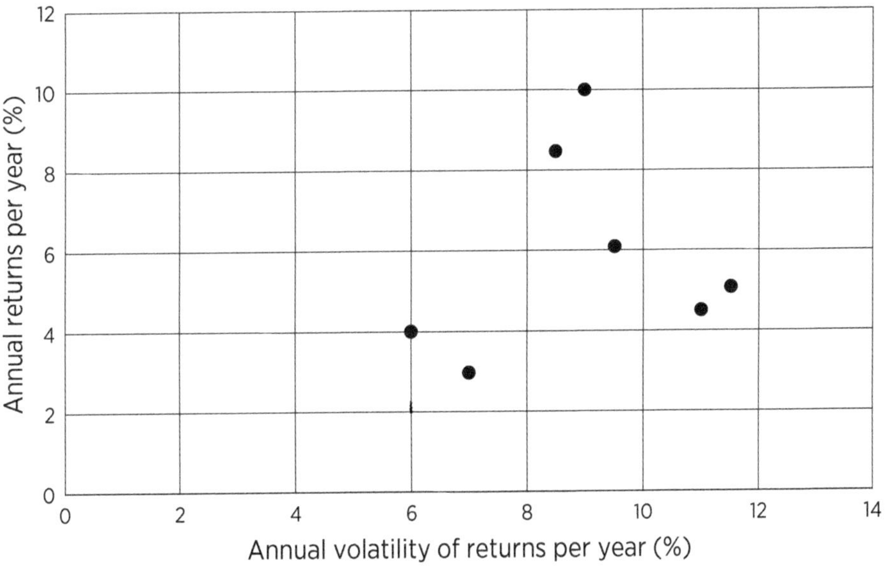

Note: Each dot represents a different portfolio.

Another way of expressing the same information is to take each manager's three-year (or five-year) average returns and divide them by the three-year (or five-year) volatility (see table 10.1). The result is known as the Sharpe ratio and it shows how much extra return a manager gives for each unit of extra volatility. If the result is positive, it means the manager has ensured their clients are rewarded for tolerating this additional volatility, so the higher the ratio, the better. The lower the ratio, the less rewarding the additional volatility has been, until the ratios become negative, which means the manager is actually doing the opposite of what is meant to happen by reducing the return while adding more volatility.

Table 10.1 Example of how to rank managers by comparing return with volatility

Manager	Return (%)	Volatility (%)	Sharpe ratio (return ÷ volatility)
Manager 1	10.8	14.6	0.7
Manager 2	10.1	9.7	1.0
Manager 3	4.3	4.7	0.9
Manager 4	5.0	8.7	0.6
Manager 5	5.4	11.6	0.5
Manager 6	3.9	9.4	0.4
Manager 7	1.3	10.0	0.1
Manager 8	−1.5	13.0	−0.1

For example, Manager 3 has returned 4.3% and Manager 6 has returned only slightly less at 3.9%. But, if you look at the volatility, Manager 6's portfolio has been twice as volatile to achieve a similar result. Why would an investor accept that additional volatility without any extra return?

Carrying out this exercise with the managers you are considering can help you to spot differences in performance that might not otherwise be obvious. But remember that if you can tolerate a higher level of unpredictability and volatility, Manager 1 might suit you best as they have made a lot more money for their clients than most of the other managers. Don't forget that the word 'risk' used in this construct does not have its natural meaning (of potential calamity), so Sharpe ratios will only ever be a guide and part of the information you might look at.

Putting performance in perspective

While good historical performance is always encouraging to see and will naturally form the cornerstone of your selection process, it can be misleading, as explained in chapter 3 – different market conditions provide tailwinds to different styles (see page 46). As such, historical performance needs to be balanced with all of the factors you have considered above, such as the manager's investment style, their level of customer service and their ability to cope with a range of different market conditions.

It is said that most managers who are fired subsequently outperform. The logic behind this statement is that a manager who has performed well will have enjoyed a tailwind, whereas an under-performing manager may have experienced a stiff headwind. Let's assume that a normal market cycle is five to seven years. In the case of the under-performing manager, by the time their clients have noticed other managers delivering higher returns and have moved their business to those other managers, what was a headwind for the original manager may very well have become a tailwind. A bold investor will appoint an under-performing manager, so long as their investment style is rigorous and credible.

Understanding fees

One of the ironic things about financial markets is that the usual market forces don't apply to them. For example, no one ever says, 'Buy my fund – it won't make you as much money but it's cheaper than the others.' Instead, everyone is a winner (until the results come in), and that is always after you've paid the fees. A higher fee does not mean a better product, just a more expensive one. It is therefore important to check your manager's fee ladder (if you put more money in, your fee level might reduce).

The only time you have any scope to negotiate fees is in advance of selecting a manager or starting a review. It is therefore best to get a good picture of the likely fees while you are still looking at a range of managers, as this will put you in the strongest possible position when it comes to negotiations later on.

How fees can affect your portfolio's returns

Industry practice is to deduct fees directly from your portfolio, which means you agree them at the outset and then rarely think about them afterwards. It is also standard to express them as a percentage of the portfolio being managed. But you can also understand fees as a percentage of how much money your investments have allowed you to spend that year. This would be like a fundraising ratio. Table 10.2 illustrates this. For example, if you paid a fee of 1% to manage a £3 million portfolio, it would cost you £30,000. If we assume your portfolio allows you to spend 4% (£120,000), the cost of raising that cash would be 25% (£30,000 ÷ £120,000).

Table 10.2 Fees on a £3 million portfolio with an income of 4% per year

Fee based on £3 million portfolio	Fee in cash terms	Fee as a percentage of your total spending
0.1%	£3,000	2.5%
0.5%	£15,000	12.5%
1.0%	£30,000	25.0%
1.5%	£45,000	37.5%

As you can see, what might look like a reasonable fee (£30,000) compared to the size of your assets (£3 million) becomes a significant cost of 25% when compared to the cash the assets are producing to spend on your purpose. If this was a fundraising ratio, what cost ratio would you accept? Investing is expensive and sometimes fundraising is just cheaper (see page 78 for a discussion around this topic).

Furthermore, the lower the amount of cash you take from your portfolio to spend, the larger the proportion spent on fees will become (because fees are not linked to income but to capital). For example, if you take out cash (including your income) worth 4% of your portfolio and you are paying fees of 1% on the portfolio, that will be equivalent to 25% of your annual expenditure (see figure 10.3). If you take out cash to spend of 2%, then half your expenditure will go on investment fees.

Figure 10.3 Effect of 1% fees on different levels of annual expenditure

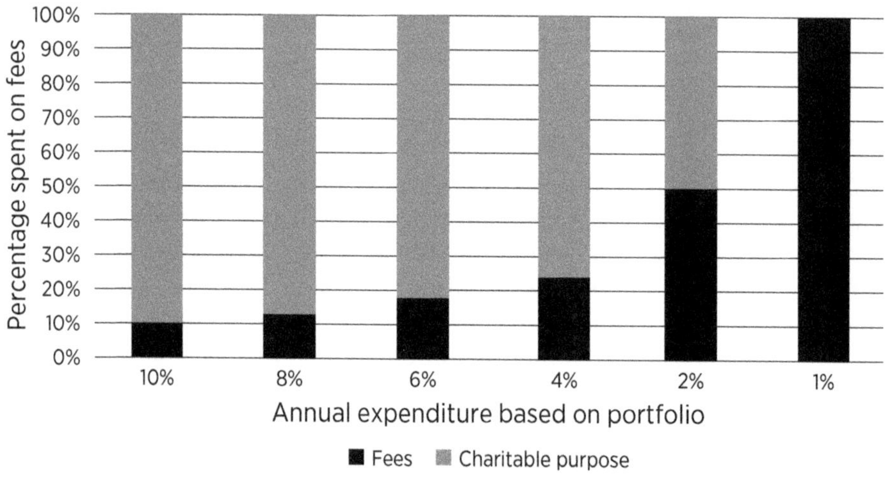

All of this means that you should not underestimate the impact fees have on what you can spend on your charitable purpose, especially over the long term, even if you are using performance fees (see below).

The ongoing charges figure

The OCF is the total fee you will be paying. You should get an approximate idea of each potential manager's OCF during the shortlisting phase, to enable you to exclude any firms that charge more than you are prepared to pay. Later, during the interview phase, you can get more precise numbers.

The OCF is the gold standard and should include *all* costs, except performance fees (see below). Do not accept other ways of quoting fees, such as the AMC, which excludes third-party charges, and certainly don't accept vagaries that simply use the word 'fees'. Such figures can exclude various costs that you will still need to pay, especially the transaction costs of buying and selling individual assets (where relevant).

The range of fees that are charged (i.e. the OCF) is wide, from about 0.2% to 2%. Below 0.6% is unusual and may warrant further investigation to ensure the level of service would be as you require. Above 1% is also rarer and would be deemed particularly expensive. You might also see fees quoted in 'basis points', or bps. A basis point is simply one hundredth of a per cent, so 0.10% can also be referred to as 10 bps.

In general, the more handholding and the higher quality of service you want, the more expensive the fee. If you want nothing but an email once a quarter from a passive manager, then that will be far cheaper. Also keep in mind that buying and holding shares in a segregated fund can be more expensive than buying a pooled fund, and both are more expensive than buying a passive fund. Generally speaking, the performances of these different legal structures will be very similar. Therefore, if you choose a more expensive option, you should be sure you understand what you are paying for.

Performance fees

Some managers offer performance fees. It is often assumed that the manager will be incentivised to perform better with such an arrangement. However, the benefit of performance fees to clients is arguable because they would probably get the same performance in any case (or not use the firm if the performance was poor).

Performance fees come in a variety of forms, but they normally include a base fee (which is always charged) and the performance element. The base fee should be sufficient to run the manager's office and the performance element is what (supposedly) provides the incentive. A reasonable base fee should be similar to that of a passive fund, so about 0.2% to 0.4%, compared to an active management fee of around 1% or so.

Following are several factors to bear in mind when considering managers that offer performance fees:

- **Agree an appropriate hurdle.** You should only expect to pay a performance fee if the manager has outstripped an agreed benchmark (normally a similar passive fund) by some margin – for example, if they have made you 2% more than the benchmark (net of fees).
- **Ensure the arrangement will be symmetrical.** A fee that rewards the manager when things go well but doesn't take account of downturns is unlikely to serve you well. For example, you won't want to pay a performance fee immediately after several straight years of bad performance. It is best to use some sort of averaging which includes several of the previous years to see if the manager has done better than the benchmark (plus the agreed percentage, such as 2%) before the manager receives the additional fee.
- **Consider that you can still pay when you've lost money.** If your portfolio has lost money over the year, but the benchmark has lost more, you will still have outperformed the benchmark and a fee will be due. That can be pretty galling when it happens, despite the logic of the arrangement.
- **Anticipate reputational danger.** If you are lucky enough to appoint a manager who outperforms the benchmark by a huge margin, you will also pay a huge additional amount in fees. This will be disclosed in your accounts, which you will need to defend to your stakeholders.

Interviewing and decision-making

By the time you have reached the end of your shortlisting process, you should have a well-researched list of three or four candidate managers (potentially including your existing manager if you are conducting a review). Now is the time to invite your shortlisted managers to meet you and your colleagues to present their proposed investment strategy for your charity. It is a good idea to set out your proposed interview date for shortlisted firms at the very outset of the process, or set a date far enough away so that you are likely to see the people who worked on your proposal (not just whoever is available at short notice).

You should see each manager separately and give each interview sufficient time. Certainly do not expect to have a useful meeting in under 30 minutes – that is barely time to introduce the two organisations and get started. An hour is good with a further 15 minutes for discussion and to catch your breath. If you have specific topics you want to cover with a manager during the meeting, such as a thorny issue that will be important, do alert the manager when sending your briefing so they have a chance to put in some thought in advance.

You should request each manager's presentation slide deck in advance so you can have a chance to read it and think about your questions before the meeting. If a manager just produces a standard presentation and doesn't respond to your questions, that itself is a weak sign. Be sure to give each manager three to four weeks to prepare a presentation for your meeting.

If you can easily visit the managers at their offices, you will get a better feeling for the business since you will often be able to meet key people who might be too senior to be able spend a day going to an external meeting with a potential client. You should be clear in advance who will chair the interview, as in any meeting. The purpose of the meeting is to get a sense of each manager's process and approach to responsible investing, the way they deal with their clients, and which manager you feel most comfortable working with.

Some questions that you might seek to have answered during the meeting include:

- Is the manager's proposed investment solution aligned with your financial objectives and goals, and is their process appropriate for your appetite for volatility?
- Is the process clear, rigorous and repeatable? How does the manager decide to sell one stock and replace it with another? How do they deal with stocks that are not performing as expected?
- Where relevant, do the firm's claims about being responsible investors stack up? For example, is there any company they would not own even if it were extremely cheap?
- What administrative support and reporting is included, including how you get cash out of your portfolio?
- What level of service will you receive?
- Who will you see and how often? Will it be the person attending the meeting now or will it be someone less central and more junior?
- Is the approach flexible enough for your purposes if your plans are liable to change?
- Are you comfortable with the firm's style and its people – do you feel you are compatible?

If a manager fails to answer your questions directly (many do), interrupt and bring them back to the point. It may be that they have genuinely misunderstood, and if not it's important to ensure you get proper answers to your questions rather than answers to the questions the manager wanted you to ask! Finally, remember that a good meeting doesn't necessarily make a good firm. It's okay to appoint a good manager after a terrible presentation as long as you're confident that they are rigorous in their process and that their style will suit your needs.

Making your decision

As with the shortlisting process, it is generally easier to start by excluding the firms that you do not want to use. If you have interviewed a series of contrasting managers, this will be much easier to do.

If the decision is not clear, then it is often sensible to go back to the relevant managers by email with additional questions. If there is a specific point about which you are uncertain, you may find that the managers can quickly offer a clarification. If necessary, you can also have a short second round of interviews, perhaps visiting the managers' offices if you did not in the first round.

Once you have a preferred candidate, this is the point at which to take up their references (who should be existing or past clients). Doing so should help you to satisfy any lingering doubts you may have about how responsive the proposed firm is to client questions and specific requirements. This is also your last chance to open negotiations about fees (see above), although you may have less power in this regard if you have already revealed they are the preferred candidate.

Providing feedback

Once you have made your decision, you should obviously tell the successful manager. However, as is often the case with interviewing generally, too often people fail to tell the unsuccessful candidates, and that reflects poorly on your charity. Managers put a great deal of work into these proposals and presentations, and they deserve proper, considered feedback.

Outline timetable for the manager selection process

It is best to assume that, at its fastest, a selection process will take about eight weeks from start to finish, depending on your meeting dates and assuming you have an up-to-date investment policy statement. It is best to identify the meeting where your board will want to confirm the arrangements and work back from there. The minimum stages in the timeline for a regular manager search with an investment committee recommending a decision to a board will be:

- one week to identify a longlist and prepare your RFP;
- three weeks for the managers to complete and return your RFP;

- one week for the investment committee to read the replies and settle on a shortlist;
- one week for the managers to prepare and return slide decks;
- one week for the investment committee to review the presentations and hold interviews;
- one week for decision, ratification and feedback.

Obviously, these time frames can be lengthened, and they usually are because of delays in finding convenient dates. The schedule can also be accelerated but it might start to eat into the quality of the process if much time is cut out.

Implementation

Once you have agreed basic terms with your new manager, you can move on to the details of implementation. These principally revolve around legalities, deciding and agreeing benchmarks, and transitioning to the new manager. If you are moving to more than one manager, the following three steps will need to be repeated for each (and usually there is no need for the different managers to know about each other). If you are moving managers, it is both common and courteous to notify your existing manager, give them authority to liaise with the new firm about transferring the assets, and ask them to keep you informed of the plan.

Legal review

Most investment agreements follow a standard format set by the FCA so there is little to be gained in seeking legal advice on them unless the value of your funds is particularly large or the firm you have chosen is very unusual (e.g. a UK charity choosing a firm based in China). Where either of these is the case, it can be worth seeking advice from a lawyer who understands both charity law and financial services, but not one who understands only one or the other.

Benchmarks

As part of your onboarding process, your manager should suggest some benchmarks that they will use to measure their performance. The next chapter goes into detail about how to use benchmarks to best effect.

Transition management

Moving assets from one place to another is expensive. There are considerable fees that can be run up in selling all your shares only to buy most of them back under a different fund's name. If you are changing to a new manager, it is possible to arrange a transfer of the shares themselves from the old manager to the new one by 'transitioning' them to the new fund 'in specie' (i.e. by transferring their ownership rather than selling and then buying them back). There are specialist (non-manager) firms that can do this for you, or your new manager may be able to arrange it on your behalf. To find out more, speak to your new manager. If this is relevant to you, it is always worth checking with both your new manager and the old how they plan to handle the transition (not all managers have the capacity to handle transitions, so they may choose to engage a specialist firm). As a rule of thumb, using a specialist service starts to become viable for portfolios worth more than £40 million, but often the old and new managers can agree this between themselves without involving a third party.

In addition, there are risks involved in being 'out of the market'. This describes the moment when you are between managers (so uninvested) and the market moves sharply up (and your holding doesn't). You can either use a specialist firm, as above, or organise the transfer in two or three tranches to reduce this risk. Again, this can be organised for you between the incoming and outgoing managers.

Ongoing review

Once your manager(s) are in place and the arrangements have settled down, you will fall into a natural cadence of meetings and reports. After some time (hopefully a long time), you will want to reassure yourself that your arrangements are still satisfactory. If all seems to be going well, you should aim to do this no more often than every five years (the chapter on governance has more to say on the topic of balancing continuity and change; see page 165). If, however, there has been a considerable change of key individuals (especially at senior levels) at your manager or if its circumstances have changed, you might want to conduct a review earlier. This will be a matter of judgement.

Some firms offer 'health checks' for potential clients at no cost. These will be interesting and informative. However, these firms can earn their keep from encouraging change (it means more work for them), and changing managers frequently is expensive in terms of lost income, time and costs.

The starting point for conducting a review will be to examine how your manager's investment strategy has performed against the benchmarks that you originally set up to help determine success. This is covered in the next chapter, on performance measurement.

Fictional case studies

Spender: Warden's Philanthropy

Founded in 1860, Warden's Philanthropy has a permanent endowment worth £40 million. It has a strong sense of social purpose, not only in how it spends but also in how it invests, not least because of its nationally recognised prize for social action.

It had enjoyed a long and untroubled relationship with its incumbent investment manager. However, as related in chapter 7, the arrival of a new chair prompted a review of the current arrangements so the trustees decided to engage an investment consultant to help them with this health check. They declined offers of free reviews from firms that would promote their own products and settled on someone recommended by their lawyer so that they could be more confident of the independence of the findings.

The review pointed out that the investment strategy had become outdated. It had been designed to deliver a high level of natural income rather than the high total return the charity had recently resolved to use. It had held over 50% in UK equities and the rest in fixed income because the previous chair believed that, as this was charitable money, the fewest possible risks should be taken with it, and the unavoidable consequence had been low levels of spending. The consultant worked with the trustees on updating the investment policy statement, especially in terms of the tolerance for volatility (they never used the word 'risk') and the need for cash rather than income. Generally, the trustees were content with their longstanding approach to responsible investing.

The trustees discussed this review with their current investment manager, who undertook to make a number of changes. However, after some reflection, the trustees decided to run a tender process, including the existing manager in the process. They outsourced this to the consultant and at the end of the process stayed with the incumbent manager, but with a renewed mandate. They declined offers from the consultant to provide monitoring services since these were already available from their manager.

Saver: Martello Tower Fund

The Martello Tower Fund is a substantial fund within the fundraising charity Preserving Our Nautical Past. It has £1 million to protect a historic coastal fort against rising sea levels.

At the fund's outset, the investment committee of the fund (which included an investment expert) knew that all they had to do was rely on the long-term growth of equities to achieve their target value, despite the ups and downs of the equity market. They therefore agreed that they did not need any sort of complicated asset allocation. Consequently, they had a fairly simple choice between using an active equity manager or a much cheaper passive one that just tracked a global equity index. They opted for the latter. The trustees agreed with this approach. The committee then visited a handful of firms it knew could fulfil this brief and chose the one that offered a responsible investing approach that showed empathy with the fund's purpose. It also offered clear reporting. The committee was confident about monitoring these reports so it did not feel the need to involve a consultant.

Spend-outer: Butterworth Music Festivals

This charity was set up in 2003 and plans to spend its entire £10 million on music festivals within ten years of its first grant. At the outset, the trustees knew that they would have to revisit their cash-flow predictions frequently because of the changing pace of their drawdowns. Although their strategy was to keep their reserves in low-risk and liquid funds, there was still room to earn a little extra if the cash was not going to be spent for some years.

After an initial false start (as related in chapter 7), they had found a reliable adviser to help them identify possible managers. They cross-referenced these suggestions with those managers who had at least advertised on charity sites or in charity magazines, because they realised this showed evidence of an interest in charity investments, which was important to them.

The trustees wrote to five managers with their investment policy statement, outlining their current plans and expectations, and asked the managers to respond to an RFP. On the basis of the responses, the trustees decided to meet three of the firms for a further discussion about how each would invest their funds, and how they would provide the required flexibility.

At the end of this process, they settled on a clear winner who they thought would be engaged, flexible, interested and responsive to their changing needs, but who would also invest cautiously to make sure they didn't incur any intolerable investment losses on the money they were meant to be spending. It helped that the firm was closely associated with sponsorship of live music performances, which presented opportunities to work together on some projects.

Conclusion

There is no 'best manager'. There are better managers and worse managers for what you are trying to achieve, but your ability to stay the course with an adequate manager is an under-rated factor. Then it is the market, the asset allocation and the governance that make the difference to your returns. No manager shoots the lights out all the time.

By asking the right questions and chasing the right answers, you can avoid mistakes and help to produce better performance. Assessing that performance is the topic of the next chapter.

Notes

1 'Key questions to ask your financial adviser' [web page], Money Helper, www.moneyhelper.org.uk/en/getting-help-and-advice/financial-advisers/key-questions-to-ask-your-financial-adviser, accessed 20 January 2024.
2 'Investing charity money: A guide for trustees (CC14)' [web page], Charity Commission for England and Wales, 2023, www.gov.uk/government/publications/charities-and-investment-matters-a-guide-for-trustees-cc14, accessed 20 January 2024.

Chapter eleven

Performance measurement

The purpose of this chapter

If you ask the right question, the right answer is usually easy to find. This chapter looks at how to use benchmarks to ask the right questions and how to interpret the answers. It aims to help you to recognise whether or not you have been successful in making and spending as much as you can. That must be the goal of every charity, even if the spending part won't happen until a future date.

The chapter begins by examining why you should measure performance, what exactly should be measured and who should carry out your day-to-day measurement activities. It then steps through four key questions that will help you to assess your performance in light of your financial objectives and goals, your spending, your overall investment strategy and your responsible investment ambitions. It then considers a series of common problems that can throw a spanner in the works of charities' measurement activities. Finally, the three case studies describe how each of the three fictional charities approach the topic of performance measurement from their own perspective.

The why, what and who of measuring performance

Why should you measure?

Measuring performance is an essential function in good financial (and investment) management. *Investing Charity Money: A guide for trustees* (CC14) requires trustees to review their investments periodically as part of their duty of care.[1] In essence, the reason to measure your performance is to see how you measure up against your original intentions – your financial objectives and goals (see chapter 2), as laid out in your investment policy statement (see chapter 8). Through the measuring process, you will also be able to answer questions such as how much money you have earned, whether it was more or less than inflation, whether you did better or worse than your peers, and perhaps how shrewd (as opposed to lucky) your manager is.

However, although these investment-related questions are important, measuring the overall financial performance of your charity is not the same as measuring the more narrowly defined performance of your investment portfolio. As a charity, your focus should always be on your financial objectives and goals, and thus whether you are meeting your obligations to your beneficiaries. As such, your reason for measuring should not only be to ascertain what you have earned but also to see what you have spent, according to whether your overall financial goal is spending, saving or spending out.

What should you measure?

Part I of this book set out the fundamentals of charity investing. It suggested that you should decide on an overall financial objective and financial goals (either for your charity as a whole or for each of your funds) and from those work out your spending policy (i.e. what you will take out) and investment strategy (i.e. what you will put in), which in turn are measured against your reserves policies. In addition, your investment strategy is heavily influenced by your values and beliefs, which are expressed (in the investment context) through your approach to responsible investing (see chapter 9). The relationships between these components are shown in figure 11.1.

Figure 11.1 The core components of charity investing

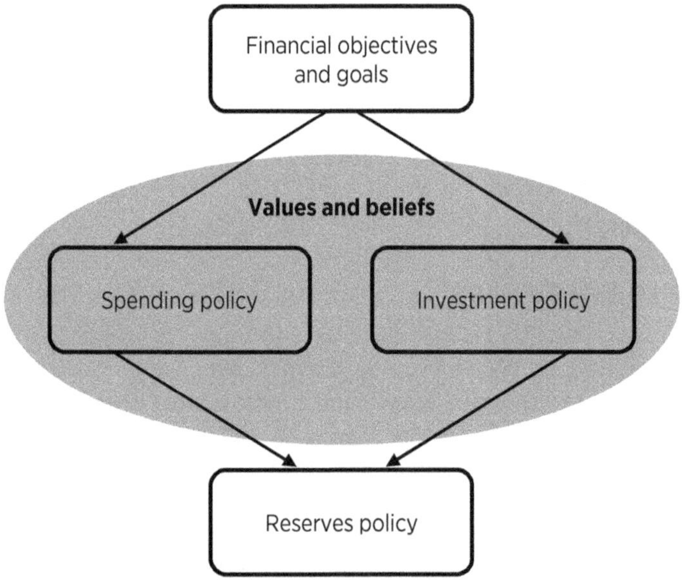

Based on these components, there are four central questions that will help you measure your success:

- Are you delivering on your financial objectives and goals (over the long term as a saver, spender or spend-outer)?
- Are you spending enough?
- Is your investment strategy delivering what you intended?
- Are you investing as responsibly as you expected?

By considering these questions, you will gain a comprehensive picture of where you have got to against your plan.

The bulk of this chapter is taken up with an exploration of how to answer these questions, but first we need to look at the role of benchmarks and briefly consider who should conduct the measuring activities.

Benchmarks

A benchmark is a standard or reference point against which performance can be compared, just like a mark on a carpenter's bench is used to record a specific length. One of the most common problems in investing for charities (and many other organisations) is using an inappropriate benchmark. Much of this chapter examines which question is best answered by which benchmark. Only with the right measuring tool will you be able to tell whether you are getting the result you want or not.

For instance, a spender charity might use a benchmark to see whether it is achieving its goal of preserving its capital over the long term after spending – in other words, to answer the question 'Are we protecting our charity against inflation?' This is the right question to ask, but if the charity's investment manager is asked to report against a benchmark such as the Consumer Prices Index (CPI) plus 4%, it won't get the right answer because the benchmark does not include the effect of spending. A CPI plus 4% benchmark only measures whether your investments have increased by the CPI plus 4%, and not whether you have grown your capital after spending.

Instead of looking at how much its *investment portfolio* has grown when compared to inflation, a spender charity that wanted to answer the question 'Are we protecting our charity against inflation?' should look at whether its *reserves* have kept pace with their target values (see chapter 6), which will include not only investment returns (i.e. what the charity puts in) but also spending (i.e. what it takes out).

Benchmarks give you a framework through which to understand your performance data, but it is crucial to pick the right benchmark for the right question. Otherwise, you might not be measuring what you think you are measuring and may get misleading answers.

Dealing with statistics

Always consider the context when you are presented with figures. A big number does not necessarily represent anything substantial, and a small number might have an impact well beyond its apparent size. For example, half a per cent off a 1% fee is a fantastic saving, but a 50% return on your gold investment is almost meaningless if you only have 1% of your portfolio in gold. Always ask if a number is big or small.

Who should do the measuring?

Of the four central questions considered in this chapter, only one – 'Is your investment strategy delivering what you intended?' – has the option of a standardised measuring process, known as the Global Investment Performance Standards (see the box below), widely considered the gold standard. You may handle this process internally, but more usually it is handled by your investment manager (if you have a single manager) or by an investment consultant or investment performance specialist (if you have more than one manager; see page 199).

In the cases of the other three central questions – which concern whether you are spending enough, whether your investment strategy is delivering what you intended and whether you are investing as responsibly as you intended – there is little standardisation around how they are measured. This is perhaps because when people think about performance measurement, they tend only to think about the performance of an investment fund (which for charities, as explained above, is only one part of the overall picture). This means you will need to either create and operate your own monitoring systems or find an amenable financial expert to help you with the calculations. Whatever route you choose, the remainder of this chapter will help to guide you towards a structure that suits your needs.

Standards for reporting on investment performance

In order to avoid subjectivity or unreliable reporting, it is best to use an established and recognised standard. Whenever your manager reports to you on performance, their calculations should comply with the Global Investment Performance Standards (GIPS), which are the global standard for performance reporting (see www.gipsstandards.org).[2] All reporting should be shown after costs and fees. Footnotes should disclose whether or not the data is GIPS compliant.

The following sections now consider the four central questions in turn. Additionally, scattered throughout the sections are boxes suggesting when each method of measurement is helpful and when you might want to use a different method.

Are you delivering on your financial objectives and goals?

Your principal measurement of success will demonstrate your progress against your overall financial objective, whether that is trying to spend fairly between generations, growing your financial base or spending it down. These are all measured by what is left in your reserves.

Chapter 6 introduced the idea of setting target values so that you can monitor your reserves and demonstrate whether you have achieved your long-term goals. Here your target value is the benchmark. For spender charities, the question will be whether you are staying close enough to the target value you have chosen for your reserves to protect your charity's long-term reserve, and so its future spending against inflation. For saver charities, it will be whether you are saving enough to reach your chosen target value or at least growing fast enough to match or outpace inflation. For spend-outers, it will be whether your spending plans are on track to hit your target value of zero reserves at the date (or rate) you have chosen.

Why does this matter?

The target value (or benchmark) for your reserves provides a framework you can use to help you understand sometimes very volatile, uncertain or even scary changes caused by movements in your investment portfolio. Too often, people assume that the maximum value of their portfolio is also its 'normal value' and if they have less than that, they have somehow 'lost money' and failed. For example, someone who currently has a portfolio of £120,000 might say that they have 'lost £30,000' but they may be using their highest ever value (£150,000) as their benchmark. People rarely use their lowest ever value – for example, the same person might equally be able to say that they have 'made £40,000' from a low point of £80,000.

Using false benchmarks in this way can lead to trustees restricting their expenditure to help them regain this random maximum value, with the inadvertent consequence that they end up imposing unnecessary austerity on their beneficiaries. In fact, it is your target value that should be your benchmark of what is normal and against which you should measure your progress against your financial objectives and goals.

If there are two constant themes in this book, they are the need to hold your nerve in testing circumstances and the need to make and spend as much as you can. Your ability to stay the course in testing times allows you to tolerate more investment volatility, and this in turn enables you to earn more money, which allows you to spend more on your charitable purpose (see chapter 8 for more on this relationship). Using target values as your principal benchmark will help you with this.

How to measure whether you are meeting your target for your overarching financial objective and goals

As explained in earlier chapters, most investors face the issue that the value of their long-term reserves will always be uncertain – they are equally likely to rise or fall the following day. It is therefore almost impossible to know precisely what your assets are worth at any given moment or what their 'normal value' is.

The best way to deal with this problem is not to worry about finding a precise answer but instead to plot your target value over time as a benchmark with a range, as shown in figure 11.2. As explained in more detail on page 113, the trajectory of the benchmark will depend on your charity's overall financial objective:

- **Spender charities** will typically have a benchmark whose line rises but only enough to keep up with inflation, and with their annual spending taken out.
- **Saver charities** will have a benchmark whose line should steadily rise towards a final target value.
- **Spend-out charities** will have a benchmark whose line steadily falls towards a final target value of nil.

Figure 11.2 shows a target value benchmark for a spender charity. The charity's long-term reserve value has steadily grown, after spending, alongside the benchmark (the target value). The actual value is above the benchmark (the target value) at the latest date, meaning that the charity is currently meeting its objective of maintaining its capital after allowing for inflation and spending.

Figure 11.2 A target value benchmark for a spender charity aiming to maintain the value of its long-term reserve after inflation and spending

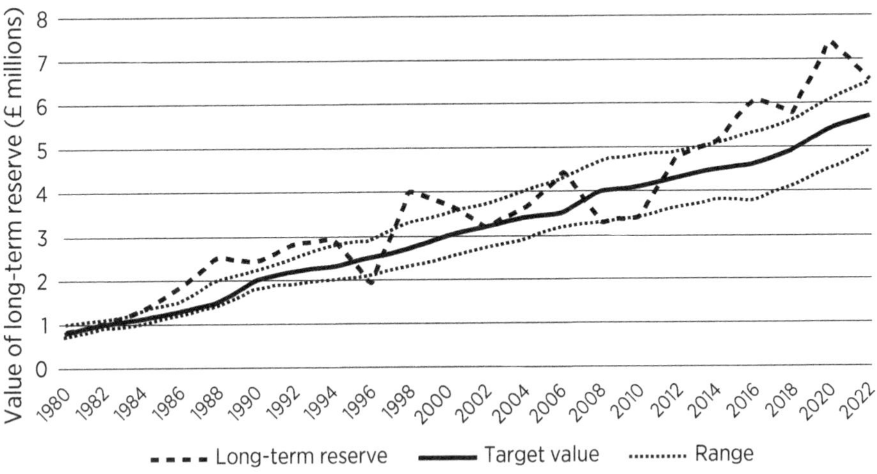

Source: Idlewild Trust

The range is helpful because it makes allowance for the inevitable volatility in long-term investing (see page 94). As shown in chapter 5, saver and spender charities are particularly likely to be affected by this volatility, but spend-out charities may also want to consider setting a range to allow for unforeseen developments. Once you have a range in place, you can be more confident about spotting when things are going wrong (or right) because there will be boundaries that serve as triggers for action. In table 11.1, the charity has set a range of plus or minus 15% of its benchmark (which is the expected volatility associated with this particular charity's investment strategy). If the actual value of the reserve fell outside these boundaries, then the charity would know that it might have to do something about it.

One way of planning how you might respond is to create a warning table based on the RAG (red, amber, green) system, as also shown in table 11.1, but with the addition of a blue level for when things are going *too* well (a RAGB system). For example, for a spender charity, the blue level means that everything is going well and you should spend freely, probably spending more. The red level means that you are below your normal range and you should at least consider reducing your spending until you are back within the desired range (which might be caused by recovering market values or by the effect of spending less).

Table 11.1 A RAGB-based trigger system for a spender charity's long-term reserves

<table>
<tr><th>Level</th><th>Trigger</th><th>Potential response</th></tr>
<tr><td>Red</td><td>Less than 85% of target value</td><td>Reduce spending</td></tr>
<tr><td>Amber</td><td>85–100% of target value</td><td rowspan="2">Spend with confidence</td></tr>
<tr><td>Green</td><td>100–115% of target value</td></tr>
<tr><td>Blue</td><td>More than 115% of target value</td><td>Consider increasing spending</td></tr>
</table>

A saver charity will have different options because it has no spending to increase or decrease (i.e. blue just means the charity is doing even better against its overarching financial goal than expected). If it is behind its benchmark (amber or red), it can try to earn more (by accepting more volatility), reduce its ultimate goal or just maintain a watchful wait without taking any specific action. A spend-outer would be unlikely to invest in such a way that would leave it so exposed to volatile assets.

Summary: measuring progress against your financial objectives and goals

Good for

- Seeing the long-term trends in how you are getting on compared to your charity's financial objectives and goals
- Understanding that losing money from your high point is not the end of the world (it is your target value that matters)
- Seeing whether you are spending too much or too little (when measured over long-enough periods)

Not good for

- Making day-to-day decisions about your investment or spending policy
- Identifying whether you are earning as much as you can

Are you spending enough?

Why does this matter?

This question applies principally to spender and spend-out charities (saver charities are unlikely to have any significant spending during the period while they are building towards their savings goal). It will be particularly relevant to you if you are a spender charity and you want to balance the interests of your current and future beneficiaries, and also ensure you are not saving too much. Spend too much now and you favour your current beneficiaries; not enough and you favour your future ones (for more on this principle – referred to as intergenerational equity – see page 57). Note that the question doesn't imply that you must spend everything possible *every year*; you can overspend one year and underspend the next, but if a trend extends over several years it begins to matter.

This question principally relates to your spending reserve, which, like the long-term reserve, was introduced in chapter 6.

How to use your spending reserve to see whether you can spend more?

There are two sub-questions that are relevant here:

- Are you spending everything that you have transferred into your spending reserve?
- Are you transferring enough into your spending reserve?

Additionally, once you have answered these two questions, you can put the information together with your findings relating to your long-term reserve to answer one more question:

- Are you effectively balancing your long-term and spending reserves?

Are you spending everything that you have transferred into your spending reserve?

Just as with your long-term reserve, you will have set a target value for your spending reserve, and this will act as a benchmark with a range (as outlined for the long-term reserve in the previous section). But instead of using a range linked to the volatility of your investments, it could be a range of what you consider an acceptable floor or ceiling for the reserve. This could be plus or minus 5%, or even 30%, but whatever it is, you will have a guide to help you identify when the balance in your spending reserve is normal or not normal. Don't forget that this is nothing to do with how much liquidity you need (see page 95); rather, it is dictated by what level of future spending you want to retain. It is an accounting question, not an investing one.

This makes the question of whether you are spending everything a fairly mechanical one to answer, because it is measured by what is left in your spending reserve. Unlike in the case of your long-term reserve, the numbers should not be subject to market volatility, so they are much easier to monitor. The question then is at what level you should set your target value benchmark for your spending reserve. Once you have decided on an appropriate target value for your spending reserve, you can again apply the RAGB-based model (see table 11.2).

Table 11.2 A RAGB-based trigger system for spending reserves (using a +/−5% range)

Level	Trigger	Action
Red	Less than 95% of target	Reduce spending or increase income
Amber	95% to 100% of target	Spend with confidence
Green	100% to 105% of target	
Blue	More than 105% of target value	Increase spending

If your spending reserve was the same as your bank account, the floor would be nil (so you didn't go overdrawn) and the target value would be something higher than that (so you had a bit of spare cash to overspend one year). The target value would lie somewhere between the floor and the ceiling. Remember that what you are measuring here is your accountability (i.e. what you have spent or not spent; covered in chapter 6), not your liquidity (which is covered in chapter 5).

Are you transferring enough into your spending reserve?

Sometimes charities transfer less into their spending reserve than their spending policy allows them to do (see chapter 3, especially page 63). This might be because they only spent part of what their policy allowed them to spend, so as a result they only needed to transfer enough to their spending reserve to maintain a positive balance in the reserve. Even if you don't spend the full amount in the year in question, you should still transfer the full amount into your spending reserve to identify it as spendable in the future. If you don't transfer the whole amount, you risk underfunding your current beneficiaries and undermining the principle of intergenerational equity. This transfer is a simple accounting exercise for your year-end accounts – you just have to reconcile what your spending policy tells you to transfer into your spending reserve with what has actually been transferred.

Are you effectively balancing your long-term and spending reserves?

Measuring the performance of your two reserves will guide you towards being able to answer the central question of your financial success: whether you are spending too much or too little for the amount you are earning. Table 11.3 provides guidelines for reflecting on how your combined reserves are working together to deliver the highest spend you can achieve (particularly important for spender charities).

Table 11.3 Measuring your long-term and spending reserves together

Long-term reserve	Spending reserve	Action
Too high	Too high	You need to increase your annual transfer (either as a one-off or by increasing your spending policy) and actually spend more (ideally all) of what is being transferred to your spending reserve.
Too high	Too low	You are spending fully but can afford to transfer more into your spending reserve to top up your spending, either as a one-off or by increasing the amount allowed by your spending policy.
Too low	Too high	You are not earning enough to sustain the transfers to your spending reserve, but nor are you spending what is available. Revisit your investment policy (to see whether you can earn more) and spending decisions (to see why you are not spending as much as you could).
Too low	Too low	You are not earning enough for what you are spending. Revisit your investment policy (to see whether you can earn more) and spending decisions (to see where you can cut back until your revised investment policy bears fruit). If both of those fail, you will have to reduce your spending ambitions.

Summary: monitoring whether you are spending as much as you can without damaging your reserves

Good for

- Ensuring that you are spending what your spending policy demands
- Demonstrating accountability for your spending
- Managing spending and budget decisions that cover multiple years
- Recognising when the pace of your spending needs to change

Not good for

- Monitoring the wisdom of what you are spending your money on
- Monitoring your spending if you only transfer part of what your spending policy requires
- Identifying whether you are earning as much as you can

Is your investment strategy delivering what you intended?

Why does this matter?

All charities will want to know the answer to one basic question: how much money have we made this quarter, year or decade? This is usually followed shortly by another question: is this better or worse than we expected? If the answers suggest the outcome is unsatisfactory, then there is a cause for concern.

How to measure whether your investment strategy is delivering what you intended

There are several approaches to understanding your investment performance and each one answers a different question. There is no single question that will tell you everything about how well you are doing, but ones that are particularly useful are:

1. How much money are you making on an absolute basis?
2. How much money are you making compared to the market?

3. How much money are you making compared to other charities (and, relatedly, could you earn more than you are currently earning)?

Each of these questions will be defined by a benchmark, at least one of which should already have been agreed with your investment manager (see page 221).

Note that these questions are all related to investing rather than accounting. Therefore, rather than looking at your long-term and spending *reserves* (covered in chapter 6), they are concerned with your long-term and short-term *portfolios* (covered in chapter 5). On most occasions, your long-term reserve will be invested in a long-term portfolio and your spending reserve will be invested in a short-term portfolio (like a bank account).

How much money are you making on an absolute basis?

'Absolute basis' means that the results are measured against some external measure, such as inflation, although the answer to this question will vary according to the benchmark chosen. Your long-term and short-term portfolios will have different benchmarks because of their different objectives:

- A suitable benchmark for a **long-term portfolio** would be inflation (often the CPI) but with an additional return of 3–5% to cover the manager's fees and what you hope to spend. The exact target will depend on how much volatility or uncertainty your portfolio is expected to have.
- With a **short-term portfolio**, you are interested principally in the return *of* your cash, and less in the return *on* cash, so you would use a cash benchmark such as SONIA (Sterling Overnight Index Average), the replacement for the discredited LIBOR (London Inter-Bank Offered Rate), which is a benchmark that underpins how interest rates are set more widely.[3]

Once you have chosen a suitable benchmark with your investment manager, you can monitor their performance against it. However, you should make sure they continue to use your agreed benchmark and do not substitute it with another unless they have your permission (and explain why). A manager is unlikely to change a benchmark if it makes a fund's comparative performance worse.

Setting a benchmark for the performance of your natural income

Natural income (explained in chapter 4) is a dangerous indicator to follow. If you set an income target for a manager, you are in effect asking them to buy stocks that will meet your income target rather than providing the best performance for the amount of risk you want to take. Nevertheless, if you do ask for a high natural income, you should use a benchmark to measure it so you can be sure you are getting the high level you requested. For example, you might use a benchmark of more than 130% of the income of the MSCI World Index or the FTSE All-Share Index.

Summary: measuring how much money you are making on an absolute basis

Good for

- Measuring your investment performance over the long term (five or more years)
- Identifying whether you are making enough money to cover your target spending level
- Monitoring your investment manager's skill

Not good for

- Measuring your progress against your financial objectives and goals
- Measuring single-year performance or performance over anything less than five years
- Measuring your natural income against a target (as in 'an above-average income')
- Measuring volatility and risk in your portfolio

How much money are you making compared to the market?

This question needs to be divided into two, depending on whether you are measuring a single-asset-class fund or a mixed-asset-class fund (see page 44), although in both cases you will still measure against an agreed benchmark.

Single-asset-class funds

To assess the performance of a single-asset-class fund, you will measure your fund against a commercially available benchmark of relevant companies. These benchmarks offer standardised measures of performance across single-asset-class funds, making comparison much easier and enabling you to tell whether your manager is performing roughly in line with the index they are meant to be following.

In the case of single-asset-class funds, the benchmark will be an index published by a firm such as Morgan Stanley Capital International (MSCI), the Financial Times Stock Exchange (FTSE), Dow Jones or S&P Global. There are many such indices, but three global indices that are very commonly used by major equity managers are:

- the MSCI World Index, covering the high-income countries (which MSCI refers to as the 'developed world');
- the MSCI All Country World Index, covering the same high-income countries together with the emerging markets but not the frontier markets (see definitions on page 39);
- the FTSE All-World index, which also covers the same high-income countries and the emerging markets but is from a different provider.

There are other indices that cover discrete regions or countries (e.g. the UK, North America or Japan), styles or 'factors' (e.g. growth, value or momentum), and sectors (e.g. technology, consumer or energy). Basically, any company listed on a stock exchange will form part of some index, somewhere, so your investment manager will always be able to help you find an index that is suitable for your investment choices.

Once you have identified a suitable index, measuring your performance is simply a case of comparing your returns with those of the index, and your investment manager should provide you with all the necessary data. Investment managers who deal in equities usually explain their performance against benchmarks by analysing their returns in two ways:

- **Asset allocation decisions:** did the manager perform well because the fund had a significant allocation to a country or industrial sector that performed better than the benchmark?
- **Stock selection decisions:** did the manager hold more successful stocks than the benchmark (or fewer unsuccessful ones)?

Bond-focused investment managers also use country and sector metrics to analyse their performance, but they also use two more metrics:

- **Credit rating:** this describes how likely a bond is to default (i.e. not repay your money). Chapter 3 goes into detail about the various credit ratings and what they mean (see page 33).
- **Duration:** this describes the risk of long-term uncertainty. A bond that will repay your capital in 12 months' time is safer than an equivalent one that will repay it in 30 years' time (because there is less room for uncertainty).

Additionally, when interpreting the data, there are some further points to bear in mind:

- **Size matters:** most indices are constructed based on the size of the companies within them, so a company that is 100 times the size of another will affect the index's values 100 times as much as the other. The danger of these so-called 'capitalisation-weighted' indices is that companies are weighted according to their size, not their prospects. Sometimes a few companies can have a disproportionate impact on the performance of an index if they are especially large.
- **Time matters too:** for example, if your investments have fallen by 3% and the index you are using as a benchmark has fallen by 5%, your investments will have outperformed the market, even though both have lost money, and that is still a good outcome. Although this seems nonsensical, over a longer time frame what matters is the aggregate result of small outperformances because they will add up to a bigger outperformance in the long run. This is why performance data is provided over various time periods, such as year to date (commonly referred to as YTD), one year, three years and five years. Ideally, these figures are annualised, so a five-year annualised return will be the average yearly return over a five-year period.

Tracking error and active share

Two further statistics that you can measure are tracking error and active share. These tell you similar things about how far a manager's returns have deviated from the index they are meant to follow. If the tracking error is a big number (say, over 5%), it means there is an increased likelihood that your returns will be quite different from the market's returns – either better or worse. If you want a manager who will take large (but measured) risks, they will probably have a high tracking error. Tracking error is considered important because you might be better off investing in a much cheaper passive fund if your manager has a low tracking error (2% is considered low).

Active share measures how the holdings in your portfolio differ from the holdings (i.e. the companies in which you own shares) in the index you are following. The higher the number, the less similar they are. An active share of 0% would mean that your portfolio and the index held exactly the same companies and in the same proportions and had no active positions at all. If this is the case, you have a passive fund, but possibly with active management fees.

Summary: measuring single-asset-class funds

Good for

- Seeing how the manager of a single-asset-class fund is performing compared to the market they are investing in
- Measuring the performance of an actively managed fund against a cheaper passive index

Not good for

- Showing whether a manager's style is suited to the current market environment
- Drawing a comparison with the performance of mixed-asset-class funds
- Comparing your performance with that of funds with different return targets or asset allocations
- Seeing how you have done against inflation

Mixed-asset-class funds

At their simplest, mixed-asset-class funds contain only two asset classes. Two common variations are 70% in equities and 30% in bonds (for portfolios intended to earn a higher return at the cost of extra volatility) and 70% in bonds and 30% in equities (for portfolios where safety is more important). In practice, most mixed funds are more complicated, as in the example shown in table 11.4. However, you will see that this example still has 30% in safer assets (cash and bonds) and 70% in higher-earning assets (property and equities).

Table 11.4 An example of a mixed-asset-class fund

Asset class	**Allocation**
Global equities	50%
UK property	20%
Fixed-income bonds	20%
Cash	10%
Total allocation	**100%**

Mixed-asset-class funds are measured using a composite benchmark made up of single-asset-class indices, each given a different weight that reflects the different asset class weights of the fund. This is sometimes referred to as the 'policy portfolio' or 'neutral allocation'. Investment portfolios with similar risk appetites will often have broadly similar asset allocation benchmarks. Variations will occur in the precise size of allocations and in the exact index that is included (such as government bonds or government and corporate bonds together).

The alpha and the beta

Investors will often refer to the return from the market as the 'beta' and the extra return from the manager's skill as the 'alpha' (both terms are derived from the language of statistics). Most of your return will come from the market (the beta) and some from the manager (the alpha). If it were the other way round (and you had a great manager), it wouldn't matter what the market did because the manager's skill would always contribute more, and asset allocation would be relatively unimportant in successful investing. (This point is discussed from the point of view of governance on page 158.)

When looking at a mixed portfolio manager's results, one of the most important things to understand is the asset allocation they are using, especially when compared to another mixed manager. One manager might make a much higher return than another, but they could well be doing so by holding more in higher-returning but more volatile assets. This is all very well when markets go up, but not when markets fall since your losses will be correspondingly greater and you may not be expecting that.

This is illustrated in figure 11.3. It shows two portfolios that have very different amounts invested in high-returning equities and therefore very different volatilities. One (the one on the right) is using a lot of volatility to make its money, while the other isn't. The point is that it is not simply about who makes the most money – you need to understand how securely that money is made by considering the volatility accompanying the returns. In short, it is not necessarily a bad thing if a manager is making you less money than another manager could, if your manager is choosing options that suit your lower risk tolerance (i.e. if they are finding the efficient frontier; see page 84).

Figure 11.3 The impacts on volatility of different asset allocations

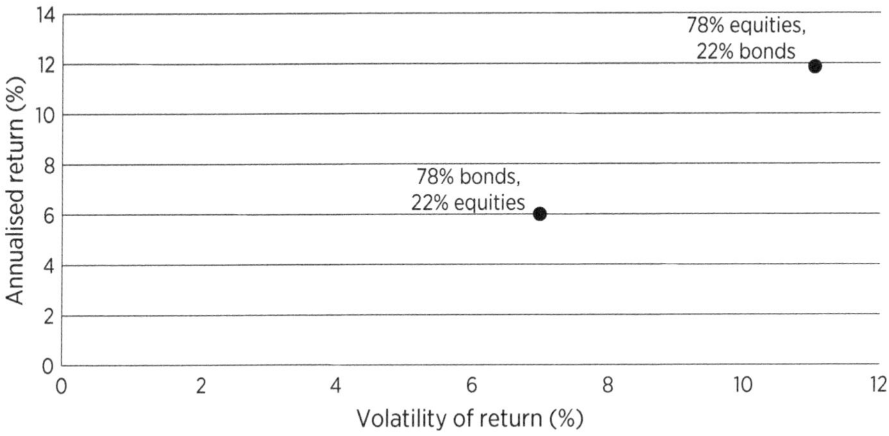

How is volatility calculated?

Volatility is an important indicator of performance in and of itself because, when it comes to your returns, it is a synonym for uncertainty and unpredictability (see chapter 5). It is measured by how much your total returns have varied over a period, normally three years. For example, cash will have a very low volatility, with the value of your cash (including the interest you earn) changing very little day by day. Compare this with an investment in a company where there are more significant daily fluctuations caused by investors changing their mind about a company's prospects and its value.

When it comes to annualised volatility, a number greater than 12% is considered to be big and a number less than 5% is considered to be small. As a rule, larger numbers are more common in equity portfolios and smaller ones in bond portfolios. A high number is good if you can deal with an unpredictable total return because it provides more opportunities to buy low and sell high (which is why it is attractive to a long-term investor). However, a low number is very important if you need to spend the money in the foreseeable future because you want to have confidence that your money is available at its face value.

All statistics only measure what they measure. Volatility is the same. If it is calculated daily, there will be many more price movements, increasing the chances of capturing higher volatility. However, if it is calculated annually or at longer intervals, there will be fewer movements and volatile assets can appear more stable. The standard is for it to be calculated on an annualised basis, and this is what your investment manager should do if asked. Volatility is widely used in the investment world; however, if you do not have to value assets every day (such as in the case of property), the statistic can be given an importance that it does not merit. Investopedia has a helpful walk-through of how to calculate volatility.[4]

Summary: measuring mixed-asset-class funds

Good for

- Comparing your performance against a manager's composite benchmark for the fund
- Comparing your performance with that of other mixed funds with similar return objectives

Not good for

- Comparing your performance with that of funds with different return targets or asset allocations
- Drawing a comparison with the performance of single-asset-class funds
- Seeing how you have done against inflation

How much money are you making compared to other charities?

Peer-group comparisons of charity funds were once the dominant way of measuring performance – did charity A perform better than charity B? The problem, however, is that not all charities are the same: different portfolios have different mixes of assets and different return aspirations, whereas peer-group comparisons assume every fund has a similar tolerance of volatility and is working to a similar timescale. In other words, the peers are not sufficiently homogenous.

If you wish to compare your charity's results against those of other charities, it is important to ensure you are comparing like with like. There are some useful peer-group benchmark providers (such as Asset Risk Consultants[5]), which organise funds by 'risk buckets' (see page 156) based on how similar a portfolio's volatility is to that of equity markets. Thus, a portfolio invested 70% in equities and 30% in bonds would be in the Steady Growth category (60–80% allocated to equity market risk), and there would be another bucket called 'Cautious' for funds with 0–40% allocated to equity risk. Such benchmarks allow you to compare your own performance to that of other, similarly invested charities.

Finally, as chapter 4 explores (see page 70), one of the most important questions you should ask is whether you are trying hard enough to make as much money as possible to spend on your beneficiaries. Sometimes it is only by looking at the investment performance (and asset allocation) of other charities with a similar operating model that you can begin to see whether you are tolerating as much risk as your peers, and therefore are earning as much as you can for your beneficiaries. Comparing yourself to a charity with a higher appetite for volatility is always a useful exercise because it helps you to understand what, if anything, is holding you back from making more money in the long run.

Summary: measuring how much money you are making compared to other charities

Good for

- Comparing your performance against that of other similar charities and commercial charity funds generally
- Checking that your investment performance is not out of step with other charities that have a similar risk profile
- Understanding whether you are being too cautious in how you invest

Not good for

- Understanding how you are doing against your own objectives
- Understanding whether your investments are performing as well as the market (or inflation)

Are you investing as responsibly as you expected?

Why does this matter?

The point of having a responsible investing policy is twofold: to make sure your charity's purpose and values are reflected in your portfolio, and to protect your reputation against inadvertently investing in something that will undermine your charitable purpose. These points are explained fully in chapter 9. In order to make sure that you are on top of both these issues, you need to know what you own, and monitor it carefully. One of the main ways of understanding how you express your approach to responsible investing is through an environmental, social and governance (ESG) lens.

How to measure whether you are investing as responsibly as you intended

Responsible investing is a rapidly developing area, but it is still young, and there are few reliable benchmarks that can be used to measure good performance. This is probably for two reasons. First, there is the difficulty of finding metrics that will adequately represent the issue you are trying to capture (especially in the social and governance categories of ESG). Second, there are differing views on what 'good' is, particularly in a global setting, where different parts of the world will have differing expectations on what is normal or fair. Nevertheless, practice will develop quickly, and meanwhile the following principles and models will help you to begin benchmarking your responsible investing performance.

Know what you own

If you are interested in advancing your mission or protecting your reputation, you will want to be confident about what you own and don't own, either directly or through your manager or any third-party funds they use. The first thing to check is that your chosen exclusions (if any) are in place and are observed. For example, if you have decided to exclude companies that use child labour, you should be able to confirm this in your manager's report.

The leading index providers, such as MSCI, London Stock Exchange Group (LSEG) and S&P Global, give companies overall ESG rankings (see table 11.5) reflecting how they perform against various criteria.[6] These scores can help to highlight the companies you might be concerned about investing in. This makes these rankings a good starting point for further investigation.

Table 11.5 MSCI's environmental, social and governance (ESG) scoring system[7]

Score	Ranking	Interpretation
AAA	Leader	Industry leader in managing ESG risks and opportunities
AA		
A	Average	Unexceptional record in managing ESG risks and opportunities
BBB		
BB		
B	Laggard	Trails its industry peers or fails to manage significant ESG risks
CCC		

A useful output from this process would be to see whether you are currently invested in any companies that are rated CCC (or equivalent) in these scoring systems. Such companies are invariably considered 'red flags' to responsible investors. Depending on your appetite for responsible investing, you might then move up the scale identifying companies in the other MSCI rankings, until you have reached a level you are happy with. You could then identify engagement activities (see page 182) which you or your investment manager could take to try to move the identified companies up the MSCI scale, or note them for future removal from your portfolio (assuming you have a segregated portfolio).

That said, just because a company has a respectable rating doesn't necessarily mean it will be attractive to charity investors. For example, British American Tobacco is at the time of writing rated as BBB, right in the middle of the range, indicating that (according to MSCI) it has an average track record of managing significant ESG risks compared to its peers. Nevertheless, your responsible investment policy may still guide you away from any company that manufactures tobacco.

Know how you are voting and engaging

Voting and company engagement are essential parts of responsible investing so it is important to measure them, but it can be tricky to identify appropriate benchmarks.

Voting

Voting is simpler to benchmark than engagement because it is easily quantifiable. Resolutions are proposed either by company management or by shareholders, and your manager will vote on these resolutions on your behalf (see page 182 for more details). Proposals put forward by shareholders (often including charities) are worth following because their existence indicates that the shareholders and management disagree about whether an idea is worthwhile (usually the background is that the idea will have been put to the management informally or semi-formally and been rejected, prompting the shareholders to put the idea into a formal proposal to try to get it implemented). Sometimes, these proposals will require the company's management to perform an action, such as report on an aspect of employment conditions or environmental considerations. Knowing this information will enable shareholders to encourage the company to adopt a better approach, if necessary. However, there can be good reasons not to support many such proposals (such as their being poorly drafted) so it is worth getting your manager's view on their merits (or otherwise).

Often managers will report on how often they voted for or against the company management's proposals. Most of these votes will be on non-controversial business, such as the reappointment of auditors or directors, but sometimes votes can be more controversial. In these situations, knowing whether your investment manager voted for or against management isn't particularly helpful because it simplifies everything into 'them' and 'us'. An alternative benchmark can be constructed by using the recommendations of one of the independent voting providers, such as Institutional Shareholder Services (ISS) or Glass Lewis (see page 183), which represent a neutral, unbiased position on how to vote as a responsible investor. So if, say, ISS recommends voting in one direction and your investment manager decides to vote the other way, you know your manager is voting actively, and you will want to understand why they didn't follow the recommended approach. The answers will tell you a great deal about how your manager thinks about responsible investing and what factors they consider to be important. Using these third-party providers as indicators of best practice also enables you to quantify your manager's voting performance according to how often they vote differently from these outsourced providers, rather than rely on anecdotal evidence.

In summary, three useful benchmarks for assessing voting records are:

- Are all your votes cast, even if it is to abstain?
- How often does your manager vote against shareholder resolutions, and why?
- How often does your manager vote against the advice of an independent voting adviser they use, and why?

Engagement

Voting is one method of engagement, but engagement more broadly is a long-term process of encouraging companies to adopt more desirable behaviours (as explained in chapter 9). This is often done behind closed doors but, on occasion, it can be done very publicly, as in the celebrated case of the 2021 ExxonMobil vote.[8] It is difficult to benchmark these interventions other than anecdotally. However, it can be helpful to get a report so you can have conversations with your manager around questions such as:

- What are your engagement priorities?
- What engagement did you undertake during the last period for each of these priorities, and what changes did you achieve?
- Whom do you collaborate with and on which engagements?

This is most useful if you ask for a brief summary and set a page limit for the response; perhaps no more than two is sufficient for a manageable overview of the key points, otherwise it is common to be sent a small forest's worth of information.

Assess your impact investments

Impact investing is a form of investing that seeks both a social and a financial return (see page 184). While it is easy to measure the financial return, it is difficult to measure the social component. One approach is based on quantifying any financial return you might be giving up and then assessing whether you would have spent the equivalent amount of money on that purpose if it were a grant.

In the worked example in table 11.6, a charity has made a loan (rather than a grant) to a beneficiary organisation as an impact investment at a concessionary rate of 3%. This is 5% less than the amount it assumes it will get from its non-impact portfolio. As a result, for every year that the loan continues, the charity has given up £2,500. Knowing this will help the trustees to decide whether they feel the social value they are getting is worth the annual cost or whether there are better projects to support.

Table 11.6 Example assessment of an impact investment consisting of a loan of £50,000

	Assumed total return	Financial return per annum
Non-impact portfolio	8%	£4,000
Loan	3%	£1,500
Financial return forgone (i.e. return from non-impact portfolio minus return from the loan)	**5%**	**£2,500**

Summary: measuring whether you are investing as responsibly as you expected

Good for

- Making a start on measuring your responsible investment activity
- Establishing areas for further examination
- Making some qualitative judgements about managers

Bad for

When it comes to measuring responsible investment, no measures are 'bad' per se but, as mentioned above, you should be aware of their limitations. Currently, there is no comprehensive quantitative approach to assessing responsible investment performance. As such, you should not expect to find a simple one-stop solution or to gain unambiguous or simplistic answers. It is therefore important to have confidence in the person to whom you are delegating these moral views.

Performance measurement problems

Setting benchmarks is fairly simple, but because it comes at the end of a long process, it is sometimes overlooked. It is crucial to have an appropriate yardstick, and not just any yardstick, to successfully measure the progress of your investments against what you expected. If you are not watchful, you can end up being so absorbed in the sunny uplands of the market outlook that you forget to measure how things have been going – or inadvertently end up relying on a measure that gives you a misleading (or wrong) answer.

Following are six problems that frequently crop up in performance measurement and suggestions on how to avoid or mitigate them.

No benchmark

While a manager is required to have a benchmark by the Financial Conduct Authority, it is remarkably common for it to fall into disuse. This means that you will have nothing meaningful to compare your performance with. Surprisingly often, trustees don't even notice the lack of a benchmark, which means that they cannot exercise one of their basic fiduciary duties: monitoring their financial performance against a target to see whether it is proceeding as expected. This is especially true of financial objectives and goals.

Wrong or irrelevant benchmark

It is also surprisingly common for an inappropriate benchmark to be chosen, or an appropriate benchmark with an inappropriate time frame (such as only the most recent quarter, rather than three or five years). For example, you might have said that you want your mixed fund measured against a benchmark of 70% in global equities and 30% in global bonds, but instead you are given something else, such as a peer-group measure or a composite benchmark, because it is easier for the manager to produce or more standard for the product you are invested in. Be specific about your required benchmark and the periods over which you want your performance to be measured.

If your manager does use a different benchmark, you should seek to understand why and in what respects it is different. For example, it may be that it is actually equivalent in most respects (rather than exactly 70% in global equities and 30% in global bonds), including the amounts held in volatile assets and in specific geographical regions. However, you should still agree this change. Table 11.7 gives an example of how a more complex manager benchmark and a simpler benchmark might actually be almost identical.

Table 11.7 Comparison of a more complex benchmark and a simpler benchmark

	Manager benchmark	**Simple benchmark**
UK equities	20%	70%
Overseas equities	40%	
Property	10%	-
Riskier assets	**70%**	**70%**
Bonds	25%	30%
Cash	5%	-
Safer assets	**30%**	**30%**
Total	**100%**	**100%**

Benchmark in a different currency

Using a benchmark in a different currency is most common if you work with international investment management firms. Returns can often be quoted in US dollars, and a UK-based client might inadvertently compare such a fund with other funds denominated in GBP. The same returns measured in different currencies will obviously not be equivalent, and this kind of comparison will give a misleading picture. This is not a reason to avoid using non-GBP funds; the point is to check what currency you are looking at because the exchange rate between any two currencies will vary throughout the benchmark period, possibly giving very different results over time. As a result, it would be misleading to translate a benchmark return from one currency into another at a single point in time, because doing so would assume that the exchange rate was the same throughout the period being reported on.

Performance shown without fee deductions

You should know whether you are being shown returns net or gross of the manager's charges. If it is not clear that the figures are net, you should assume the returns are gross (i.e. shown before any deductions for your manager's fees). In such cases, you should deduct 1% (if you don't know what fees you are paying), as your returns may otherwise be overstated. See page 215 for more information on manager fees.

Too short a time period

Successful managers will get more decisions right than wrong, but no manager gets everything right all the time so you will need to allow time for their skill to emerge. Decent indications of longer-term performance do not begin to emerge for some time, usually three years or so, and you will only get the true measure of the performance of a manager after at least one market cycle has passed (usually considered to be seven years or so). If performance is measured over too short a period, you may draw the wrong conclusions. If you are confident in the manager's process, have confidence in their future performance.

Misleading charts

Take care when looking at charts. Many charts are used as a substitute for an explanation, encouraging you to infer something that may or may not be there. Confusion commonly arises from an inappropriate or unusual axis being used to make a point, such as when the message is about the long term, but the chart only goes back two or three years. Where you start the data from also matters, as explained in chapter 6 in the discussion on setting a start point for your target value for your long-term reserve (see page 115). It is therefore important to clearly understand why a particular start point has been chosen.

Fictional case studies

Spender: Warden's Philanthropy

The investment strategy of Warden's Philanthropy is to earn as much as it can to spend on its charitable purpose, and consequently the trustees have accepted that they will have to be tolerant of a volatile investment portfolio. Armed with their new knowledge of their investments following the completion of their review (see chapters 7 and 10), the trustees had two principal questions they wanted answered: were they maintaining their long-term reserve in line with inflation, and were they earning and spending as much as their tolerance for uncertainty allowed? They used three benchmarks to answer these questions.

The first question was answered by using a benchmark of their agreed target value, which recorded how much the long-term reserve should have been had the charity's value kept pace with inflation. They relied on a RAGB-based table with ranges of plus or minus 15% (the portfolio's expected volatility) to work out whether they were within the range that would allow them to continue to spend normally.

The second question (about how much they were earning and spending) was in two parts. First, to make sure they were earning as much as they could, they compared their own investment returns to a benchmark made up of a portfolio with a similar asset allocation (or 'risk bucket'). In their case this was an index constructed as shown in table 11.8.

Table 11.8 Warden's Philanthropy's benchmark

Asset class	Allocation
Global equities	65%
UK property	20%
Bonds	10%
Cash	5%
Total allocation	**100%**

If their returns (after costs) were as good as those of the similar portfolio of about 85% in equity-type assets, then they were earning at the level they had agreed was optimum for their chosen level of volatility. If the long-term reserve was not growing at or above the green level in its RAGB triggers, then the spending was keeping pace with what was available.

The second part looked to see if the spending reserve was still within its RAGB range of plus or minus 5% of its target value, after the full amount had been transferred into it (which was simpler when it was just income, rather than a mix of income and some capital gains).

At their six-monthly meetings with their investment manager, the trustees quickly reviewed the data for the previous six months, and analysed where any differences had arisen between the performance of their benchmarks and their portfolio. The meetings also involved a review of the portfolio for any holdings that attracted low scores in their ESG rating system. Finally, they looked annually at how many times the manager had voted against its proxy adviser and shareholder resolutions, and then discussed the reasons for these decisions.

Saver: Martello Tower Fund

The Martello Tower Fund (MTF) is the most substantial restricted fund of the fundraising charity Preserving Our Nautical Past, which is established as a charitable incorporated organisation. It is accumulating a fund large enough to build a wall to protect a fort from rising sea levels, and possibly create a longer-term fund with the excess.

The MTF uses two benchmarks. The first is its target value, which is based on the cost of the planned renovation work. So long as the value of the fund is higher than the cost of the renovation, the fund is succeeding. At the moment, the fund is significantly ahead of this benchmark (so the trustees could start the refurbishment at any time if they chose).

The second benchmark aims to see whether the MTF's passive fund is giving it the same return as the index it has chosen to track. As its assets are invested in global equities, the investment committee has asked the fund's manager for a benchmark that reflects the index that the passive fund tracks. In the initial reports, the manager offered a variety of different benchmarks as a way of selling new products which it regarded as more attractive solutions. This irritated the investment committee, which insisted that only the passive fund benchmark be used, which it then was. The results of this comparison told the committee that the fund was performing in line with the chosen index (FTSE All-World Index), with a small lag for fees (which the index doesn't pay).

Spend-outer: Butterworth Music Festivals

Butterworth Music Festivals must spend its entire £10 million within ten years and has decided to keep all its money in a short-term portfolio but with a slightly higher risk appetite than would be usual. They took this risk in the form of a wider-than-usual range of credit quality but with a more careful selection of duration. They also used some absolute return funds and a small portion of equities.

In terms of measuring performance, the most important benchmark they used was their spend-out target value of zero. Were they going to be able to spend all the money in the required time frame? They tracked this using their target value projections, which were influenced by their investment returns, but principally by how quickly they could spend the money. They were finding this quite difficult to do well and had delayed their plans once already.

They had allowed their manager to invest up to 20% of their portfolio in some carefully selected equities to enhance their returns, and they wanted to check they were getting value from this. The trustees asked the manager to provide sufficient information so they could monitor the proportion and nature of the equities against this rule of holding no more than 20%. The reports they received showed that they were making a good absolute return against cash (which they aimed to exceed by 1%) and CPI inflation (which they aimed to match) once the manager's fees were deducted.

Conclusion

This chapter began by emphasising the importance of asking the right question. Once you have identified the right question, the appropriate benchmark will be easier to find and the answer easier to see. Another central thread running through this chapter is that whereas in the investment world performance assessment only applies to managers, in the charity world it should apply as much (perhaps even more) to trustees, because trustees set the goals and limits around what can be earned and what is spent. If they are unambitious, they will produce disappointing results for their beneficiaries, who may rely heavily upon them. In this spirit, performance assessment should be as central to charity investors as evaluating the impact of their spending. They are two sides of the same coin and equally essential parts of good charity financial management.

The next chapter brings the book to a conclusion by drawing together the threads developed in each of the previous chapters and by revealing how each of the fictional case study charities turned out.

Notes

1 'Investing charity money: A guide for trustees (CC14)' [web page], Charity Commission for England and Wales, 2023, www.gov.uk/government/publications/charities-and-investment-matters-a-guide-for-trustees-cc14, accessed 20 January 2024.
2 For further information see James Chen, 'Global Investment Performance Standards (GIPS): Definition and uses' [web article], Investopedia, www.investopedia.com/terms/g/gips.asp, 15 December 2020.
3 'SONIA interest rate benchmark' [web page], Bank of England, 2023, www.bankofengland.co.uk/markets/sonia-benchmark, accessed 20 January 2024.
4 See Adam Hayes, 'Volatility: Meaning in finance and how it works with stocks' [web article], Investopedia, www.investopedia.com/terms/v/volatility.asp, 31 March 2023.
5 See 'Charity investment performance in perspective' [web page], Asset Risk Consultants, www.assetrisk.com/solutions/charities/arc-charity-indices-funds, accessed 20 January 2024.
6 See 'What is an MSCI ESG rating?' [web page], MSCI, www.msci.com/our-solutions/esg-investing/esg-ratings, accessed 20 January 2024.
7 Ibid.

8 See Jillian Ambrose, 'ExxonMobil and Chevron suffer shareholder rebellions over climate' [web article], *The Guardian*, www.theguardian.com/business/2021/may/26/exxonmobil-and-chevron-braced-for-showdown-over-climate, 26 May 2021.

Chapter twelve

Conclusion

This book begins with one of Aesop's fables, where the moral is that the point of money is to use it, not to bury it, although using it involves putting it at risk. Nothing has really changed since the time of Aesop because what makes you charitable is what you spend, not what you keep. If there is one lesson to take from this book, that is it.

For your charity to be successful, it is not enough just to have the biggest investment returns you can achieve – you should aim to have the highest spending you can manage. This means being ambitious about your investment returns (even if that can be uncomfortable) and then being ambitious about spending as much of those returns as possible.

Too often the default among charities is to err on the side of caution both when investing and when spending. It is far better (and more charitable) to err on the side of spending a little too much for a little too long than to watch a series of wonderful opportunities pass you by. Even if you overspend, this book explains how simple it can be to remedy any damage, ensuring it is only a temporary problem.

Although charities carry a weighty responsibility for being good stewards of their resources, in many ways the money is not morally theirs but belongs to their beneficiaries. If you want to spend it all, you usually can. If you want to use some or all of your portfolio to deliver your purpose directly, you usually can. It is not for an investment manager to tell you that you shouldn't – it is for the trustees to decide that there are good reasons not to. Investment managers can advise on the consequences of different options, but a good trustee will always encourage spending more where they can. Only trustees are in a position to see all sides of this argument.

A great deal of this book is about risk, or more accurately unpredictability, and how to manage it successfully. Sometimes you can manage it by creating and using clear frameworks; other times you will do so by understanding that something you are told is a risk in fact isn't a risk for you, even though it might be for other types of investor. Investing is a skill just as fundraising or charity trading is a skill, and all are accompanied by their own jargon. The difference is the confidence and ambition that trustees have in these different environments. If you set out with the idea that you are a charity and therefore cannot take risks, you are destined to fail.

Even if you only adopt some of the principles explained in this book, they are likely to make your charity a more successful and deliberate investor. The best investment is in understanding how you apply these principles, and, of course, remembering that what makes you charitable is what you spend, not what you save. After all, it's not your money – it's for someone else. What's best for them?

Fictional case studies

Spender: Warden's Philanthropy

Founded in 1860, Warden's Philanthropy had a permanent endowment worth £40 million. It had a strong sense of social purpose, not only in how it spent but also in how it invested, partly because of its nationally recognised prize for social action.

As the charity approached its 200th anniversary, it was able to reflect that its donor, Mr Gilbert, would likely have been reasonably pleased that the charity had been assiduous in making sure that all its investment returns were spent as soon as possible on its charitable purpose, and not held back just so the charity could become bigger. Over that time, other newer charities had been set up which were much larger and spent much more. However, because of the age and integrity of Warden's Philanthropy, it retained an influence far greater than its assets would suggest, not least because its annual prize had become so prestigious it barely mattered to the recipients how modest the award had become.

Saver: Martello Tower Fund

The Martello Tower Fund was a substantial fund within the fundraising charity Preserving Our Nautical Past. It had £1 million to protect a historic coastal fort against rising sea levels. The trustees had decided to try to grow the £1 million as quickly as possible so there would be enough money not only to build the sea wall but also to leave a surplus for other projects. They needed to build their wall within 30 years.

The investment committee appointed by the trustees to manage the fund turned out to be very shrewd. Because they were so volatility tolerant, the money started to pile up, albeit with ups and downs. Within 15 years the fund had enough money to build the sea wall, with a good surplus. So impressed were the trustees of Preserving Our Nautical Past that they asked the committee to stay invested to earn even more to create a larger fund to pay for some of their long-cherished pet projects. Greed overcame fear, and soon enough construction inflation took hold at the same time as returns started to go backwards. Soon, the charity was racing to make sure they had enough money just to complete the basics of the original brief, which they just about managed.

Spend-outer: Butterworth Music Festivals

This charity was set up in 2003 and planned to spend its entire £10 million on music festivals within ten years of its first grant.

Well, they did it! They managed to spend the £10 million within ten years, although at times it was a little more chaotic than they might have wished. Because of a slower than expected start, their music festivals became bigger and more elaborate, and they were able to spend more than they had expected on ensuring they were using green, sustainable approaches. They began to receive national attention, with the last festival attracting so many people that special trains had to be laid on to the local station. Just before the ten-year deadline, the charity wound up by giving its remaining assets (worth £250,000) to another charity that put on live concerts, and then settled its outstanding costs. The trustees commissioned an author to capture their recollections in a small report reflecting the sheer joy of their mission. What they didn't know was that apart from the concerts bringing immense pleasure to a huge number of people, one of the attendees – a child at the time – went on to become a world-class musician and would cite one of these concerts as having sparked their lifelong love of music.

Appendix one

Specimen investment policy statements for the three fictional charities

There is no set format or wording for an investment policy statement, and these examples are deliberately broad to incorporate the ideas covered in this book. Therefore, these three examples can be regarded as templates to show the ideas you may wish to include.

Warden's Philanthropy

1. Introduction
   1.1. This document summarises Warden's Philanthropy's financial objectives and investment policies.
   1.2. Warden's Philanthropy is a grant-making charity, sustained by its permanent endowment. Its focus is on access and opportunity, in whatever form, for people in the Barchester area. It is currently worth £40 million and has a strong sense of social purpose in how it invests its money and delivers its services. It also awards a prestigious annual prize recognising effective social action, which gives the charity a high public profile.
   1.3. The charity has no other income and has a perpetual time horizon. Accounting expenditure of £1.6 million includes a series of one-, two- and three-year grants, which are accounted for when awarded. The balance is used to run the charity and monitor its activities. The current grant budget is 85% of total expenditure. The annual cash outflow is easily controlled by reducing new commitments. The trustees wish to maintain a balance between current and future beneficiaries as far as possible and intend to be prudent in their approach, not cautious.

2. Financial objectives and goals

2.1. The charity's overarching financial objective is to balance its spending and investments so as to maximise its spending on its beneficiaries.

2.2. The trustees have agreed three financial goals for the charity (including its investment portfolio):

2.2.1. to grow the charity's assets in line with inflation over the long term;

2.2.2. to provide a stable level of annual expenditure, sustainable into the future;

2.2.3. to invest with careful regard to the charity's values and reputation.

3. Spending policy

3.1. The trustees spend based on a total return drawn from a mixture of capital and income.

3.2. Their policy is to spend £1.6 million per year, which they will keep under review in the context of the charity's long-term reserves.

3.3. The £1.6 million will be increased annually in line with inflation as measured by the Consumer Prices Index (CPI).

4. Investment policy

4.1. Warden's Philanthropy has two investment mandates, each with different appetites for volatility and uncertainty. All assets can be invested widely and in line with Charity Commission guidance and best practice.

4.2. A **long-term portfolio** seeks to produce a high financial return to fund long-term expenditure.

4.3. The long-term portfolio's characteristics include:

4.3.1. The portfolio will aim to maximise returns, even though this means a high level of volatility (similar to that of equities).

4.3.2. At least 70% is likely to be invested in property and equities.

4.3.3. All funds should be available for withdrawal with no more than six months' notice.

4.3.4. Hedging is permitted only for efficient portfolio purposes and not for speculation.

4.3.5. The base currency is sterling.

4.4. A **short-term portfolio** seeks to keep safe money that has been earmarked for spending by avoiding anything but temporary and marginal capital losses. It can be invested in a bank account or a portfolio designed to preserve capital and deliver a stable return, or a combination of both.

4.5. The short-term portfolio's characteristics include:
  - 4.5.1. It is unlikely to hold more than 30% in equities or property.
  - 4.5.2. Investments should be deposited with investment-grade institutions or in diversified money market funds with similar ratings.
  - 4.5.3. Deposits should be spread by counterparty.
  - 4.5.4. The base currency is sterling.

5. Responsible investing

5.1. It is the trustees' intention to make a positive impact on people and the planet by avoiding harm through environmental, social and governance (ESG) integration and exclusions, benefitting stakeholders through responsible business activities and contributing to solutions through influence and investing for impact.

5.2. The trustees therefore ask the manager(s) to make the following commitments:
  - 5.2.1. Integrate ESG factors within the selection process, across all asset classes.
  - 5.2.2. Seek to influence companies, both through engagement and voting, to encourage them to be responsible employers and citizens.
  - 5.2.3. Avoid investing in companies that are harmful to the environment or society.
  - 5.2.4. Collaborate with other charity investors to identify areas of mutual concern.

5.3. These exclusions apply to both portfolios (as far as possible), covering all assets to minimise reputational risk:
  - 5.3.1. indiscriminate weaponry (<5% of revenues);
  - 5.3.2. civilian firearms (<5% revenues);
  - 5.3.3. controversial fossil fuels, such as shale or thermal coal (<5% of revenues);
  - 5.3.4. tobacco (<10% revenues);
  - 5.3.5. gambling (<10% revenues).

6. Investment powers

6.1. Warden's Philanthropy has general powers of investment.

6.2. It passed a resolution permitting spending based on a total return on 24 April 2021. The investment fund was valued on that date at £35 million. It has chosen CPI as its preferred measure of inflation, beginning on 1 January 2022. The unapplied total return has been divided between the long-term and spending reserves.

6.3. Investment management will be delegated to a professional investment manager, authorised and regulated by the Financial Conduct Authority.

7. Governance

7.1. The trustees set the overall financial objectives and goals, including the investment objectives for the long-term and spending reserves, the target values, and the responsible investment policy.

7.2. It delegates these to the finance committee:

- 7.2.1. appointing the manager(s) and consultants;
- 7.2.2. deciding the ranges for the long-term and short-term portfolios;
- 7.2.3. ongoing monitoring of the portfolios.

8. Reserves policy and target values

8.1. The charity has divided its reserves into a long-term reserve (with an indefinite time horizon) and a spending reserve.

8.2. The **spending reserve** separates all money allocated to be spent in the near future. The target value for this reserve is £1 million.

8.3. The **long-term reserve** represents all other assets. Its target value is £32 million, to be increased annually in line with CPI inflation from 2022.

9. Management, reporting and monitoring

9.1. The charity will itself calculate its reserves position relative to its target values.

- 9.1.1. If the long-term reserve is within a range of +/−15% of the target value, no action is required. If it is outside this range, the trustees should consider increasing or reducing their spending policy.
- 9.1.2. If the spending reserve is outside a range of +/−50%, the trustees should increase or reduce their actual spending (not necessarily change the policy).

9.2. The manager will provide the following information on a quarterly basis for each portfolio:

- 9.2.1. A table showing:
  - 9.2.1.1. opening valuation;
  - 9.2.1.2. any additions and subtractions by the client;
  - 9.2.1.3. fees paid to the manager;
  - 9.2.1.4. gains or losses;
  - 9.2.1.5. closing valuation.

9.2.2. Actual annualised portfolio performance (on a Global Investment Performance Standards basis) for the year to date, 12 months, 3 years and 5 years. All four measures of performance will be compared with:
9.2.2.1. CPI + 4%;
9.2.2.2. an 80% equity, 20% bond index;
9.2.2.3. the ARC Sterling Steady Growth index.
9.2.3. Average volatility for the past three years compared to the ARC Sterling Steady Growth ACI index.

9.3. On an annual basis, the manager will supply details for the long-term portfolio of:
9.3.1. the proportion of its votes cast against its proxy voting adviser's recommendations;
9.3.2. the proportions of assets invested in any of the excluded categories above;
9.3.3. the names of any companies whose ESG credentials are rated BBB by Morgan Stanley Capital International;
9.3.4. a summary of the material engagements on ESG and any details of material collaborations with other investors.

9.4. The short-term spending reserves will be monitored by the charity against prevailing cash rates and CPI inflation + 0% (after costs).

10. Approval and review

10.1. This investment policy statement has been prepared to provide a framework for the management of the charity's reserves. It will be reviewed annually to ensure its continuing appropriateness.

Approved by the Board of Trustees

Signed ____________________________ (Chair/Treasurer)

Dated ____________________________

Martello Tower Fund

1. Introduction

1.1. This document summarises the financial objectives and investment policies for the Martello Tower Fund (MTF), a restricted fund within the charity Preserving Our Nautical Past (PONP). The charity's main income comes from fundraising and membership, but the MTF is PONP's most substantial investment asset.

1.2. The MTF was established with an endowment of £1 million from the government to preserve a historic coastal fort. When it was set up, its endowment was given specifically so that the trustees would have sufficient money to build a sea wall at some future point to protect the fort against rising tides caused by climate change. It has been left up to the trustees to decide when will be the best time to do this, as long as the wall is completed within 30 years. The timing will depend on whether MTF's assets grow faster than the building costs. If the assets grow well, the trustees have the option to create a lump sum that could be spent on some other project to celebrate the nautical past. Alternatively, if growth is less than planned, they may need to do a slightly less good job on the wall. In the meantime, the fund will have minimal spending, principally focused on monitoring efforts to check whether to build now or later.

2. Financial objectives and goals

2.1. The charity's overarching financial objective is to grow through the acquisition of new properties. For this restricted fund, the goal is to grow the value of the fund at a rate high enough to enable the sea wall to be built within 30 years.

2.2. The trustees have agreed four financial goals for the charity (including its investment portfolio):

2.2.1. to maximise the fund's growth over 30 years;

2.2.2. to exceed the rate of the construction industry's inflation over 30 years;

2.2.3. to be able to liquidate the portfolio with five years' notice;

2.2.4. to invest while recognising the naval engineering roots of the fund.

3. Spending policy

3.1. The MTF does not have any significant spending requirements (other than investment fees and occasional updates on the eventual cost of the work), so its policy is to spend on an ad hoc basis, drawing cash from its portfolios as required. When it reaches the point when it will start its building work, it will become a spend-out fund and have a spending policy appropriate for that sort of model.

4. Investment policy

4.1. While the fund has well over five years left to run, it will remain invested in its long-term portfolio, which will be invested entirely in passively managed global equities.

4.2. As the time approaches when it might start spending, it will establish a short-term portfolio and start to move money into that portfolio as its need for certain asset values begins to become much clearer.

4.3. The base currency of both portfolios is sterling.

5. Responsible investing

5.1. The MTF has a responsible investment policy which must be both consistent with the aims of a nautical charity and respectful of high-quality engineering enterprises. As a result, it expects its managers to engage on issues of climate change and the health of the seas. It welcomes investments in the defence industries.

5.2. Investments in companies significantly involved with controversial fossil fuels, such as shale gas or thermal coal (more than 5% of revenues), are to be excluded from this mandate.

6. Investment powers

6.1. PONP has general powers of investment, including a capacity to make social investments.

6.2. Investment management will be delegated to a professional investment manager, authorised and regulated by the Financial Conduct Authority.

7. Governance

7.1. The trustees of PONP set the overall financial objectives and goals, including the target values for the long-term reserves and the responsible investment policy. They retain responsibility for any mixed-motive or programme-related investments.

7.2. They have appointed a committee of experts to advise them on investment and other decisions relating to the MTF.

7.3. The trustees will decide when to spend out the fund.

7.4. The trustees delegate to the investment committee:

7.4.1. appointing the manager(s);

7.4.2. monitoring progress and responsible investment activity.

8. Reserves policy and target values

8.1. The investment committee of the MTF has an agreed target of how much money it needs to deliver to fund the building work in today's prices (based on a quinquennial review of costs).

8.2. All the fund's assets and any liabilities are currently designated as part of the charity's long-term reserve.

9. Management, reporting and monitoring

9.1. The charity will itself calculate the fund's reserve position relative to its target values.

9.2. The manager will provide the following information on a quarterly basis:

9.2.1. A table showing:

9.2.1.1. opening valuation;

9.2.1.2. any additions and subtractions by the client;

9.2.1.3. fees paid to the manager;

9.2.1.4. gains or losses;

9.2.1.5. closing valuation.

9.2.2. Actual annualised portfolio performance (on a Global Investment Performance Standards basis) for the year to date, 12 months, 3 years and 5 years. All four measures of performance will be compared with:

9.2.2.1. construction industry inflation;

9.2.2.2. a 100% global equity index;

9.2.2.3. average volatility for the past three years compared to the global equity index.

9.3. On an annual basis, the manager will be asked to supply details for the long-term portfolio of:

9.3.1. the proportion of its votes cast against its proxy voting adviser's recommendations;

9.3.2. the proportion of assets invested in the excluded category above and a report on any investments in the defence and other engineering industries;

9.3.3. the names of any companies whose environmental, social and governance (ESG) credentials are rated CCC by Morgan Stanley Capital International;

9.3.4. a summary of the material engagements on ESG and any details of material collaborations with other investors.

10. Approval and review

10.1. This investment policy statement has been prepared to provide a framework for the management of the charity's reserves. It will be reviewed annually to ensure its continuing appropriateness.

Approved by the Board of Trustees

Signed ______________________________ (Chair/Treasurer)

Dated ______________________________

Butterworth Music Festivals

1. Introduction

1.1. This document summarises the financial objectives and investment policies for Butterworth Music Festivals, which is a spend-out charity.

1.2. Its purpose is to spend £10 million on bringing music to communities that otherwise might not enjoy any live performances. There are no instructions beyond this. The trustees therefore have wide discretion in how to use this money, but they have to spend it all within ten years of their first grant (expected to be made this year). Any residue at the end of ten years will be gifted to the government to advance general social well-being.

2. Financial objectives and goals

2.1. The charity's overarching financial objective is to spend out the value of the fund within ten years of the first grant being made.

2.2. The trustees have agreed four financial objectives and goals for the charity (including its investment portfolio):

2.2.1. to spend all the assets within ten years;

2.2.2. to maintain the value against inflation;

2.2.3. to have high and reliable liquidity;

2.2.4. to be able to spend quickly, wisely and decisively.

3. Spending policy

3.1. The policy is to be as flexible as possible, spending income and capital without distinction. The expected spend rate will accelerate over the life of the fund and expected cash outflows are regularly prepared.

3.2. When they get near the end of the ten-year spending term, the trustees have decided to bequeath any remaining investments to one or two of their preferred beneficiaries to make sure the £10 million (together with any additional income) has been fully spent, but without them having to spend out to an exact zero balance. This will give the trustees the greatest flexibility in closing down in an orderly way.

4. Investment policy

4.1. This short-term portfolio is to be invested mainly in cash and bonds but also in some equities, absolute return funds and infrastructure.

4.2. An active discretionary manager with good service is preferred so the trustees can keep in close touch with the manager about how their spending plans might change, potentially rapidly.

4.3. The base currency of the portfolio is sterling.

5. Responsible investing

5.1. The investments (be they in equities, bonds or cash) should exclude a broad range of 'sin stocks', and the manager should demonstrate active engagement with companies in a number of areas, but with a particular focus on protecting the environment.

6. Investment powers

6.1. Butterworth Music Festivals has normal, wide-ranging investment powers that are in line with the Trustee Act 2000, giving it plenty of flexibility in how it invests its money.

6.2. Investment management will be delegated to a professional investment manager, authorised and regulated by the Financial Conduct Authority.

7. Governance

7.1. The trustees do not have a specialist investment committee and they want to remain close to the investments, which they will be drawing on regularly.

7.2. The trustees require quarterly calls and meetings with their manager as their expenditure plans develop and emerge over the years, enabling everyone to have a clear idea of how much cash will be needed and when.

8. Reserves policy and target values

8.1. The charity has a simple metric of having to spend all its assets within ten years of making its first grant. Its target value is nil – but not less.

8.2. All assets are part of a single spending reserve.

9. Management, reporting and monitoring

9.1. The charity will itself calculate its reserve position relative to its target value.

9.2. The manager will provide the following information on a quarterly basis for each portfolio:

9.2.1. A table showing:

9.2.1.1. opening valuation;

9.2.1.2. any additions and subtractions;

9.2.1.3. fees paid to the manager;

9.2.1.4. gains and losses;

9.2.1.5. closing valuation.

9.2.2. Actual annualised portfolio performance (on a Global Investment Performance Standards basis) for the year to date, 12 months, 3 years and 5 years. All four measures of performance will be compared with:

9.2.2.1. inflation as measured by the Consumer Prices Index;

9.2.2.2. a money market rate (SONIA (Sterling Overnight Index Average)).

9.3. On an annual basis, the manager will be asked to supply details for the short-term portfolio of:

9.3.1. the proportion of its votes cast against its proxy voting adviser's recommendations (if any);

9.3.2. the names of any companies whose environmental, social and governance (ESG) credentials are rated CCC by Morgan Stanley Capital International (if any);

9.3.3. a summary of the material engagements on ESG and any details of material collaborations with other investors (if any).

10. Approval and review

10.1. This investment policy statement has been prepared to provide a framework for the management of the charity's reserves. It will be reviewed annually to ensure its continuing appropriateness.

Approved by the Board of Trustees

Signed ______________________ (Chair/Treasurer)

Dated ______________________

Appendix two

How to do total return accounting

Chapter 4 introduces the principles of total return accounting and explores why you might want to make use of it in your charity. This appendix goes into more detail about why and how to employ total return accounting, both with and without a permanent endowment. Total return accounting for charities is a necessary complement to total return investing.

Why should you consider total return accounting?

Formal charity accounting, as set out in the Charities Statement of Recommended Practice (SORP), is based on reporting across two separate domains: income and expenditure, and capital gains or losses.[1] The first records 'operating' movements (e.g. donations received less salaries paid) and the second 'capital' movements (e.g. investment gains less investment losses and fees).

Consider a charity that has decided to spend £75,000 per year on a total return basis, even though its natural income (see page 59) is only £50,000. Table A2.1 shows what this charity's financial activities would look like using 'standard rules' (i.e. natural income) accounting.[2] Note that there is an operating loss of £25,000 but an overall surplus (total movement) of £3,000.

Table A2.1 Example of accounting using natural income

	Standard rules accounting (£)
Income: natural	50,000
Expenditure	(75,000)
Operating surplus/(deficit)	**(25,000)**
Capital gains/losses	28,000
Total movement	**3,000**
Opening funds	1,000,000
Closing funds	**1,003,000**

Note: brackets signify losses.

It looks like the charity has a significant operating deficit for the period (of £25,000) because the capital part of the total return is not included in the first part of the calculation. It is possible to simply accept the apparent discrepancy and continue using standard rules accounting, but this is not intuitive to most people. Trustees and staff may require training and retraining to understand that an operating loss is not, per se, a bad thing (as long as the total movement is positive over a number of years). Operating deficits can be an integral part of using total return. What matters is the position of the reserves compared to their target values.

In contrast to the standard rules, total return accounting ignores the separation of natural income and capital. This is done through the introduction of total return transfer lines, as shown in table A2.2. Because £30,000 is transferred from the capital section to the income section, the charity now has a healthy operating surplus of £5,000. However, because of the accounting rules, once a charity has taken money out of an endowment, it cannot be put back in, so it is a one-way transfer. Note too that there is no change in the closing funds compared to the natural income method (see table A2.1).

Table A2.2 Accounting using total return

	Total return accounting (£)
Income: natural	50,000
Income: transfer from capital	*30,000*
Expenditure	(75,000)
Income surplus/(deficit)	**5,000**
Capital gains/losses	28,000
Transfer to income (above)	*(30,000)*
Subtotal	**(2,000)**
Total movement	**3,000**
Opening funds	1,000,000
Closing funds	**1,003,000**

Note: brackets signify losses.

In this way, the total return accounting approach supports your spending policy by clearly showing your operating or income surplus or deficit for the year (and not the arbitrary difference between your careful decision about what to spend and what natural income your portfolio has achieved).

How to set up total return accounting

As a starting point, you should first ascertain that total return is appropriate for your charity and in the interests of your beneficiaries – both current and future. For example, if you have a permanent endowment which is entirely invested in a community hall, then it would not be possible to operate on a total return basis because you could not sell little bits of the hall every year to supplement your income.

Next, it is important to understand the different accounting and legal implications of implementing total return accounting. The accounting side is designed for permanent endowments but also works with expendable endowments, whereas the legal side is only relevant to charities with permanent endowments.

Accounting treatment

Increased complexity

Total return accounting is slightly more complicated to operate than standard rules accounting. The advantages and disadvantages of total return are covered in chapter 4 (see page 61).

Using total return accounting alongside the Charities SORP and the Statement of Financial Activities

The Charities SORP, which regulates charity accounting, is designed according to the traditional division of an investment return into natural income and capital gains, with natural income being the measure of what can be spent. This makes the Charities SORP cumbersome as a way of telling a charity's financial story, because the standard rules are incompatible with the spirit of total return investing.

More specifically, the problem lies in how the Charities SORP treats charities' profit-and-loss account, known as the Statement of Financial Activities (SOFA). The SOFA calculates a charity's surplus by deducting expenditure from income (in line with the method in table A2.1). This is very clear if you are only spending your natural income, but what happens if you want to use some (but not all) of your capital gains? The capital you will use to supplement your natural income cannot be shown as income in the SOFA, so you will always see an operating deficit, which may give an inaccurate impression of poor financial management.

There is no perfect solution here – you will have to accept that while your internal accounting more clearly reflects your charity's actual financial health (using the method in table A2.2), the Charities SORP will look different. The Charities SORP allows you to use your trustees' annual report to link your spending activities with the funding sources used to finance them, and this is the best place to explain any apparent discrepancy in the context of your overall financial objectives.[3]

Legal treatment (only for charities with permanent endowments)

If your charity has a permanent endowment, you are required to complete a formal process if you wish to spend the capital from that permanent endowment. If you have a permanent endowment and you do not complete this process, you must spend only your natural income. All your other income is unaffected by these provisions, which only relate to permanent endowments.

The Charity Commission's guidance *Total Return Investment for Permanently Endowed Charities* summarises all of the relevant legislation and processes.[4]

Trusts (Capital and Income) Act 2013

Historically, charities with permanent endowments could only use total return accounting with the permission of the Charity Commission. However, the Trusts (Capital and Income) Act 2013 allowed such charities to move towards using total return rather than natural income. The process requires such charities to determine the value of their permanent capital (which should not be spent), called the 'investment fund', and separate it from the remainder (which can be spent if they so choose), called the 'unapplied total return' (UTR) (because it has not been applied to your charitable purpose yet).[5]

You can do this by passing a board resolution; you do not need to obtain prior permission from the Charity Commission, although it is wise to take advice first. In addition, if your permanent endowment is less than £25,000 (increased from £10,000 by the Charities Act 2022), your trustees can resolve to spend the entire sum on the purpose for which the endowment was given and thereby extinguish the endowment.[6]

Determining the new value of your long-term permanent endowment

As part of moving to total return, as a one-off process, you have to determine the new value of your investment fund. This involves identifying how much of your current endowment will be the new capital base of your charity and how much you will no longer consider as permanent, and instead make available for spending (now or in the future). In effect, this allows you to reassess the value of your permanent endowment to reflect the impact of historical inflation.

For example, imagine that your charity was given a permanent endowment of £100 during the French Revolution, in 1789. Your first step is to check what the endowment would be worth currently if it had kept up with inflation. You can do this using the Bank of England's inflation calculator, which shows that if your original £100 had grown in line with inflation, it would have been worth £12,664 by the end of 2023.[7] Let's say that the actual current value of your charity's endowment is £92,664, or £80,000 more than the Bank of England's figure. If you choose, you can pass a board resolution to agree that £12,664 is the current value of your permanent endowment (the investment fund) and decide to spend some or all of the rest.

Maintaining your investment fund into the future

After this, your investment fund should never fall below the value you agree (£12,664 in the above example). If the value of the investment fund falls below this level, you cannot continue to spend until it has recovered to this historical value (legally you do not have to include growing the fund in line with inflation), although you can borrow from the fund under a process called 'recoupment'.[8]

The remaining funds (£80,000 in our example) represent the proportion of the endowment that is yet to be used: the UTR. It is good practice to divide this pot into two:

- **Cushion:** you could keep back some or all of the UTR as part of your long-term reserve so your charity remains roughly the size that your stakeholders have come to expect. This also helps to prevent the investment fund falling below its floor, requiring you to have to stop spending, because you will have a cushion. In our example, with a hard floor of £12,664, you might choose to keep a cushion of £70,000, so your long-term reserves would be £82,664. You might then set your target value slightly lower (say, £75,000) if you felt that the market was very highly valued at present and due to fall. You would then be able to see whether you were fulfilling your intergenerational equity obligations under the total return order, but from this new, higher starting level, accepting and not spending the historic gains.
- **Balance:** you can then identify the balance (£92,664 – £82,664 = £10,000) as being available to fund your future spending by placing it in your spending reserve.

Recognising and recording your income

The final piece of this jigsaw is money that has been received as dividends or interest and is clearly income. In the regulations, this goes into something called the 'income fund' or in legal terms, the 'trust for application',[9] which is best thought of as your spending reserve – or, under the standard rules, the income account. If you don't wish to spend it all, you can if you wish add this income to your cushion and increase your target level for your long-term reserve (if you have reason to grow your reserves). Your investment return cannot be added to your investment fund except to increase it by the required amount of inflation (if you wish to).

Building your investment fund into your reserves

In practice, you can build these provisions into your normal reserves structure for your long-term and short-term spending (see chapter 6). You will also need to separately disclose the value of the investment fund in your accounts and the date of your total return resolution.

In practice, your reserves might look something like table A2.3 (incorporating the target values for your reserves, again discussed in chapter 6). As you can see, our example charity is now able to release some of the value that was previously locked up if it so wishes, and this can be spent on advancing the charity's purpose. In the example, the trustees have set a target of reducing their spending reserve to £5,000, and they will not be unduly worried if market volatility reduces the long-term fund to £75,000. They will reduce their spending reserve over time by spending most of the surplus £5,000 in their spending reserve on their charitable purpose through a series of exciting new projects.

Table A2.3 Using total return in relation to your reserves

Internal reporting (£)		**Formal accounting (£)**		**Target values (£)**
Long-term reserve	82,664	Investment fund	12,664	75,000
		UTR (cushion)	70,000	
Spending reserve	10,000	UTR (spending) plus income fund	10,000	5,000
Total assets	**92,664**	**Total assets**	**92,664**	**80,000**

UTR: unapplied total return.

It will be a matter for you to decide to allocate the UTR between your long- and short-term funds. You can maintain your charity at a similar size (as in our example above), or you can take a more radical approach and spend a substantial amount of the UTR on your beneficiaries' needs.

Using total return accounting for multiple funds

Chapter 6 suggests that you should divide your reserves into a long-term reserve and a spending reserve. It then outlines how you can reconcile this split with the Charities SORP's requirement to report the values of individual funds (endowments, restricted funds, designated funds and unrestricted funds) (see page 121).

The format in table A2.4 is useful for monitoring what is going on within each fund. This approach is consistent with the format required by the Charities SORP for permanent endowments, and expendable endowments are included to show a similar approach.

Table A2.4 Example of how to show multiple funds in total return accounting, with a long-term reserve and a spending reserve (£000s)

Reserve/fund	Opening balance	Income	Expenses	Gains	Transfers	Closing balance	Target values
Long term							
Permanent endowment	83	3	(2)	5	(5)	**84**	*75*
Expendable endowment	5,119	160	(236)	340	(500)	**4,883**	*4,800*
Restricted fund 1	983	30	(5)	60	(50)	**1,018**	*1,000*
	6,185	193	(243)	405	(555)	**5,985**	*5,875*
Spending reserve							
Restricted fund 1	10	-	(60)	-	50	**-**	*0*
Restricted fund 2	17	20	(31)	-	-	**6**	*0*
General fund	380	460	(850)	-	505	**495**	*150*
	407	480	(941)	-	555	**501**	*150*
Total funds	**6,592**	**673**	**(1,184)**	**405**	**-**	**6,486**	*6,025*

Note: The value of the investment fund (shown in the 'Permanent endowment' row) is £12,664.

Table A2.4 summarises what has been going on with each of these funds over the year. In the long-term reserve:

- The **endowments** (permanent and expendable together), whose closing balances total just under £5 million, generated an income of £163,000, incurred investment management fees of £238,000, and had gains of £345,000 during the year. The trustees decided to move £505,000 of this to the general fund spending reserve in line with their target values for both endowments. A footnote discloses the value of the investment fund for the permanent endowment for compliance purposes.
- **Restricted fund 1**, as specified by the donor, can be spent at any time. However, the trustees have decided to treat it as a long-term fund and just spend the income. The spending policy for the fund transfers

£50,000 to the spending reserve every year. This year the total return has been higher than that (£30,000 + £60,000). However, since the value of the fund is still above the target value, the trustees have decided to stick with the current spending policy and not revisit it. Should there be any investment losses in the future, the trustees would look at the target value to see how far short the fund was from this goal before deciding what action to take.

The combination of the two endowments and the long-term restricted fund gives a value for the long-term reserve of £5,985,000, only slightly more that the target value of £5,875,000.

The balance on the spending reserve of £501,000 is due to be spent in the near future down to £150,000, the target level specified for it in the charity's reserves policy. The table shows how the spending reserve is subdivided into different funds:

- **Restricted fund 1** is at its target value of zero. The other part of this fund is shown in the long-term reserve since it is not expected to be spent for some years, as it is a quasi-endowment.
- **Restricted fund 2** has no long-term aspirations so all the money will be spent imminently. It is therefore shown as part of the spending reserve with a target value of nil.
- The **general fund** represents the income (from all other sources) that is available for spending, or that is kept to provide ballast should there be a shortfall in income or unexpected expenditure in one year. In this example, its target is to keep £150,000, the level specified in the reserves policy for this fund. As explained above, £505,000 has been transferred in from the endowments because they were significantly above target so could afford to fund more spending. As a result, this reserve is significantly above its target level; however, the trustees are spending faster than normal to bring the balance back to target.

As explained in chapter 6, you will have different investment strategies for your long-term and spending reserves, as your long-term reserves will be much better able to withstand volatile asset prices because you do not need to spend them immediately. You should always make sure that you only invest money in volatile assets if you can tolerate that unpredictability. In this way, the investing, spending and accounting considerations in your various funds should be correctly aligned. If you are transferring money from a long-term to a short-term reserve, you should also consider transferring it from your long-term to your short-term portfolio (see chapter 5).

Case study

Here we will consider just one of the fictional case study charities to provide a further example of how total return accounting works in practice.

Spender: Warden's Philanthropy

Warden's Philanthropy had been set up in 1860 with a permanent endowment of £200,000, which the charity had calculated should have been worth £18 million in 2022 if it had kept pace with inflation. The charity was currently worth £40 million, giving the trustees a UTR cushion of £22 million and an investment fund of £18 million.

The trustees were very conscious of the fact that the founding principle of the charity was to make sure that as much of its income was spent as possible. They had accidentally saved considerable amounts in real terms that they could have spent, giving a large UTR of £22 million, all of which could now be spent if the trustees agreed. However, the local community had grown to expect a certain level of support into the future, so the trustees settled on a balance (at the beginning of the year) between these two completing demands by dividing up their £40 million between £35 million in their long-term reserve and £5 million in their spending reserve.

They agreed a target value for their long-term reserve of £32 million (they had been advised that the current market value of £35 million was likely to fall soon) and a spending reserve target of £1 million, leaving them £4 million to spend in the foreseeable future. They did this by dividing the UTR into two parts: £17 million (£35 million – £18 million) was allocated to the long-term reserve, which when combined with the investment fund gave it a balance of £35 million. The remainder of the UTR (£5 million) went into the spending reserve.

They had decided on a spending policy of 5% of their long-term target of £32 million, giving them £1.6 million a year to spend. Since their target value would increase in line with the Consumer Prices Index (CPI) every year, their spending would also increase in line with the CPI. This constant growth spending model (see page 65) was in keeping with their desire for stable annual budgets, and as an ambitious level of spending it was matched by their high-returning (but volatile) investment strategy.

The accounting was straightforward and is illustrated in table A2.5.

Table A2.5 Annual accounting for total return (£ million)

	Brought forward	Income	Capital gains or losses	Total return	Expenditure inc. fees	Transfer	Total movement	Carried forward	Target value
Long-term reserve									
Investment fund	18	–	–	–	–	–	–	18	
UTR cushion	17	2	3	5	(0.4)	(1.6)	(2)	20	
Subtotal	**35**	2	3	**5**	(0.4)	(1.6)	**(2)**	**38**	**32**
Spending reserve inc. UTR balance subtotal	**5**	–	–	**-**	(2.0)	1.6	**(0.4)**	**4.6**	**32**
Total	**40**	2	3	**5**	(2.4)	–	**(2.4)**	**42.6**	**33**

UTR: unapplied total return.

The key transactions at the end of the year (and reported in their accounts) are:

- All the income, gains (or losses) and investment fees are allocated to the long-term reserve.
- The target value of £32 million increased only modestly because inflation for the year was 0.7% (an increase of £224,000).
- The £1.6 million expenditure budget (arising from the spending policy of 5% of the target value of the long-term reserve) is transferred from the long-term reserve to the spending reserve using the 'Transfers' column.
- Actual spending is charged against the spending reserve.

Notes

1 *Charities SORP (FRS 102)* [PDF], 2nd edition, Chartered Institute of Public Finance and Accounting, 2019, www.gov.uk/government/publications/charities-sorp-2005, accessed 20 January 2024.
2 'Total return investment for permanently endowed charities' [web page], Charity Commission for England and Wales, 2023, www.gov.uk/government/publications/total-return-investment-for-permanently-endowed-charities/total-return-investment-for-permanently-endowed-charities, accessed 20 January 2024.
3 *Charities SORP (FRS 102)* [PDF], 2nd edition, Chartered Institute of Public Finance and Accounting, 2019, www.gov.uk/government/publications/charities-sorp-2005, s. 1.12, accessed 20 January 2024.
4 'Total return investment for permanently endowed charities' [web page], Charity Commission for England and Wales, 2023, www.gov.uk/government/publications/total-return-investment-for-permanently-endowed-charities/total-return-investment-for-permanently-endowed-charities, accessed 20 January 2024.
5 Ibid.
6 Charities Act 2011, s. 282 (as amended); see also Lucy Rhodes, 'The Charities Act 2022 explained: Permanent endowment and restricted funds' [web article], Bates Wells, https://bateswells.co.uk/updates/the-charities-bill-explained-permanent-endowment-and-restricted-funds, 15 June 2023.
7 See www.bankofengland.co.uk/monetary-policy/inflation/inflation-calculator.
8 'Total return investment for permanently endowed charities' [web page], Charity Commission for England and Wales, 2023, www.gov.uk/government/publications/total-return-investment-for-permanently-endowed-charities/total-return-investment-for-permanently-endowed-charities, s. 5.5, accessed 20 January 2024.
9 Ibid., s. 2.2.

Index